The
Master's Perspective
on
PASTORAL
MINISTRY

The Master's Perspective Series
Volume 3

The

Master's Perspective
on
PASTORAL
MINISTRY

RICHARD L. MAYHUE
ROBERT L. THOMAS
general editors

Kregel
Academic & Professional

In most cases the endnotes in this work have been left as they originally appeared in *The Master's Seminary Journal.*

Library of Congress Cataloging-in-Publication Data
The Master's perspective on pastoral ministry / editors, Richard L. Mayhue and Robert L. Thomas.
    p. cm. — (The Master's perspective series; v. 3)
    Includes bibliographical references and indexes.
    1. Pastoral theology. I. Mayhue, Richard. II. Thomas, Robert L. III. Series.

BV4011.3 .M37 2002   253—dc21   2001050857

ISBN 0-8254-3183-2

Contents

Foreword

The Bible reveals not only the full truth of the gospel but also the means for its proclamation through the church.

The New Testament is the manual for ministry. It contains the design of God for the people of God to fulfill the Great Commission. A biblical ecclesiology is no less the mandate of God than is a biblical Christology or soteriology. One of the strange features of contemporary evangelicalism is that it often seeks to frame the ministry of the church along cultural rather than biblical paths and then congratulates itself for that unbiblical achievement, offering its superficial success as proof that it has discerned the model that all churches should follow.

In this volume, the reader will find some clear, biblical insight bearing on the most initial element of a biblical ministry—the divinely designed role of the pastor. If the church is to be obedient to Scripture in the full range of its ministry, it must begin with obedience to the biblical pattern for the men who lead the church.

—John F. MacArthur Jr.

Introduction

Pastoring God's flock (i.e., shepherding the people of God on earth) is a noble, time-honored labor. The ultimate Shepherd is God Himself; one psalmist declared, "The LORD is my shepherd . . ." (Ps. 23:1) while another recognized God as the Shepherd of Israel (80:1).

The NT speaks of our Lord Jesus Christ as the Shepherd. He is the Good Shepherd who lays down His life for the sheep (John 10:11). As the Great Shepherd, Christ died the atoning death and arose on the third day (Heb. 13:20). And lest there be any mistake about the matter of rank, Peter refers to Christ as the Chief Shepherd (1 Peter 5:4).

God has delegated this worthy but difficult task of pastoring to human shepherds, who will in the end be accountable to Him for their efforts (Heb. 13:17). Charles Jefferson offers the following realistic perspective on pastoring, which all of us who are in ministry would do well to remember:

> The shepherd's work is a humble work; such it has been from the beginning and such it must be to the end. A man must come down to do it. A shepherd cannot shine. He cannot cut a figure. His work must be done in obscurity. The things which he does do not make interesting copy. His work calls for continuous self-effacement. It is a form of service which eats up a man's life. It makes a man old before his time. Every good shepherd lays down his life for the sheep. If a man is dependent on the applause of the crowd, he ought never to enter the ministry. The

finest things a minister does are done out of sight, and never get reported. They are known to himself and one or two others, and to God. His joy is not that his success is being talked about on earth, but that his name is written in heaven. The shepherd in the East had no crowd to admire him. He lived alone with the sheep and the stars. His satisfactions were from within. The messengers of Christ must not expect bands of music to attend them on their way. Theirs is a humble, unpretentious, and oftentime unnoticed labor, but if it builds souls in righteousness it is more lasting than the stars.[*]

The following articles on various features of pastoring are offered with the prayer that Christ's under-shepherds will distinguish themselves before the flock and God as men who took seriously their spiritual assignment on earth, who did not lord it over the flock but proved to be examples, and who went about their shepherdly duties, not under compulsion, but according to the will of God. May God's flock flourish under the spiritual leadership of godly pastors, and may God's received glory be great as the outcome.

The analysis of each area of discussion is the position of the contributor and does not necessarily represent the opinion of The Master's Seminary, its administration, or its faculty. Each analysis, however, is a proposal that is recommended for consideration by readers of this volume.

English translations used in this volume are those of the individual contributors unless otherwise indicated.

We want to express our thanks to Mr. Mark Axelson for his help in compiling the indexes for this volume.

—Richard L. Mayhue and
Robert L. Thomas, general editors

---

*Charles Jefferson, *The Minister As Shepherd* (1913; reprint, Hong Kong: Living Books for All, 1973), 32–33.

About *The Master's Seminary Journal*

For readers who are unfamiliar with *The Master's Seminary Journal,* a word of introduction is in order. *TMSJ* began publication in 1990 with the following statement of purpose:

> With this issue, *The Master's Seminary Journal* launches its career as a medium for the publication of scholarly articles dealing with the biblical text, Christian theology, and pastoral concerns. As you have noted, or will note, it also contains reviews of current and significant books and occasionally, of articles, relating to these issues. With these emphases in mind, technical articles dealing with such issues as the philosophy of religion, linguistics, or archaeology, will not be included unless they clearly, directly, and significantly contribute to the understanding or application of God's written revelation—the Holy Bible. The editors desire that all articles be understandable, not only by seminary professors and other professional scholars, but also by pastors, and, indeed, by any serious students of Scripture.
>
> While most of the articles will be contributed by the faculty members of The Master's Seminary, the editors will solicit articles and reviews from recognized evangelical scholars, will evaluate voluntary contributions for possible inclusion, and will

occasionally include outstanding historical selections from the public domain.

It is our fervent prayer that our Lord Jesus Christ will be honored and exalted, either directly or indirectly, on every page of this publication, and that every article and review will contribute to the understanding or application of the Holy Scriptures as we await His return. (Excerpted from "Editorial," *TMSJ* 1, no. 1 [1990]: 1–2).

The *Journal* has continued without interruption since that time, endeavoring to fulfill the purpose established at its beginning. Readers interested in a subscription to *TMSJ* may contact Professor James F. Stitzinger, *The Master's Seminary Journal,* 13248 Roscoe Blvd., Sun Valley, CA 91352, or by e-mail <jstitzinger@tms.edu>.

As a matter of policy, in its fall issue each year, *TMSJ* publishes the annual Faculty Lecture Series delivered to The Master's Seminary student body in January and February of that year. The fall 1999 issue covered the subject of the biblical covenants, the fall 2000 issue dealt with Christian ethics, and the fall 2001 issue dealt with the "openness of God" position. Besides these topics, of course, other issues have treated a wide variety of biblical, theological, and practical subjects. Articles from past issues are available on The Master's Seminary Web site at <www.tms.edu>.

The following issues of *TMSJ* are the sources of *The Master's Perspective on Pastoral Ministry:*

- volume 1 (1990)—one chapter (chap. 7),
- volume 2 (1991)—one chapter (chap. 8),
- volume 3 (1992)—one chapter (chap. 11),
- volume 4 (1993)—one chapter (chap. 12),
- volume 5 (1994)—one chapter (chap. 10),
- volume 6 (1995)—three chapters (chaps. 1, 2, 4),
- volume 7 (1996)—two chapters (chaps. 5, 6),
- volume 8 (1997)—one chapter (chap. 3), and
- volume 9 (1998)—one chapter (chap. 9).

Contributors

John M. Koessler, D.Min.
Professor of Pastoral Studies
Moody Bible Institute

John F. MacArthur Jr., D.D.
President, Professor of Pastoral Ministries
The Master's Seminary

Wayne A. Mack, D.Min.
Adjunct Professor of Biblical Counseling
The Master's College

Richard L. Mayhue, Th.D.
Senior Vice President and Dean
Professor of Pastoral Ministries and Theology
The Master's Seminary

James E. Rosscup, Th.D.; Ph.D.
Professor of Bible Exposition
The Master's Seminary

John Sherwood, D.Min.
Associate Director
UFM International

James F. Stitzinger, Th.M.
Associate Professor of Historical Theology
The Master's Seminary

Benjamin B. Warfield, D.D.
Professor of Systematic Theology (1887–1921)
Princeton Theological Seminary

George J. Zemek, Th.D.
Adjunct Professor of Theology
The Master's Seminary

CHAPTER ONE

Read by next week

The Religious Life
of Theological Students

Benjamin B. Warfield

A minister must be both learned and religious. It is not a matter of choosing between the two. He must study, but he must study as in the presence of God and not in a secular spirit. He must recognize the privilege of pursuing his studies in the environment where God and salvation from sin are the air he breathes. He must also take advantage of every opportunity for corporate worship, particularly while he trains in the theological seminary. Christ Himself leads in exemplifying the importance of participating in the religious life of the community. Ministerial work without taking time to pray is a tragic mistake. The two must be combined if the servant of God is to give a pure, clear, and strong message.

This message was first delivered by Benjamin Breckinridge Warfield (1851–1921) at the Autumn Conference of Princeton Theological Seminary on October 4, 1911. It later appeared in *Selected Shorter Writings of Benjamin B. Warfield,* ed. John E. Meeter (Nutley, N.J.: Presbyterian and Reformed, 1970), 1:411–25; and in booklet form under the same title as this chapter (Nutley, N.J.: Presbyterian and Reformed, 1970). Warfield stands as one of America's most notable Reformed theologians. He taught theology at Princeton Theological Seminary from 1887 until his death in 1921. See *The Works of Benjamin B. Warfield,* 10 vols. (1927–1932; reprint, Grand Rapids: Baker, 1991), for his major writings.

* * * * *

I am asked to speak to you on the religious life of the student of theology. I approach the subject with some trepidation. I think it the most important subject which can engage our thought. You will not suspect me, in saying this, to be depreciating the importance of the intellectual preparation of the student for the ministry. The importance of the intellectual preparation of the student for the ministry is the reason of the existence of our theological seminaries. Say what you will, do what you will, the ministry is a "learned profession"; and the man without learning, no matter with what other gifts he may be endowed, is unfit for its duties. But learning, though indispensable, is not the most indispensable thing for a minister. "Apt to teach"—yes, the minister must be "apt to teach"; and observe that what I say—or rather what Paul says—is "apt to *teach*." Not apt merely to exhort, to beseech, to appeal, to entreat; nor even merely to testify, to bear witness; but to *teach*. And teaching implies knowledge: He who teaches must know. Paul, in other words, requires of you, as we are perhaps learning not very felicitously to phrase it, "instructional," not merely "inspirational," service. But aptness to teach alone does not make a minister; nor is it his primary qualification. It is only one of a long list of requirements which Paul lays down as necessary to meet in him who aspires to this high office. And all the rest concern, not his intellectual, but his spiritual fitness. A minister must be learned, on pain of being utterly incompetent for his work. But before and above being learned, a minister must be godly.

Nothing could be more fatal, however, than to set these two things over against one another. Recruiting officers do not dispute whether it is better for soldiers to have a right leg or a left leg: Soldiers should have both legs. Sometimes we hear it said that ten minutes on your knees will give you a truer, deeper, more operative knowledge of God than ten hours over your books. "What!" is the appropriate response. "Than ten hours over your books, on your knees?" Why should you turn from God when you turn to your books, or feel that you must turn from your books in order to turn to God? If learning and devotion are as antagonistic as that, then the intellectual life is in itself accursed, and there can be no question of a religious life for a student, even of theology. The mere fact that he is a student inhibits religion for him. That I am asked to speak to you on the religious life of the student of theology proceeds on the recognition of the absurdity of such antitheses. You are students of theology; and, just because you are students of theology, it is understood that you are religious men—especially religious men, to whom the cultivation of your religious life is a matter of the profoundest concern—of such concern that you will wish above all things to be warned of the dangers that may assail your religious life, and be pointed to the means by which you may strengthen and enlarge it. In your case there can be no "either-or" here—either a student or a man of God. You must be both.

Perhaps the intimacy of the relation between the work of a theological student and his religious life will nevertheless bear some emphasizing. Of course you do not think religion and study incompatible. But it is barely possible that there may be some among you who think of them too much apart—who are inclined to set their studies off to one side, and their religious life off to the other side, and to fancy that what is given to the one is taken from the other. No mistake could be more gross. Religion does not take a man away from his work; it sends him to his work with an added quality of devotion. We sing—do we not?—

> Teach me, my God and King,
> In all things Thee to see—
> And what I do in anything,
> To do it as for Thee.

> If done t' obey Thy laws,
> E'en servile labors shine,
> Hallowed is toil, if this the cause,
> The meanest work divine.

It is not just the way George Herbert wrote it. He put, perhaps, a sharper point on it. He reminds us that a man may look at his work as he looks at a pane of glass—either seeing nothing but the glass, or looking straight through the glass to the wide heavens beyond. And he tells us plainly that there is nothing so mean but that the great words "for thy sake" can glorify it:

> A servant, with this clause,
> Makes drudgery divine,
> Who sweeps a room as for Thy laws,
> Makes that, and the action, fine.

But the doctrine is the same, and it is the doctrine, the fundamental doctrine, of Protestant morality, from which the whole system of Christian ethics unfolds. It is the great doctrine of "vocation," the doctrine, to wit, that the best service we can offer to God is just to do our duty—our plain, homely duty, whatever that may chance to be. The Middle Ages did not think so; they cut a cleft between the religious and the secular life, and counseled him who wished to be religious to turn his back on what they called "the world," that is to say, not the wickedness that is in the world—"the world, the flesh and the devil," as we say—but the work-a-day world, that congeries of occupations which forms the daily task of men and women, who perform their duty to themselves and their fellowmen. Protestantism put an end to all that. As Professor Doumergue eloquently puts it, "Then Luther came, and, with still more consistency, Calvin, proclaiming the great idea of 'vocation,' an idea and a word which are found in the languages of all the Protestant peoples—*Beruf, Calling, Vocation*—and which are lacking in the languages of the peoples of antiquity and of medieval culture. 'Vocation'—it is the call of God, addressed to every man, whoever he may be, to lay upon him a particular work, no matter what. And the calls, and therefore also the called, stand on a complete equality with one another. The burgomaster is God's burgomaster; the physician is God's physician; the merchant is God's merchant; the laborer is God's laborer. Every vocation, liberal, as we call it, or manual, the humblest and the vilest in appearance as truly as the noblest and the most glorious, is of divine right." Talk of the divine right of kings! Here is the divine right of every workman, no one of whom needs to be ashamed, if only he is an honest and good workman. "Only laziness," adds Professor Doumergue, "is ignoble, and while Romanism multiplies its mendicant orders, the Reformation banishes the idle from its towns."

Now, as students of theology your vocation is to study theology; and to study it diligently, in accordance with the apostolic injunction:

"Whatsoever ye do, do it heartily, as to the Lord."[1] It is precisely for this that you are students of theology; this is your "next duty," and the neglect of duty is not a fruitful religious exercise. Dr. Charles Hodge, in his delightful autobiographical notes, tells of Philip Lindsay, the most popular professor in the Princeton College of his day—a man sought by nearly every college in the Central States for its presidency—that "he told our class that we would find that one of the best preparations for death was a thorough knowledge of the Greek grammar." "This," comments Dr. Hodge, in his quaint fashion, "was his way of telling us that we ought to do our duty." Certainly, every man who aspires to be a religious man must begin by doing his duty, his obvious duty, his daily task, the particular work which lies before him to do at this particular time and place. If this work happens to be studying, then his religious life depends on nothing more fundamentally than on just studying. You might as well talk of a father who neglects his parental duties, of a son who fails in all the obligations of filial piety, of an artisan who systematically skimps his work and turns in a bad job, of a workman who is nothing better than an eye-servant, being religious men as of a student who does not study being a religious man. It cannot be: You cannot build up a religious life except you begin by performing faithfully your simple, daily duties. It is not the question whether you like these duties. You may think of your studies what you please. You may consider that you are singing precisely of them when you sing of "e'en servile labors," and of "the meanest work." But you must faithfully give yourselves to your studies, if you wish to be religious men. No religious character can be built up on the foundation of neglected duty.

There is certainly something wrong with the religious life of a theological student who does not study. But it does not quite follow that therefore everything is right with his religious life if he does study. It is possible to study—even to study theology—in an entirely secular spirit. I said a little while ago that what religion does is to send a man to his work with an added quality of devotion. In saying that, I meant the word *devotion* to be taken in both its senses—in the sense of "zealous application," and in the sense of "a religious exercise," as the standard dictionary phrases the two definitions. A truly religious man will study anything which it becomes his duty to study with "devotion" in both of these senses. That is what his religion does for him: it makes him do his duty, do it thoroughly, do it "in the Lord." But in the case of many branches of study, there is nothing in the topics studied which tends directly to feed the religious life, or to set in movement the religious emotions, or to call out specifically religious reaction. If we study them "in the Lord," that is only because we do it "for his sake," on the principle which makes "sweeping a room" an act of worship. With theology it is not so. In all its branches alike, theology has as its unique end to make God known: The student of theology is brought by his daily task into the presence of God, and is kept there. Can a religious man stand in the presence of God, and not worship? It is possible, I have said, to study even theology in a purely secular spirit. But surely that is possible only for an irreligious man, or at least for an unreligious man. And here I place in your hands at once a touchstone by which you may discern your religious state, and an instrument for the quickening of your religious life. Do you prosecute your daily tasks as students of theology as "religious exercises"? If you do not, look to yourselves: It is surely not all right with the spiritual condition of that man who can busy himself daily with divine things, with a cold and impassive heart. If you do, rejoice. But in any case, see that you do! And that you do it ever more and more abundantly. Whatever you may have done in the past, for the future make all your theological studies "religious exercises." This is the great rule for a rich and wholesome religious life in a theological student. Put your heart into your studies; do not merely occupy your mind with them, but put your heart into them. They bring you daily and hourly into the very presence of God; his ways, his dealings with men, the infinite majesty of his Being form their very subject matter. Put the shoes from off your feet in this holy presence!

We are frequently told, indeed, that the great danger of the theological student lies precisely in his constant contact with divine things. They may come to seem common to him, because they are customary. As the average man breathes the air and basks in the sunshine without ever a thought that it is God in his goodness who makes his sun to rise on him, though he is evil, and sends rain to him, though he is unjust; so you may come to handle even the furniture of the sanctuary with never a thought above the gross earthly materials of which it is made. The words which tell you of God's terrible majesty or of his glorious goodness may come to be mere words to you—Hebrew and Greek words, with etymologies, and inflections, and connections in sentences. The reasonings which establish to you the mysteries of his saving activities may come to be to you mere logical paradigms, with premises and conclusions, fitly framed, no doubt, and triumphantly cogent, but with no further significance to you than their formal logical conclusiveness. God's stately stepping in his redemptive processes may become to you a mere series of facts of history, curiously interplaying to the production of social and religious conditions, and pointing mayhap to an issue which we may shrewdly conjecture: but much like other facts occurring in time and space, which may come to your notice. It *is* your great danger. But it is your great danger, only because it is your great privilege. Think of what your privilege is when your greatest danger is that the great things of religion may become common to you! Other men, oppressed by the hard conditions of life, sunk in the daily struggle for bread perhaps, distracted at any rate by the dreadful drag of the world upon them and the awful rush of the world's work, find it hard to get time and opportunity so much as to pause and consider whether there be such things as God, and religion, and salvation from the sin that compasses them about and holds them captive. The very atmosphere of your life is these things; you breathe them in at every pore; they surround you, encompass you, press in upon you from every side. It is all in danger of becoming common to you! God forgive you, you are in danger of becoming weary of God!

Do you know what this danger is? Or, rather, let us turn the question—are you alive to what your privileges are? Are you making full use of them? Are you, by this constant contact with divine things, growing in holiness, becoming every day more and more men of God? If not, you are hardening! And I am here today to warn you to take seriously your theological study, not merely as a duty, done for God's sake and therefore made divine, but as a religious exercise, itself charged with religious blessing to you; as fitted by its very nature to fill all your mind and heart and soul and life with divine thoughts and feelings and aspirations and achievements. You will never prosper in your religious life in the theological seminary until your work in the theological seminary becomes itself to you a religious exercise out of which you draw every day enlargement of heart, elevation of spirit, and adoring delight in your Maker and your Savior.

I am not counseling you, you will observe, to make your theological studies your sole religious exercises. They are religious exercises of the most rewarding kind; and your religious life will very much depend upon your treating them as such. But there are other religious exercises demanding your punctual attention which cannot be neglected without the gravest damage to your religious life. I refer particularly now to the stated formal religious meetings of the seminary. I wish to be perfectly explicit here, and very emphatic. No man can withdraw himself from the stated religious services of the community of which he is a member without serious injury to his personal religious life. It is not without significance that the apostolic writer couples together the exhortations to "hold fast the confession of our hope, that it waver not,"[2] and to forsake not "the assembling of ourselves together."[3] When he commands us not to forsake "the assembling of ourselves together," he has in mind, as the term he employs shows, the stated, formal assemblages of the community, and means to lay upon the hearts and consciences of his readers their duty to the church of which they are the supports, as well as their duty to themselves. And when he adds, "as the custom of some is," he means to put a lash into his command. We can see his lip curl as he says it. Who are these people, who are so vastly strong, so supremely holy, that they do not need the assistance of the common worship for themselves; and who, being so strong and holy, will not give their assistance to the common worship?

Needful as common worship is, however, for men at large, the need of it for men at large is as nothing compared with its needfulness for a body of young men situated as you are. You are gathered together here for a religious purpose, in preparation for the highest religious service which can be performed by men—the guidance of others in the religious life; and shall you have everything else in common except worship? You are gathered together here, separated from your homes and all that home means; from the churches in which you have been brought up, and all that church fellowship means; from all the powerful natural influences of social religion—and shall you not yourselves form a religious community, with its own organic religious life and religious expression? I say it deliberately, that a body of young men, living apart in a community life, as you are and must be living, cannot maintain a healthy, full, rich religious life individually, unless they are giving organic expression to their religious life as a community in frequent stated diets of common worship. Nothing can take the place of this common organic worship of the community as a community, at its stated seasons, and as a regular function of the corporate life of the community. Without it, you cease to be a religious community and lack that support and stay, that incitement and spur, that comes to the individual from the organic life of the community of which he forms a part.

In my own mind, I am quite clear that in an institution like this the whole body of students should come together, both morning and evening, every day, for common prayer and should join twice on every Sabbath in formal worship. Without at least this much common worship, I do not think the institution can preserve its character as a distinctively religious institution—an institution whose institutional life is primarily a religious one. And I do not think that the individual students gathered here can, with less full expression of the organic religious life of the institution, preserve the high level of religious life on which, as students of theology, they ought to live. You will observe that I am not merely exhorting you "to go to church." "Going to church" is in any case good. But what I am exhorting you to do is go to your own church—to give your presence and active religious participation to every stated meeting for worship of the institution as an institution. Thus you will do your part to give to the institution an organic religious life, and you will draw out from the organic religious life of the institution a support and inspiration for your own personal religious life which you can get nowhere else, and which you cannot afford to miss—if, that is, you have a care to your religious quickening and growth. To be an active member of a living religious body is the condition of healthy religious functioning.

I trust you will not tell me that the stated religious exercises of the seminary are too numerous, or are wearying. That would only be to betray the low ebb of your own religious vitality. The feet of him whose heart is warm with religious feeling turn of themselves to the sanctuary, and carry him with joyful steps to the house of prayer. I am told that there are some students who do not find themselves in a prayerful mood in the early hours of a winter morning, and are much too tired at the close of a hard day's work to pray, and therefore do not find it profitable to attend prayers in the late afternoon; who think the preaching at the regular service on Sabbath morning dull and uninteresting, and who do not find Christ at the Sabbath afternoon conference. Such things I seem to have heard before, and yours will be an exceptional pastorate if you do not hear something very much like them before you have been in a pastorate six months. Such things meet you every day on the street; they are the ordinary expression of the heart which is dulled or is dulling to the religious appeal. They are not hopeful symptoms among those whose life should be lived on the religious heights. No doubt, those who minister to you in spiritual things should take them to heart. And you who are ministered to must take them to heart, too. And let me tell you straight out that the preaching you find dull will no more seem dull to you if you faithfully obey the Master's precept: "Take heed [what] ye hear";[4] that if you do not find Christ in the conference room it is because you do not take him there with you; that, if after an ordinary day's work you are too weary to unite with your fellows in closing the day with common prayer, it is because the impulse to prayer is weak in your heart. If there is no fire in the pulpit it falls to you to kindle it in the pews. No man can fail to meet with God in the sanctuary if he takes God there with him.

How easy it is to roll the blame of our cold hearts over upon the shoulders of our religious leaders! It is refreshing to observe how Luther, with his breezy good sense, dealt with complaints of lack of attractiveness in his evangelical preachers. He had not sent them out to please people, he said, and their function was not to interest or to entertain; their function was to teach the saving truth of God, and, if they did that, it was frivolous for people in danger of perishing for want of the truth to object to the vessel in which it was offered to them. When the people of Torgau, for instance, wished to dismiss their pastors, because, they said, their voices were too weak to fill the churches, Luther simply responded, "That's an old song: better have some difficulty in hearing the gospel than no difficulty at all in hearing what is very far from the gospel." "People cannot have their ministers exactly as they wish," he declares again, "they should thank God for the pure word," and not demand St. Augustines and St. Ambroses to preach it to them. If a pastor pleases the

Lord Jesus and is faithful to him, there is none so great and mighty but he ought to be pleased with him, too. The point, you see, is that men who are hungry for the truth and get it ought not to be exigent as to the platter in which it is served to them. And they will not be.

But why should we appeal to Luther? Have we not the example of our Lord Jesus Christ? Are we better than He? Surely, if ever there was one who might justly plead that the common worship of the community had nothing to offer him it was the Lord Jesus Christ. But every Sabbath found Him seated in His place among the worshiping people, and there was no act of stated worship which He felt himself entitled to discard. Even in His most exalted moods, and after His most elevating experiences, He quietly took His place with the rest of God's people, sharing with them in the common worship of the community. Returning from that great baptismal scene, when the heavens themselves were rent to bear Him witness that He was well pleasing to God; from the searching trials of the wilderness, and from that first great tour in Galilee, prosecuted, as we are expressly told, "in the power of the Spirit"; He came back, as the record tells, "to Nazareth, where He had been brought up, and"—so proceeds the amazing narrative—"He entered, as His custom was, into the synagogue, on the Sabbath day."[5] "As His custom was!" Jesus Christ made it His habitual practice to be found in His place on the Sabbath day at the stated place of worship to which He belonged. "It is a reminder," as Sir William Robertson Nicoll well insists, "of the truth which, in our fancied spirituality, we are apt to forget—that the holiest personal life can scarcely afford to dispense with stated forms of devotion, and that the regular public worship of the church, for all its local imperfections and dullness, is a divine provision for sustaining the individual soul." "We cannot afford to be wiser than our Lord in this matter. If any one could have pled that his spiritual experience was so lofty that it did not require public worship, if any one might have felt that the consecration and communion of his personal life exempted him from what ordinary mortals needed, it was Jesus. But He made no such plea. Sabbath by Sabbath even He was found in the place of worship, side by side with God's people, not for the mere sake of setting a good example, but for deeper reasons. Is it reasonable, then, that any of us should think we can safely afford to dispense with the pious custom of regular participation with the common worship of our locality?" Is it necessary for me to exhort those who would fain be like Christ, to see to it that they are imitators of Him in this?

But not even with the most assiduous use of the corporate expressions of the religious life of the community have you reached the foundation-stone of your piety. That is to be found, of course, in your closets, or rather in your hearts, in your private religious exercises, and in your intimate religious aspirations. You are here as theological students; and if you would be religious men, you must do your duty as theological students; you must find daily nourishment for your religious life in your theological studies, you must enter fully into the organic religious life of the community of which you form a part. But to do all this, you must keep the fires of religious life burning brightly in your heart; in the inmost core of your being, you must be men of God. Time would fail me, if I undertook to outline with any fullness the method of the devout life. Every soul seeking God honestly and earnestly finds Him, and, in finding Him, finds the way to Him. One hint I may give you, particularly adapted to you as students for the ministry: Keep always before your mind the greatness of your calling, that is to say, these two things: the immensity of the task before you, the infinitude of the resources at your disposal. I think it has not been idly said, that if we face the tremendous difficulty of the work before us, it will certainly throw us back upon our knees; and if we worthily gauge the power of the gospel committed to us, that will certainly keep us on our knees. I am led to single out this particular consideration because it seems to me that we have fallen upon an age in which we very greatly need to recall ourselves to the seriousness of life and its issues, and to the seriousness of our calling as ministers to life. Sir Oliver Lodge informs us that "men of culture are not bothering," nowadays, "about their sin, much less about their punishment," and Dr. Johnston Ross preaches us a much needed homily from that text on the "lightheartedness of the modern religious quest." In a time like this, it is perhaps not strange that careful observers of the life of our theological seminaries tell us that the most noticeable thing about it is a certain falling off from the intense seriousness of outlook by which students of theology were formerly characterized. Let us hope it is not true. If it were true, it would be a great evil; so far as it is true, it is a great evil. I would call you back to this seriousness of outlook, and bid you cultivate it, if you would be men of God now, and ministers who need not be ashamed hereafter. Think of the greatness of the minister's calling; the greatness of the issues which hang on your worthiness or your unworthiness for its high functions; and determine once for all that with God's help you will be worthy. "God had but one Son," says Thomas Goodwin, "and He made Him a minister." "None but He who made the world," says John Newton, "can make a minister"—that is, a minister who is worthy.

You can, of course, be a minister of a sort, and not be God-made. You can go through the motions of the work, and I shall not say that your work will be in vain—for God is good and who knows by what instruments He may work His will of good for men? Helen Jackson pictures far too common an experience when she paints the despair of one whose sowing, though not unfruitful for others, bears no harvest in his own soul.

> O teacher, then I said, thy years,
>   Are they not joy? each word that issueth
> From out thy lips, doth it return to bless
>   Thine own heart manyfold?

Listen to the response:

> I starve with hunger treading out their corn,
>   I die of travail while their souls are born.

She does not mean it in quite the evil part in which I am reading it. But what does Paul mean when he utters that terrible warning: "Lest . . . when I have preached to others, I myself should be a castaway?"[6] And there is an even more dreadful contingency. It is our Savior Himself who tells us that it is possible to compass sea and land to make one proselyte, and when we have made him [so,] to make him twofold more a child of hell than we are ourselves.[7] And will we not be in awful peril of making our proselytes children of hell if we are not ourselves children of heaven? Even physical waters will not rise above their source: The spiritual floods are even less tractable to our commands. There is no mistake more terrible than to suppose that activity in Christian work can take the place of depth of Christian affections.

This is the reason why many good men are shaking their heads a little today over a tendency which they fancy they see increasing among our younger Christian workers to restless activity at the apparent expense of depth of spiritual culture. Activity, of course, is good: Surely in the cause of the Lord we should run and not be weary. But not when it is substituted for inner religious strength. We cannot get along without our Marthas. But what shall we do when, through all the length and breadth of the land, we shall search in vain for a Mary? Of course, the Marys will be as little admired by the Marthas today as of yore. "Lord," cried Martha, "dost thou not care that my sister hath left me to serve alone?"[8] And from that time to this the cry has continually gone up against the Marys that they waste the precious ointment which might have been given to the poor, when they pour it out to God, and are idle when they sit at the Master's feet. A minister, high in the esteem of the churches, is even quoted as declaring—not confessing, mind you, but publishing abroad as something in which he gloried—that he has long since ceased to pray: He *works*. "Work and pray" is no longer, it seems, to be the motto of at least ministerial life. It is to be all work and no praying; the only prayer that is prevailing, we are told, with the same cynicism with which we are told that God is on the side of the largest battalions—is just work. You will say this is an extreme case. Thank God, it is. But in the tendencies of our modern life, which all make for ceaseless—I had almost said thoughtless, meaningless—activity, have a care that it does not become your case; or that your case—even now—may not have at least some resemblance to it. Do you pray? How much do you pray? How much do you love to pray? What place in your life does the "still hour," alone with God, take?

I am sure that if you once get a true glimpse of what the ministry of the cross is, for which you are preparing, and of what you, as men preparing for this ministry, should be, you will pray, "Lord, who is sufficient for these things?" Your heart will cry, and your whole soul will be wrung with the petition, "Lord, make me sufficient for these things."

Old Cotton Mather wrote a great little book once to serve as a guide to students for the ministry. The not very happy title which he gave it is *Manductio ad Ministerium.*[9] But by a stroke of genius he added a subtitle which is more significant. And this is the subtitle he added: *The angels preparing to sound the trumpets.* That is what Cotton Mather calls you, students for the ministry: the angels, preparing to sound the trumpets! Take the name to yourselves, and live up to it. Give your days and nights to living up to it! And then, perhaps, when you come to sound the trumpets the note will be pure and clear and strong, and perchance may pierce even to the grave and wake the dead.

Endnotes

1. Colossians 3:23 (KJV).
2. Hebrews 10:23 (ASV).
3. Hebrews 10:25 (KJV).
4. Mark 4:24 (ASV).
5. Luke 4:16 (ASV).
6. 1 Corinthians 9:27 (KJV).
7. Matthew 23:15 (paraphrased).
8. Luke 10:40 (KJV).
9. Cotton Mather, *Manductio ad Ministerium: The angels preparing to sound the trumpets* (Boston: Thomas Porter, 1726).

CHAPTER TWO

Rediscovering Pastoral Ministry

Richard L. Mayhue

Current unbiblical changes that are beginning to overtake the church could negatively mark the twenty-first-century church if they continue unchecked. A growing number of respected evangelicals believe that the contemporary redirection of the church toward being less biblical and more acceptable to society ultimately will lead to a Christ-condemned church. However, by using Scripture to answer the questions "What is a pastor to be and do?" and "How can contemporary ministry be shaped by biblical mandates?" the church can be revived and obediently realign herself with God's revealed purposes for the bride of Christ. Thus, it is possible to achieve a biblically balanced, complementary relationship for understanding God's will for the church, engaging in relevant pastoral ministry, and preparing a new generation of pastors for ministry as outlined by God's Word.

This essay, in a slightly different form, appears in John F. MacArthur Jr., *Rediscovering Pastoral Ministry* (Dallas: Word, 1995), 3–18. It is used by permission. Quotations are from the *New American Standard Bible* unless otherwise noted.

* * * * *

Crossroads. Transition. Crisis. Uncertainty. Restlessness.

These unsettling words express the pessimistic perception voiced by many evangelicals regarding the immediate state of the church and pastoral ministry. Few would disagree that a call for redirection is necessary for the evangelical church as the twenty-first century has begun. However, no current consensus exists on which route the church should take to get back on track.

Consider, for example, John Seel's 1992 survey of twenty-five prominent evangelical leaders.[1] The leaders expressed their less-than-optimistic views on the general state of American evangelicalism at the end of the twentieth century. Eight dominant themes emerged from their responses:

1. Uncertain identity—A widespread confusion over what defines an evangelical.
2. Institutional disenchantment—A perceived ministry ineffectiveness and irrelevance.
3. Lack of leadership—A lament over the paucity of leadership in the church.
4. Pessimism about the future—A belief that the future of evangelicalism hangs in the balance.
5. Growth up, impact down—A confusing paradox without immediate clear explanations.
6. Cultural isolation—A complete arrival of the post-Christian era.
7. Belief that political and methodological responses provide the solution—A drift toward unbiblical approaches to ministry.
8. Shift from truth-orientation to market-response ministry—A redirection away from the eternal and toward the temporal to be viewed as relevant.

David F. Wells has reached essentially the same conclusion:

I have written this book because, like the students who participated in our survey, I believe the vision of the evangelical church is now clouded, its internal life greatly weakened, its future very uncertain, and I want something better for it. I want the evangelical church to be *the church*. I want it to embody a vibrant spirituality. I want the church to be an alternative to postmodern culture, not a mere echo of it. I want a church that is bold to be different and unafraid to be faithful, a church that is interested in something better than using slick marketing techniques to swell the numbers of warm bodies occupying sanctuaries, a church that reflects an integral and undiminished confidence in the power of God's Word, a church that can find in the midst of our present cultural breakdown the opportunity to be God's people in a world that has abandoned God.

To be the church in this way, it is also going to have to find in the coming generation leaders who exemplify this hope for its future and who will devote themselves to seeing it realized. To lead the church in the way that it needs to be led, they will have to rise above the internal politics of the evangelical world and refuse to accept the status quo where that no longer serves the vital interests of the kingdom of God. They will have to decline to spend themselves in the building of their own private kingdoms and refuse to be intimidated into giving the church less and other than what it needs. Instead, they will have to begin to build afresh, in cogently biblical ways, among the decaying structures that now clutter the evangelical landscape. To succeed, they will have to be people of large vision, people of courage, people who have learned again what it means to live by the Word of God, and, most importantly, what it means to live before the holy God of that Word.[2]

The Master's Seminary acknowledges these alarming trends, believing that decisions made now and in the near future will reshape the American evangelical church for much of the present century. Thus, the future direction of the contemporary church is a legitimate, preeminent consideration. Unquestionably, the twenty-first-century church faces a defining moment.[3] The real contrast in competing ministry models, however, is not the "traditional" versus the "contemporary" but rather the *scriptural* in contrast to the *unscriptural*.

The Moment of Decision

Having arrived at the proverbial "fork in the road," evangelicals must decide between two alternatives. The first is an approach to ministry that is characteristically, but not exclusively, need based, man centered, consumer driven, and culturally defined. These emphases generally depend on and change with the latest directions in the behavioral sciences, which, after attempted integration as alleged coequals with Scripture, supposedly provide a scientifically validated, relevant ministry for our contemporary computer/media-oriented society.

The second option features a God-focused, redemptively centered, biblically defined, and scripturally prioritized ministry. The Master's Seminary champions this latter model, which looks to the sufficiency of Scripture as the revelation of past, present, and future works of God the Father, God the Son, and God the Holy Spirit, which have the utmost relevance—now and forever. The church must look to the Scriptures and address the challenge of "shaping contemporary ministry with biblical mandates."

Arguably, no other time in church history has more closely approximated the first-century beginnings of the church than the present. Our ancient brethren faced a pagan, pre-Christian, and premodern culture. Similarly, the contemporary church encounters a pagan, post-Christian, and postmodern world. The essential biblical model of ministry of the first century has never been more appropriate than it is today.

This essay attempts to balance the tensions between temporal and eternal considerations and between divine and human factors in ministry. God's character, revelation, and will have not changed, although time and culture have. How should a balanced ministry reconcile the two sides? We reason that the timeless should define any particular moment in time, not the reverse. Christ has been and will remain the Chief Shepherd (1 Peter 5:4), the Good Shepherd (John 10:11, 14), and the Great Shepherd (Heb. 13:20). Pastors will always be His undershepherds and laborers in the church, which He purchased with His own precious blood (Acts 20:28) and continues to build (Matt. 16:18).

Pastors assume a huge responsibility when they accept the overwhelming task of exhorting and reproving on Christ's behalf (Titus 1:9). Paul's word about this stewardship to the Corinthian church almost two thousand years ago is sobering:

Let a man regard us in this manner, as servants of Christ, and
stewards of the mysteries of God. In this case, moreover, it is
required of stewards that one be found trustworthy. But to me
it is a very small thing that I should be examined by you, or by
any human court; in fact, I do not even examine myself. I am
conscious of nothing against myself, yet I am not by this acquitted; but the one who examines me is the Lord. Therefore
do not go on passing judgment before the time, but wait until
the Lord comes who will both bring to light the things hidden
in the darkness and disclose the motives of men's hearts; and
then each man's praise will come to him from God (1 Cor.
4:1–5).

The twenty-first-century church generally and pastors particularly face
the following very crucial questions. What is the pastor to be and do?
How should the church respond to a rapidly changing culture? What
does God consider relevant? How concerned is Christ with the traditional and/or the contemporary? Are the Scriptures an adequate basis of
ministry today? What are a pastor's ministry priorities? Under whose
authority does a pastor stand? How shall we distinguish between the
God-called pastor and the counterfeit? Who defines the need for ministry—God or men? What direction does Christ want for His church in the
twenty-first century? And foremost, when we stand before the Lord of
glory and give account of our stewardship, what will we say and, far
more importantly, what will *He* say?

We submit that God will use His Word as the benchmark by which He
commends or condemns our labors in His church. He will not inquire
whether a ministry was "traditional" or "contemporary" but will ask,
"Was it biblical?" Our ministry will be either in accord with His will or
contrary to it. This Scripture expresses Christ's reference point for rightly
building the church: "All Scripture is inspired by God and profitable for
teaching, for reproof, for correction, for training in righteousness; that
the man of God may be adequate, equipped for every good work" (2 Tim.
3:16–17).

The Church on the Wrong Way

We could reasonably expect that after two thousand years of existence, the church should know and understand exactly what God intended
her to be. Yet just the opposite seems to be true.[4]

Apparently, the way of religion in American culture has become the
way of the church—a wrong way. Jeffery Sheler concludes that culture
is having its sway with Christianity instead of Christianity having a more
decided influence on culture:

> The social critics among us, and the consciences within us, in-
> creasingly wonder if we have lost our moral compass and for-
> saken our spiritual heritage. Yale professor Stephen Carter, in
> his recent book, *The Culture of Disbelief,* blames this cultural
> decay on what he believes has been a growing exclusion of reli-
> gion from public life. "We have pressed the religiously faithful
> . . . to act as though their faith does not matter," Carter argues.[5]

Francis Schaeffer called this phenomenon "the great evangelical disaster." He succinctly summarized the situation as follows:

> Here is the great evangelical disaster—the failure of the evan-
> gelical world to stand for truth as truth. There is only one word
> for this—namely *accommodation:* the evangelical church has
> accommodated to the world spirit of the age. First, there has
> been accommodation on Scripture, so that many who call them-
> selves evangelicals hold a weakened view of the Bible and no
> longer affirm the truth of all the Bible teaches—truth not only in
> religious matters but in the areas of science and history and
> morality. As part of this, many evangelicals are now accepting
> the higher critical methods in the study of the Bible. Remember,
> it was these same methods which destroyed the authority of the
> Bible for the Protestant church in Germany in the last century,
> and which have destroyed the Bible for the liberal in our own
> country from the beginning of the century. And second, there
> has been accommodation on the issues, with no clear stand be-
> ing taken even on matters of life and death.[6]

Encouragingly, in recent years we have seen an increase in the number of books calling the church back to the primacy of God and Scripture. They strongly warn that the church is slowly but surely being culturalized. For example, David F. Wells, the Andrew Mutch Professor of Historical and Systematic Theology at Gordon-Conwell Theological Seminary, recently wrote a landmark analysis of American evangelicalism in the 1990s in which he notes,

> The disappearance of theology from the life of the Church, and the orchestration of that disappearance by some of its leaders, is hard to miss today but, oddly enough, not easy to prove. It is hard to miss in the evangelical world, in the vacuous worship that is so prevalent, for example, in the shift from God to self as the central focus of faith, in the psychologized preaching that follows this shift, in the erosion of its conviction, in its strident pragmatism, in its inability to think incisively about the culture, in its reveling in the irrational.[7]

Wells argues that the influential and liberal preacher Harry Emerson Fosdick popularized the twentieth-century ministry philosophy that begins with man's needs rather than God's will.[8] He traces the lineage forward to Norman Vincent Peale and then to Robert Schuller.[9] Furthermore, Schuller seems to have significantly influenced Bill Hybels, currently the most visible evangelical proponent of a "church the unchurched" philosophy of ministry.[10] In a sense, Fosdick's philosophy of ministry lives on long after his death.

Noted historian George Marsden warns evangelicals of the encroachments of humanism on the church. He concludes that "while fundamentalists and their evangelical heirs have erected doctrinal barriers against theological liberalism, more subtle versions of similar sub-Christian values have infiltrated behind their lines."[11]

John MacArthur sees the church becoming like the world.[12] In a positively provocative fashion, he compares the many similarities between the decline of the church in England during Spurgeon's time a century ago and the faltering American church in our day. MacArthur notes the parallel path and common distinction of spiritual deadness shared by the liberal modernists of a century ago and evangelical pragmatists today. They both have an unhealthy aversion to doctrine.

Os Guinness provides several probing analyses of the modern church and evangelicals.[13] They include *The Gravedigger File, No God but God,* and *Dining with the Devil.* In these three works, he writes about the secularization of the church, idolatry in the church, and the modern church growth movement, respectively.

"Selling Out the House of God?," a recent *Christianity Today* interview of Bill Hybels, illustrates the tensions existing in today's church.[14] The increase of hard, probing questions that pastors want to ask this very visible, "consumer-oriented" church pastor about his ministry basis and style occasioned the article. Our fear is that if the next generation takes the path that Hybels now travels, it eventually will arrive at the same destination as the modernist movement did earlier in the twentieth century in America.

Consider the following recent warning:

> Evangelical pastors and theologians can learn from the mainline experience of placing relevance above truth. We must avoid the lure of novelty and soft sell, which, we are told, will make it easier for moderns to believe. Methods may change, but never the message. . . . We are called to be faithful stewards of a great and reliable theological heritage. We have truths to affirm and errors to avoid. We must not try to make these truths more appealing or user friendly by watering them down. We must guard against a trendy "theological bungee-jumping" that merely entertains the watching crowd.[15]

Interestingly, this clear call to a biblically sound ministry does not come from the conservative wing of evangelism. Rather, it is a warning to evangelical churches from one who is attempting to bring revival within the liberal, mainline United Methodist Church. He cautions the church to avoid the "user friendly" route of church ministry because the end is predictable: Within a generation or two, churches will lose their spiritual direction and life.

Identity Crisis

As a result of a confusing maze of cultural attractions, the natural corollary to the church's spiritually disastrous detour from the biblical mainstream is a corresponding loss of pastoral identity and consequent debate over how to revise ministerial training. Not surprisingly then, as the church succumbs to cultural and secular pressures, biblically defined pastoral roles and the Scripture-oriented content of ministerial training have experienced a serious challenge also.

Pastoral Identity

This confusion is not entirely new to the church. As early as the first century, Paul felt compelled to articulate carefully the role of the pastor. All succeeding generations have experienced this tension too, with the corresponding need to reaffirm the biblical absolutes of ministry. Culbertson and Shippee notice this ongoing tension:

> Pastoral theology is for the most part a field without a clear definition: its precise meaning and component parts seem to vary widely from one denomination to the next and from one seminary to the next. The how-to of pastoral care and the component elements in the process of clergy character formation seem to be equally slippery. In all three fields, however, constitutive material seems to be taught either from a strictly scriptural base, or from a base of modern psychological and sociological theory as it has been appropriated by the church, or through a combination of Scripture and modern scientific insight—but rarely does the teaching of pastoral formation make direct reference to the fascinating history and tradition of the early church.[16]

H. Richard Niebuhr documented the confusion that prevailed during the early and middle twentieth century.[17] Thomas Oden updated the dilemma into the 1980s.[18] He laments that the entire twentieth century has evidenced confusion over the role of the church and the pastor.[19] Oden strongly calls for a return to Scripture to understand the pastoral office and role:

Scripture provides the primary basis for understanding the pastoral office and its functions. We will treat Scripture as the church's book, rather than as the exclusive turf of the historian or social theorist. Pastoral wisdom has lived out of the key *locus classicus* texts that have enjoyed a rich history of interpretation long before the advent of modern historical research. We are free to learn from and use that research without being handcuffed by some of its reductionist assumptions.

Pastoral theology lives out of Scripture. When the pastoral tradition has quoted Scripture, it has viewed it as an authoritative text for shaping both its understanding and its practice of ministry. We do not put Scripture under our examination, according to criteria alien to it, in order to understand ministry. Rather, Scripture examines our prior understandings of ministry. It puts them to the test.[20]

Ministerial Training

Redefining the church inevitably leads to redefining the pastoral role. The latter reorientation then spills over into pastoral training at the seminary level. Predictably, a seemingly endless flood of current literature is calling for radical restructuring of seminary education.

In 1990, *The Atlantic* published a striking general assessment of American seminaries. This comprehensive study concluded,

If they are to succeed, this generation of seminarians must, of course, be educationally and spiritually sound, politically aware, as conversant with demography as they are with morality. They must be sensitive to race, ethnicity, gender, and sexuality, but they must not drive us up still another wall with their convictions. We have been flogged enough; we know our shortcomings. When our future clerics speak, we want to hear powerful yet measured voices bringing out the moral dimension of life, and not only the politics of the left wing of the Democratic Party or the right of the Republican, masquerading as religious belief.

We want them to be people who in some tiny way reflect the mercy and goodness of God we want to know, not only His judgment. We want them to be people who see the goodness in us that we have yet to unleash, the potential within us to transcend our differences. In the end, I think, we are looking for those who will help us find that voice deep within us which is not our own, but calls us to do what is right.[21]

"Consumer appeal" in both ministry and pastoral training clearly marks the conclusion to this quoted article and reflects much of the current literature.

A 1993 study commissioned by seven well-known American seminaries concluded,

The church, in order to maintain relevancy to its constituency, has had to devise new ways of doing ministry or be faced with closing the doors. . . . This report . . . calls for a major restructuring of the seminary—form and function.[22]

If we carry the consumer paradigm to its logical conclusion, it will be brilliantly consistent with prevailing contemporary theories but sadly unscriptural. In effect, it reasons, "What the people want, the church should provide. What the church provides, pastors should be trained to deliver." Taking it one step further, the ultimate result will be that "what pastors are trained to deliver (i.e., what the people want), the church will provide. When the church provides what the people want, people will want more." This approach eventually will create a virtually unstoppable cause-and-effect cycle that will render the American church impotent and thus condemned by Christ.

However, before seminaries capitulate, they should study the history of seminaries and seminary education in America. Notable among many such seminaries are Andover Seminary and Princeton Seminary, founded in 1807 and 1812, respectively.[23] Both started strong with seemingly unshakable biblical foundations, but with time and for various reasons, each succumbed to the demand to go beyond the Scriptures for both their doctrine and their practice. Conservatives agree that both schools long ago outlived their usefulness to the gospel ministry because they shifted away from their initial high view of God and the Scriptures.

Any given seminary might effectively change many things to make itself more useful to the church and ultimately the cause of Christ, but its emphasis upon biblical truth as the core of the curriculum should never change. David Dockery, former vice president for Academic Administration at Southern Seminary, recently summarized seminary education for a new century thus:

> We want to be able to teach the Scriptures in a creative and relevant way that models for our students that the Bible is normative and authoritative for the contemporary church—for their lives individually and for the church corporately. The Bible is an ancient document that is written to specific people in specific times in specific context. It nevertheless transcends those times and contexts because it is inspired by the Spirit of God, so it is both a divine and human document. It is a time-related document as well as an eternal document. Therefore, it speaks beyond its context and we want faculty who live out of deep commitment to the full truthfulness and complete authority of God's inspired word.
>
> Biblical authority is a much maligned and misunderstood concept in our contemporary world. People ask how can you believe that a book written 2,000 years ago has authority and relevance where we are now? The answer is because of its source. Its source is not just in the prophets and the apostles; it is in God Himself, who has actually breathed out this Word to us to study, to believe, and obey.[24]

Taking a Biblical Approach

At The Master's Seminary, we unequivocally believe that Paul made an absolute assertion with undeniable implications when he wrote to Timothy, "All Scripture is inspired by God and profitable for teaching, for reproof, for correction, for training in righteousness; that the man of God may be adequate, equipped for every good work" (2 Tim. 3:16–17). This passage teaches not only a high view of Scripture's authority but also its sufficiency, especially in formulating ministry plans and priorities. It demands that we begin with God and the Bible rather than man and culture to understand God's will in ministry.

The ministry tensions, problems, and questions that our generation faces are not new, as these biblical examples indicate. Malachi indicted Israel because they exchanged the glory of God for the way of the culture. Paul confronted the Corinthians, and Christ condemned the Laodicean elders. Jeremiah and Ezekiel warned against the proliferation of false shepherds in the OT, as did Peter and Jude in the New.

The contemporary pastor must pay close attention to the lessons of biblical history, for they will surely be repeated in his generation. Therefore when we ask, "What is a pastor to be and do?" we must look to God's Word for answers and not to the latest fads or theories that find their source more in society rather than in Scripture, or primarily in culture and not in Christ.

To be biblically specific, God has given several defining passages explaining who a pastor is to be and what a pastor is to do (e.g., 1 Timothy 3:1–7; Titus 1:6–9; and 1 Peter 5:1–5). But perhaps the most explicit books in the NT regarding the work of the ministry are 1 and 2 Thessalonians. A careful analysis of these "pastoral" epistles leads to this basic "ministry description." A pastor's primary activities include the following:

1. Praying	1 Thessalonians 1:2–3; 3:9–13
2. Evangelizing	1 Thessalonians 1:4–5, 9–10
3. Equipping	1 Thessalonians 1:6–8
4. Defending	1 Thessalonians 2:1–6
5. Loving	1 Thessalonians 2:7–8
6. Laboring	1 Thessalonians 2:9
7. Modeling	1 Thessalonians 2:10
8. Leading	1 Thessalonians 2:11–12
9. Feeding	1 Thessalonians 2:13
10. Watching	1 Thessalonians 3:1–8
11. Warning	1 Thessalonians 4:1–8
12. Teaching	1 Thessalonians 4:9–5:11
13. Exhorting	1 Thessalonians 5:12–24
14. Encouraging	2 Thessalonians 1:3–12
15. Correcting	2 Thessalonians 2:1–12
16. Confronting	2 Thessalonians 3:6, 14
17. Rescuing	2 Thessalonians 3:15

Paul exemplifies the *character* of a pastor and how that character relates to ministry *conduct* (1 Thess. 2:1–6). He describes the *nature* of pastoral leadership in terms of a mother (2:7–8), a laborer (2:9), a family member (2:10), and a father (2:11–12). Although these texts do not exhaust the subject, they unmistakably point to Scripture as the appropriate source from which to answer contemporary questions about ministry.

Christ's letters to the seven churches in Revelation 2–3 raise the relevant question, "If Christ were to write a letter to the American church in 2001, what would He say?" Although this inquiry is purely hypothetical and will not happen because the time of written, divine revelation has passed, the first-century truths of Revelation 2–3 are still applicable to the twenty-first-century church because they represent the unchanging mind of Christ regarding His church. We know both what He would *commend* and what He would *condemn*.

The bottom line is simply this: Will we seek to be fruitful in ministry by depending on the power of God's Word (Rom. 1:16–17; 1 Cor. 1:22–25; 1 Thess. 2:13) and God's Spirit (Rom. 15:13; 2 Tim. 1:8) or on the power of man's wisdom? Consider how Paul instructed the Corinthian church, whose curious preoccupation with their culture paralleled the contemporary evangelical church's comparable fascination:

> For consider your call, brethren, that there were not many wise according to the flesh, not many mighty, not many noble; but God has chosen the foolish things of the world to shame the wise, and God has chosen the weak things of the world to shame the things which are strong, and the base things of the world and the despised, God has chosen, the things that are not, that He might nullify the things that are, that no man should boast before God. But by His doing you are in Christ Jesus, who became to us wisdom from God, and righteousness and sanctification, and redemption, that, just as it is written, "Let him who boasts, boast in the Lord" (1 Cor. 1:26–31).

Rediscovering Pastoral Ministry

The Master's Seminary remains convinced that God's Word provides the timeless defining paradigm for the nature and particulars of pastoral ministry. Scripture outlines what God wants a pastor to be and what God wants a pastor to do. Contemporary ministry in any generation should be shaped by biblical mandates.

We set before our peers the assertion that Christ must build His church His way (Matt. 16:18).[25] If we desire to see God-pleasing fruit in our ministry, it must come from planting the good seed of God's Word in the rich soil of diligent pastoral labor according to the Scriptures.

For those who would question the content or conclusions of this essay, please do not misinterpret the preceding discussion. The statements in this essay are *not* calling for

- a user-*unfriendly* church,
- a culturally *ignorant* church, or
- a seeker-*insensitive* church.

We have no desire to *"unchurch the unchurched"* or to promote an irrelevant dinosaur of a church.

On the other hand, neither do we want to substitute the latest theories in sociology and psychology for the truth of Scripture. We do not want to confuse the common sense benefit of demographic statistics and analysis of culture with the far more important understanding of God's will for the church—for both Christians and non-Christians. We ardently desire to let the important consideration—God and His revealed will in Scripture—be the major focus.

A significant segment of evangelical churches and a growing proportion of evangelical literature seem to be distancing themselves from biblical priorities. Unbiblical imbalances among contemporary evangelicals are showing up in the following growing tendencies:

1. overemphasis on man's reasoning and a corresponding underemphasis on God's revelation in Scripture,
2. overemphasis on human need as defined by man and a corresponding underemphasis on God's definition of man's need,
3. overemphasis on earthly relevance and a corresponding underemphasis on spiritual relevance,

4. overemphasis on the temporal side of life and a corresponding underemphasis on the eternal, and
5. overemphasis on satisfying contemporary culture and a corresponding underemphasis on God's pleasure.

Because of these escalating trends, the church is increasingly in danger of equating religion with Christianity and "going to church" with salvation. The church increasingly substitutes human power for God's power and replaces talk that centers on God directly with mere peripheral talk about Him. The church increasingly confuses emotion with worship in spirit and truth and looks toward the cleverness of man's words rather than the power of the gospel. If the evangelical church remains on its present course, we fear that the next generation may, by popular demand, replace true Christianity with an impotent, idolatrous religion, as did the ancient churches of Pergamum, Thyatira, Sardis, and Laodicea.

More could be written on these present dangers and deceits facing the evangelical church and ministry. However, we conclude by urging all of Christendom, both in America and around the world, to rediscover pastoral ministry as outlined in Scripture. Here you will find ministry that is biblically based, *not* demographically defined; Spirit led, *not* market driven; Christ centered, *not* man directed; and God focused, *not* consumer oriented.

Being About the Father's Business

As Jesus engaged in His Father's work, so must we. An anonymous writer vividly captured the essence of pastoral stewardship before the Lord with the following exhortation to do God's work God's way according to God's Word:

> Stick with your work. Do not flinch because the lion roars; do not stop to stone the devil's dogs; do not fool away your time chasing the devil's rabbits. Do your work. Let liars lie, let sectarians quarrel, let critics malign, let enemies accuse, let the devil do his worst; but see to it nothing hinders you from fulfilling with joy the work God has given you.

He has not commanded you to be admired or esteemed. He has never bidden you defend your character. He has not set you at work to contradict falsehood (about yourself) which Satan's or God's servants may start to peddle, or to track down every rumor that threatens your reputation. If you do these things, you will do nothing else; you will be at work for yourself and not for the Lord.

Keep at your work. Let your aim be as steady as a star. You may be assaulted, wronged, insulted, slandered, wounded and rejected, misunderstood, or assigned impure motives; you may be abused by foes, forsaken by friends, and despised and rejected of men. But see to it with steadfast determination, with unfaltering zeal, that you pursue the great purpose of your life and object of your being until at last you can say, "I have finished the work which *Thou* gavest me to do."

Endnotes

1. John Seel, *The Evangelical Forfeit* (Grand Rapids: Baker, 1993), 48–65.
2. David F. Wells, *God in the Wasteland* (Grand Rapids: Eerdmans, 1994), 214–15; cf. Charles Haddon Spurgeon, "The Evils of the Present Time," in *An All-Round Ministry* (1900; reprint, Pasadena, Tex.: Pilgrim, 1983), 282–314.
3. Four of the top five books in *Christianity Today's* "Reader's Choice" Book-of-the-Year survey addressed these issues with a strong call for a return to a God-centered, biblically based ministry ("1994 Book Awards," *Christianity Today* 38, no. 4 [4 April 1994]: 39). These four books are Charles Colson, *The Body* (Dallas: Word, 1992); David F. Wells, *No Place for Truth or Whatever Happened to Evangelical Theology* (Grand Rapids: Eerdmans, 1993); John F. MacArthur Jr., *Ashamed of the Gospel: When the Church Becomes Like the World* (Wheaton: Crossway, 1993); Hank Hanegraaff, *Christianity in Crisis* (Eugene, Ore.: Harvest House, 1993).
4. This confusion is not as apparent when one reads standard theology offerings or specific volumes dealing with the theology of the church, such as Gene A. Getz, *Sharpening the Focus of the Church* (Chicago: Moody, 1974); Alfred F. Kuen, *I Will Build My Church* (Chicago: Moody, 1971); John F. MacArthur Jr., *Body Dynamics* (Wheaton: Victor, 1982); Earl D. Radmacher, *What the Church Is All About* (Chicago: Moody, 1978). The problem arises in volumes that deal with translating one's theology into contemporary practices in the church or in those that ignore Scripture when establishing practices in the church.

5. Jeffery L. Sheler, "Spiritual America," *U.S. News and World Report* 116, no. 13 (4 April 1994): 48.

6. Francis A. Schaeffer, *The Great Evangelical Disaster* (Westchester, Ill.: Crossway, 1984), 37. Also see Harold Lindsell, *The New Paganism* (San Francisco: Harper and Row, 1987), 211–32, in which he asserts that the West is now in a "post-Christian" era of paganism and then discusses the role of the church in this type of culture. For a decisive analysis of the battle between fundamentalism and liberalism in the early 1900s, see J. Gresham Machen, *Christianity and Liberalism* (1923; reprint, Grand Rapids: Eerdmans, 1992). George Marsden, *Understanding Fundamentalism and Evangelicalism* (Grand Rapids: Eerdmans, 1991), provides a historical background to Machen's era. James Davison Hunter, *Evangelicalism: The Coming Generation* (Chicago: University of Chicago, 1987), discusses the profile of late twentieth-, early twenty-first-century evangelicalism. For further reading, consult John Fea, "American Fundamentalism and Neo-Evangelicalism: A Bibliographic Survey," *Evangelical Journal* 11, no. 1 (spring 1993): 21–30.

7. Wells, *No Place for Truth*, 95.

8. Ibid., 178. It is most interesting that Leith Anderson et al., *Who's in Charge?* (Portland, Ore.: Multnomah, 1992), 100, identifies Fosdick as his mentor. Anderson, who is widely read and respected by a large segment of evangelicalism, also points to Fosdick as a preaching model in *A Church for the 21st Century* (Minneapolis: Bethany, 1992), 213–14.

9. Ibid.

10. Bill Hybels on several occasions has been a prominent speaker at Robert Schuller's institutes for pastors. Like Fosdick, Hybels has a penchant for "needs based" preaching to reach the consumer in the pew as is evident in Bill Hybels, et al., *Mastering Contemporary Preaching* (Portland, Ore.: Multnomah, 1989), 27.

11. George Marsden, "Secular Humanism Within the Church," *Christianity Today* 30, no. 1 (17 January 1986): 14I–15I.

12. MacArthur, *Ashamed of the Gospel*. Almost two decades ago, MacArthur wrote of the dangers then facing the church in "Church Faces Identity Crisis," *Moody Monthly* 79, no. 6 (February 1979): 123–26.

13. Os Guinness, *The Gravedigger File* (Downers Grove, Ill.: InterVarsity, 1983); Os Guinness and John Seel, eds., *No God but God* (Chicago: Moody, 1992); and Os Guinness, *Dining with the Devil* (Grand Rapids: Baker, 1993).

14. Michael G. Maudlin and Edward Gilbreath, "Selling Out the House of God?" *Christianity Today* 38, no. 8 (18 July 1994): 20–25. Contrast Hybels's approach with the far more biblical course recommended by Bill Hull, *Can We Save the Evangelical Church?* (Grand Rapids: Baker/Revell, 1993). Douglas D. Webster, *Selling Jesus: What's Wrong with Marketing the Church?* (Downers Grove, Ill.: InterVarsity, 1992), provides an insightful analysis of the contemporary church's market orientation.

15. James V. Heidinger II, "Toxic Pluralism," *Christianity Today* 37, no. 4 (5 April 1993): 16–17.

16. Philip L. Culbertson and Arthur Bradford Shippee, *The Pastor: Readings from the Patristic Period* (Minneapolis: Fortress, 1990), xi.

17. H. Richard Niebuhr, *The Purpose of the Church and Its Ministry* (New York: Harper and Brothers, 1956), 51.

18. Thomas C. Oden, *Pastoral Theology: Essentials of Ministry* (San Francisco: Harper, 1983).

19. Ibid., x–xii.

20. Ibid., 11.

21. Paul Wilkes, "The Hand That Would Shape Our Souls," *The Atlantic* 266, no. 6 (December 1990): 59–88.

22. Carolyn Weese, *Standing on the Banks of Tomorrow* (Granada Hills, Calif.: Multi-Staff Ministries, 1993): 3, 53. Other recent pieces include Michael C. Griffith, "Theological Education Need Not Be Irrelevant," *Vox Evangelica* 20 (1990): 7–19; Richard Carnes Ness, "The Road Less Traveled; Theological Education and the Quest to Fashion the Seminary of the Twenty-First Century," *The Journal of Institute for Christian Leadership* 20 (winter 93–94): 27–43; Bruce L. Shelly, "The Seminaries' Identity Crisis," *Christianity Today* 37, no. 6 (17 May 1993): 42–44; Timothy C. Morgan and Thomas S. Giles, "Re-Engineering the Seminary," *Christianity Today* 38, no. 12 (24 October 1994): 74–76.

23. Steven Meyeroff, "Andover Seminary: The Rise and Fall of an Evangelical Institution," *Covenant Seminary Review* 8, no. 2 (fall 1982): 13–24; and Mark A. Noll, "The Princeton Theology," in *The Princeton Theology,* ed. David F. Wells (Grand Rapids: Baker, 1989), 14–35, present convincing accounts of these two institutions. George C. Fuller, "Practical Theology: The State of the Art," in *Practical Theology and the Ministry of the Church,* ed. Harvie M. Conn (Phillipsburg, N.J.: Presbyterian and Reformed, 1990), 109–28, adds to the discussion.

24. David Dockery, "Ministry and Seminary in a New Century," *The Tie: Southern Seminary* 62, no. 2 (spring 1994): 20–22.

25. John F. MacArthur Jr., "Building His Church His Way," *Spirit of Revival* 24, no. 1 (April 1994): 21–24.

CHAPTER THREE

In Defense of Integrity

John F. MacArthur Jr.

Spurgeon's defense of the truth and concern for integrity follow the pattern set by Paul in dealing with his opponents in Corinth. In 2 Corinthians, Paul's response to criticism consisted of a defense of his integrity, without which his ministry would have been ineffective. He placed before his readers a number of reasons to reassure them of his integrity, including his reverence for the Lord, his concern for the church, his devotion to the truth, his gratitude for Christ's love, his desire for righteousness, and his burden for the lost. In defending his integrity, he risked being called proud by his enemies, so he also displayed several marks of his humility: an unwillingness to compare oneself with others, a willingness to minister within limits, an unwillingness to take credit for others' labors, a willingness to seek only the Lord's glory, and an unwillingness to pursue anything but eternal commendation. Paul had right motives, and he defended them for the right reasons, that is, to glorify God and to promote the truth of the gospel and Christ's church.

The source of this essay is the volume titled *The Power of Integrity,* by John F. MacArthur Jr. (Wheaton, Ill.: Crossway, 1997). It is adapted and used here by permission. Quotations are from the *New American Standard Bible* unless otherwise noted.

* * * * *

Charles Haddon Spurgeon, the gifted nineteenth-century London preacher, said this in one of his later sermons, "I feel that, if I could live a thousand lives, I would like to live them all for Christ, and I should even then feel that they were all too little a return for His great love to me."[1]

Spurgeon was a pastor and Christian leader who clearly loved the Lord and defended His cause with integrity. That fact never exhibited itself more clearly than during the late 1880s, just a few years before his death. He was then a central figure in a major British church struggle known as the Downgrade Controversy. This doctrinal debate began within the Protestant churches of England (most notably the Baptist Union) when Spurgeon could no longer refrain from criticizing the church's alarming departure from sound doctrine and practice. Many churches and their pastors, who previously had been firmly conservative and evangelical, became more tolerant of theories that undermined the authority of Scripture and its view of man. Spurgeon also observed a deviation from the great Reformation doctrines and the proper role played by God's sovereign grace in salvation. From his pulpit and the pages of his magazine, *The Sword and the Trowel,* he courageously and consistently spoke out for the truth and urged average believers to resist false teaching and stand firm on the fundamentals of Christianity.

However, the tide of doctrinal declension among the churches in Charles Spurgeon's day continued, and his godly conscience constrained him to leave the Baptist Union. Shortly after his death in 1892, some of Spurgeon's supporters formed a new society called the Bible League to continue the battle for doctrinal purity and practical orthodoxy among evangelical churches. During the months of controversy, Spurgeon received harsh criticism from his opponents, but he never wavered from his defense of the truth. The following excerpt from a sermon titled "Something Done for Jesus" preached during the Downgrade reveals the true nature of Spurgeon's righteous motives and proper integrity.

We love our brethren for Jesus' sake, but He is the chief among ten thousand, and the altogether lovely. We could not live without Him. To enjoy His company is bliss to us: for Him to hide

His face from us is our midnight of sorrow. . . . Oh, for the power to live, to die, to labour, to suffer as unto Him, and unto Him alone! . . . If a deed done for Christ should bring you into disesteem, and threaten to deprive you of usefulness, do it none the less. I count my own character, popularity, and usefulness to be as the small dust of the balance compared with fidelity to the Lord Jesus. It is the devil's logic which says, "You see I cannot come out and avow the truth because I have a sphere of usefulness which I hold by temporizing with what I fear may be false." O sirs, what have we to do with consequences? Let the heavens fall, but let the good man be obedient to his Master, and loyal to his truth. O man of God, be just and fear not! The consequences are with God, and not with thee. If thou hast done a good work unto Christ, though it should seem to thy poor bleared eyes as if great evil has come of it, yet hast thou done it, Christ has accepted it, and He will note it down, and in thy conscience He will smile thee His approval.[2]

Paul's Defense of His Integrity

Charles Spurgeon's defense of the truth and concern for integrity aligned with the legacy of the apostle Paul. Throughout his ministry, Paul faced opposition from those who hated the gospel and wanted to pervert its proclamation for their own purposes. Most of the opposition came from a group of false teachers in Corinth. They accused him of being incompetent, unsophisticated, unappealing, and impersonal. As a consequence, Paul was obliged, much against his normal preferences, to defend himself and his ministry. He did not seek to glorify himself, but he knew that he had to defend the gospel and the name of the Lord from those who sought to destroy the truth.

It soon became clear to the false teachers in Corinth that if they were going to redirect the Corinthian believers toward error and a false gospel, in addition to getting rich and gaining power and prestige, they would have to destroy Paul's integrity. Because he had established and taught the church at Corinth, the false teachers would have to undermine the church's confidence in Paul if they were going to replace his teaching with their own.

If his opponents at Corinth could destroy his integrity, they could also do away with Paul's usefulness, fruitfulness, and ability to serve the Lord. Therefore Paul had to maintain his integrity. Although he had acknowledged his own humility in ministry—"We have this treasure in earthen vessels" (2 Cor. 4:7)—he also understood the real issue at stake in defending his integrity: "that the surpassing greatness of the power may be of God and not from ourselves" (v. 7).

An essential goal for any spiritual leader is to gain people's trust through genuine integrity. Like Paul, a leader's conduct must be trustworthy and consistent with his words. But once a leader proves to be hypocritical in any area of ministry, no matter how seemingly insignificant, he loses everything he has labored for in ministry and sees his credibility destroyed. That is what Paul feared as he confronted the rumors and lies of the false teachers at Corinth.

Paul used his second letter to the Corinthians, and certain passages in particular, to defend his integrity to the church. Second Corinthians 5:11 begins one of those passages, where Paul says, "We persuade men, but we are made manifest to God; and I hope that we are made manifest also in your consciences." Paul wanted the church to understand and accept his sincerity in all things, as God had.

As Paul began this defense of his integrity, common sense dictated that he not expend any more time or energy in further self-promotion (2 Cor. 5:12)—the Corinthians were already well aware of his consistent character and what he had done. Nevertheless, because of the insidious, persistent, and often vicious nature of his enemies' attacks, Paul outlined several reasons the Corinthians could look to for reassurance regarding his integrity.

Paul's Reverence for the Lord

The first reason Paul offered in defense of his integrity was his "fear of the Lord" (2 Cor. 5:11). *Fear* in this context does not mean "being afraid" but "worship" and "reverence." The following Scriptures easily illustrate this truth:

The fear of the LORD is the beginning of wisdom, And the knowledge of the Holy One is understanding. (Proverbs 9:10)

So the church throughout all Judea and Galilee and Samaria enjoyed peace, being built up; and, going on in the fear of the Lord
and in the comfort of the Holy Spirit, it continued to increase.
(Acts 9:31)

Therefore, having these promises, beloved, let us cleanse ourselves from all defilement of flesh and spirit, perfecting holiness in the fear of God. (2 Corinthians 7:1)

Having the fear of the Lord means holding God in such awe that a
person is wholeheartedly motivated to pursue His holiness and His service. Without question, that was true of Paul. He was so committed to
the glory of God that it grieved him even to consider the possibility of
dishonoring the Lord's name. Paul's intense reverence for God was therefore a powerful incentive for him to convince others of his integrity.

People sometimes ask me what is most difficult about receiving false
criticism. I tell them that what is deeply disturbing and disconcerting is
that the unfair criticism can lead others to believe that I am misrepresenting God. That is what upset Paul about the allegations from the false
teachers at Corinth—he knew that they were misrepresenting him to the
Corinthian believers.

A reverential knowledge of God's greatness is what characterized Paul.
How else could he make this powerful declaration about God's attributes:
"Now to the King eternal, immortal, invisible, the only God, be honor
and glory forever and ever. Amen" (1 Tim. 1:17)?

Paul's life was summed up in the exhortation he gave to the Roman
Christians: "Present your bodies a living and holy sacrifice, acceptable
to God, which is your spiritual service of worship" (Rom. 12:1). His
reverence for the Lord was complete, and he was grieved when enemies
of the truth sought to undermine his integrity and threaten his ability to
teach and preach. Therefore, Paul felt constrained to launch a defense of
his integrity, not for his sake, but for God's.

Paul's Concern for the Church

Paul's concern for the church at Corinth was well established (cf.
1 Cor. 1:10). And potential harm from false teachers had freshly aroused

his interest in her spiritual welfare. He was concerned that the false teachers would eventually gain converts and more influence within the fellowship, leading to an ideological war between their faction and Paul and his supporters. That would shatter the unity of the church, which would yield other negative results such as a discredited leadership, stunted spiritual growth among church members, and a hindered outreach to the surrounding community.

Paul's response to this array of threats against the Corinthian church is instructive for all who strive for integrity. Rather than jumping into the rhetorical trenches and answering each criticism and lie of the false teachers, Paul took a wiser, more judicious approach: "We . . . are giving you an occasion to be proud of us, that you may have an answer for those who take pride in appearance, and not in heart" (2 Cor. 5:12). The apostle knew that in spite of all of the dangers to the church, to mount a personal defense directly before his foes was not prudent. Instead, Paul armed the people to whom he ministered so they might ably defend him and his integrity.

In the long run, that is a much sounder method to contend for truth and integrity with one's enemies rather than trying to answer every charge personally. As Paul discovered, one can go to his opponents repeatedly and present the best-reasoned, most balanced defense of the truth and his integrity, yet all they will do is twist what he has said and use it to tear him down some more.

A person is better off to let his friends be his defenders because those who have something against him are not as likely to feel the same way toward his friends. The Corinthians certainly experienced Paul's consistent behavior and integrity, so they had no reason not to defend him.

So Paul appealed to the brethren in the Corinthian church because he was passionately concerned with their unity and growth. In the end, he could leave the results of his efforts with God: "But he who boasts, let him boast in the Lord. For not he who commends himself is approved, but whom the Lord commends" (2 Cor. 10:17–18).

Paul's Devotion to the Truth

A few years ago, I was invited to speak in a philosophy class at one of the state universities located near my home church in southern California.

I began my remarks by saying, "I'm here to tell you about the truth you've been searching for all your life. It is all the truth you need to know."

My approach dumbfounded the students in the class. Students in such classes invariably spend the entire term considering various views of the truth but never reach any conclusions. Quite likely, they leave the course not ever expecting to find the truth. That is why I went against the conventional wisdom and expounded the truth of the gospel.

Whenever you are dogmatic, affirmative, and absolute in speaking the truth, as I was in that classroom, the world thinks that you have lost your reason. That is how Paul's adversaries in Corinth characterized him. His passionate zeal and devotion to the truth became another reason for defending his integrity: "For if we are beside ourselves, it is for God; if we are of sound mind, it is for you" (2 Cor. 5:13). The Corinthian believers did not need to question Paul's reason—they came to Christ through his preaching, grew in their sanctification under his teaching, and, as a result, loved Paul and trusted in God. His sound mind was obvious to everyone. But the false teachers and their "converts," in their attempt to overthrow Paul's scriptural teachings with their own self-centered, erroneous views, charged that Paul had lost control of his senses.

But the apostle made abundantly clear that he and his fellow ministers were beside themselves for God (5:13). The phrase *beside ourselves* refers to his passion and devotion to God's truth. The term does not refer to a person who is clinically deranged, but it can describe someone, such as Paul, who is dogmatically committed to truth. And Paul could be more dogmatic than anyone else because he was dealing with direct revelation from the Lord.

Nevertheless, Paul's enemies insisted and persisted in labeling him a dogmatic extremist who was off balance mentally. But dogmatism has always had a negative connotation for the world, as the apostle discovered on other occasions. Notice what happened when Paul gave an earnest, straightforward presentation of the gospel before the Roman official, Festus:

> "And so, having obtained help from God, I stand to this day testifying both to small and great, stating nothing but what the

Prophets and Moses said was going to take place; that the Christ was to suffer, and that by reason of His resurrection from the dead He should be the first to proclaim light both to the Jewish people and to the Gentiles." And while Paul was saying this in his defense, Festus said in a loud voice, "Paul, you are out of your mind! Your great learning is driving you mad." But Paul said, "I am not out of my mind, most excellent Festus, but I utter words of sober truth." (Acts 26:22–25)

Once again, the solid thread of integrity is evident in Paul's ministry. He was in complete control and possessed a sound, sober mind. Both at Caesarea before Festus and at the church in Corinth, Paul's message was passionate and zealous because the truth of the gospel was at stake. But he also knew how to be humble and well reasoned so that people would receive and apply the truth. In the end, the issue was the same—he defended his integrity so he could continue to proclaim God's truth unhindered.

Paul's Gratitude for Christ's Love

Another reason Paul was so concerned to defend his integrity was his thankfulness for the Savior's love for him. He told the Corinthians, "The love of Christ controls us, having concluded this, that one died for all, therefore all died" (2 Cor. 5:14). Paul defended his ministry and offered its richness to Christ as an act of gratitude.

To emphasize the strength of this motivation, Paul used the Greek word translated "controls." The simplest, clearest meaning of this word is "a pressure that causes action." The gratitude Paul had for Christ's love for him exerted great pressure on him to offer his life and ministry to the Lord. And the overriding factor for Paul was the Lord's substitutionary death and the application of that death to him. The essence of Christ's substitution is summarized well in Romans 5: "For while we were still helpless, at the right time Christ died for the ungodly. For one will hardly die for a righteous man; though perhaps for the good man someone would dare even to die. But God demonstrates His own love toward us, in that while we were yet sinners, Christ died for us" (vv. 6–8).

The death of Christ is meaningless apart from an understanding of its substitutionary impact—if Christ didn't die in our place, then we would have to die for our sins, and that would result in eternal death.

That fact certainly should be motivation enough for all of us to strive for integrity in our ministries and all other aspects of our lives. After all, everyone who died in Christ receives forever the saving benefits of His substitutionary death (cf. Rom. 3:24–26; 6:8). That's the conclusion to which Paul is referring in the second part of 2 Corinthians 5:14 when he says, "One died for all, therefore all died." The truth of our Lord's substitution is both a comfort and a motivation for thanksgiving, for both Paul and us: "I shall not be put to shame in anything, but that with all boldness, Christ shall even now, as always, be exalted in my body, whether by life or by death. For to me, to live is Christ, and to die is gain" (Phil. 1:20–21).

Paul's Desire for Righteousness

The great eighteenth-century English hymn writer Isaac Watts composed the following stanzas about the pursuit of righteousness and obedience to God's Word:

> Blest are the undefiled in heart, whose ways are right and clean,
> who never from the law depart, but fly from ev'ry sin.
> Blest are the men who keep thy Word and practice thy commands;
> with their whole heart they seek the Lord, and serve thee with
> their hands.
> Great is their peace who love thy law; how firm their souls abide!
> Nor can a bold temptation draw their steady feet aside.
> Then shall my heart have inward joy, and keep my face from shame,
> when all thy statutes I obey, and honor all thy Name.

Those words, based on Psalm 119:1, could easily have been uttered by the apostle Paul as a way of declaring his all-out desire to live righteously. His desire flowed logically from his tremendous gratitude for Christ's love and was another reason Paul so vigorously defended his integrity to the Corinthians. Paul told them, "He died for all, that they who live should no longer live for themselves, but for Him who died and rose again on their behalf" (2 Cor. 5:15).

In defending his integrity, Paul wanted the Corinthians to know that his old, self-centered life was finished. Against all of the distorted accusations from the false teachers, he wanted his brethren to be persuaded that his motives in ministry were completely pure. And Paul had a strong case because, by God's grace, he was without self-promotion, self-aggrandizement, pride, or greed as he labored to plant and nourish local churches among the people of Asia Minor.

The Corinthians should never have doubted Paul's integrity. He had already instructed them about the spiritual lifestyle they ought to adopt: "Whether, then, you eat or drink or whatever you do, do all to the glory of God. Give no offense either to Jews or to Greeks or to the church of God; just as I also please all men in all things, not seeking my own profit, but the profit of the many, that they may be saved. Be imitators of me, just as I also am of Christ" (1 Cor. 10:31–11:1).

Paul's beliefs and motivations had not changed, no matter what his hypocritical opponents were accusing him of. He still lived for Christ and for the sake of righteousness, not for himself. Any other standard was unacceptable to him. So Paul defended his integrity because he desired to live boldly for the Lord and did not want anyone to think his motivation in life was anything less than that. Paul's example should be an encouragement to all of us to cultivate and defend our integrity; without it, we cannot minister effectively for the Lord.

Paul's Burden for the Lost

Paul was extremely passionate when it came to reaching the lost for Christ. Seeing people converted by the sovereign power of the gospel message was the ultimate reason for him to continue in ministry. Therefore, Paul's burden for the lost is the last of his reasons for defending his integrity.

Acts 17:16–17 illustrates the intensity of Paul's evangelistic burden:

> Now while Paul was waiting for them at Athens, his spirit was being provoked within him as he was beholding the city full of idols. So he was reasoning in the synagogue with the Jews and the God-fearing Gentiles, and in the market place every day with those who happened to be present.

Paul writes about his passion for the unsaved in Romans 1:13–16:

> I do not want you to be unaware, brethren, that often I have
> planned to come to you (and have been prevented thus far) in
> order that I might obtain some fruit [converts] among you also,
> even as among the rest of the Gentiles. I am under obligation
> both to Greeks and to barbarians, both to the wise and to the
> foolish. Thus, for my part, I am eager to preach the gospel to
> you also who are in Rome. For I am not ashamed of the gospel,
> for it is the power of God for salvation to every one who be-
> lieves, to the Jew first and also to the Greek.

Later in his letter to the Roman believers, in perhaps the most telling
statements he ever wrote about his burden for lost souls, Paul says,

> I am telling the truth in Christ, I am not lying, my conscience
> bearing me witness in the Holy Spirit, that I have great sorrow
> and unceasing grief in my heart. For I could wish that I myself
> were accursed, separated from Christ for the sake of my breth-
> ren [the Jews], my kinsmen according to the flesh. . . . Brethren,
> my heart's desire and my prayer to God for them [the Jews] is
> for their salvation. (Rom. 9:1–3; 10:1)

As he continued to defend his integrity to the Corinthians, Paul said,
"Therefore from now on we recognize no man according to the flesh"
(2 Cor. 5:16). This connects back to verse 15 and simply means that,
since his transformation in Christ, Paul no longer evaluated people by
external, worldly standards. He had a new priority, and that was to meet
the spiritual needs of the people of God.

Before our transformation, we used to assess others by only external
criteria: Physical appearance, outward behavior, social and economic
orientation, and engaging personality were our old yardsticks. But when
a person comes to faith in Christ, he begins to evaluate people by a new
set of criteria. And the central issue we want to determine when we meet
someone is his relationship to God. Does he know Christ?

Perhaps you have a neighbor who is kind and considerate, who helps you out often and is especially available when you have an illness or emergency. As is often the case, you develop a warm and friendly relationship with someone like that. But if you are honest, you can never be content in your friendship until you are sure that he has a right relationship to God. In fact, the more you build your relationship with your neighbor or anyone else, the more burdened you become for his spiritual welfare.

Paul gives believers no option but to think of the unsaved and everything in life from a transformed perspective: "Therefore if any man is in Christ, he is a new creature; the old things passed away; behold, new things have come" (2 Cor. 5:17). Paul had certainly experienced complete change in his life—from self-centered Pharisee to dedicated apostle of Christ—and he knew such transformation would happen to anyone who became a Christian.

Is it any wonder that Paul defended his integrity so ardently? If any of his enemies could destroy it, he would lose his credibility and influence in preaching the gospel and thus his entire reason for living. If only every Christian could have the same passion and purpose as did the apostle Paul!

Paul Reveals His Humility

Time and again as Paul defended his integrity, he risked being labeled proud by the false teachers at Corinth. Yet, such a designation could not have been more unfair or untrue. Paul had already, by the sovereign plan of God, distinguished himself as the most noble, most influential, most effective earthly servant the church had ever seen, apart from the Lord Jesus Himself. Yet, undergirding all of his strong character qualities and various motives for defending his integrity was the all-important characteristic of humility.

Scripture demonstrates that Paul was aware of his weaknesses and shortcomings. In Romans 7:18, he says, "For I know that nothing good dwells in me, that is, in my flesh." In 2 Corinthians 4:7, Paul describes himself in the lowliest of terms: "We have this treasure [the light of the gospel] in earthen vessels [garbage pails]." Finally, the apostle's humble self-analysis is seen very clearly in what he wrote to Timothy: "Christ Jesus came into the world to save sinners, among whom I am foremost of all" (1 Tim. 1:15).

No Christian virtue is more cherished than humility. Micah 6:8 says, "He has told you, O man, what is good; and what does the LORD require of you but to do justice, to love kindness, and to walk humbly with your God?" Humility is best defined as a true and genuine sense of conviction that one is utterly and completely unworthy of the goodness, mercy, and grace of God and incapable of anything of value apart from those divine gifts.

Paul culminates his defense of his integrity before the Corinthians with a thorough presentation of the marks of humility (2 Cor. 10:12–18). In this passage, he continues to contrast his pure motives and righteous goals in ministry with the impure motives and unholy agendas of the false teachers. Paul was certain that his humility would be convincing proof to his readers of his true integrity.

An Unwillingness to Compare Oneself with Others

The first mark of humility for the godly teacher and leader is an unwillingness to compare himself with others and claim superiority over them. False teachers typically elevate themselves. But Paul had a different approach. He told the Corinthians, "We are not bold to class or compare ourselves with some of those who commend themselves" (2 Cor. 10:12).

Those who invaded the Corinthian church with error used glib speech, a superior attitude, and a hypocritical front to appear better than everyone else, especially Paul. But he refused to lower himself to their childish, ego-centeric games. In fact, he did not even consider such a strategy, saying, "To me it is a very small thing that I should be examined by you, or by any human court; in fact, I do not even examine myself. I am conscious of nothing against myself, yet I am not by this acquitted; but the one who examines me is the Lord" (1 Cor. 4:3–4).

Paul was concerned only with comparing his credentials with God's standards. He did not use man-centered criteria to boast of his successes. Instead, he was more inclined to boast of his suffering, such as the sadness, tears, imprisonment, pain, and persecution he endured—all for the love of Christ (cf. 2 Cor. 11:23–31).

In contrast, those who are proud and without integrity will establish these standards for success: charm, flattering personality, authoritarian bearing, rhetorical skills, and mystical spiritual experiences. They invent the standards, measure themselves by them, and commend themselves for superior "success."

Paul's standards were objective and God centered. The false teachers' standards were subjective and worldly. Based on that simple comparison, it is easy to determine what pattern one should follow in pursuit of genuine integrity.

A Willingness to Minister Within Limits

The humble servant of God will also have a willingness to minister within limits. That was not the attitude of Paul's opponents at Corinth. They overextended and overstated everything they did in an effort to widen their influence, enhance their prestige, and increase their fortune. They exaggerated everything so that they would look better than they actually were.

We do not know exactly what the false teachers told the Corinthian believers about their battle with Paul, but undoubtedly they portrayed themselves as more powerful, more sophisticated, more articulate, and more successful than him. And they had to lie to make that case.

How did Paul respond to those claims? Again, he refused to engage in the same dishonest tactics of his enemies but simply told the Corinthians, "We will not boast beyond our measure, but within the measure of the sphere which God apportioned to us as a measure, to reach even as far as you" (2 Cor. 10:13). Paul was concerned with only one thing: to portray accurately the reality of his ministry.

Paul always understood the principle of ministering within limits. He mentions it at both the beginning and the end of his letter to the Romans:

> Through whom we have received grace and apostleship to bring about the obedience of faith among all the Gentiles, for His name's sake. (1:5)

> Therefore in Christ Jesus I have found reason for boasting in things pertaining to God. For I will not presume to speak of anything except what Christ has accomplished through me, resulting in the obedience of the Gentiles by word and deed. . . .

And thus I aspired to preach the gospel, not where Christ was
already named, that I might not build upon another man's foundation. (15:17–18, 20)

Pride and overstatement were not characteristic of Paul. He spoke of
only what Christ had done through him and supported his statements by
objective, truthful evidence. God had sovereignly gifted Paul and given
him a specific commission to fulfill. He was completely content to preach
the gospel in the Gentile world and found churches and train leaders in
those unreached regions. He did not need to be more important than
God intended him to be; he just wanted to be faithful to God's plan and
carry it out with a depth of excellence that would please the Lord.

What is remarkable about Paul's pattern for ministry is that he simply
followed Jesus' example. We often forget that Christ willingly functioned
within the narrow limits that His Father established.

First, Jesus' ministry was limited by God's will. In John 5:30, Jesus
told the Jewish leaders, "I can do nothing on My own initiative. As I
hear, I judge; and My judgment is just, because I do not seek My own
will, but the will of Him who sent Me." Second, Jesus obeyed the Father's
will according to His timetable only (Matt. 26:45; Luke 22:14; John 2:4;
4:23; 5:25; 7:30; 17:1). Third, Jesus limited His ministry to God's people
and to those who recognized their need for salvation (Matt. 15:24; Luke
5:31–32). Fourth, Jesus limited His ministry by God's plan. He preached
the gospel to a small group of people first (including the disciples) before extending it beyond the regions of Judea. Never did Christ allow
Himself to get sidetracked onto other issues, and neither did Paul.

An Unwillingness to Take Credit for Others' Labors

Plagiarism has been a problem in the world for centuries. *Plagiarize*
means "to steal and pass off (the ideas or words of another) as one's
own." A truly humble person with real integrity will avoid plagiarism,
and that was true of Paul. He never displayed a willingness to take credit
for others' labors.

His deference for others contrasted with the false teachers' desire to
take credit for things they had never achieved, such as their contribu-
tions to the spiritual progress of the Corinthian church. But Paul could

confidently and accurately tell the Corinthians how God had used him in their lives:

> We are not overextending ourselves, as if we did not reach to you, for we were the first to come even as far as you in the gospel of Christ; not boasting beyond our measure, that is, in other men's labors, but with the hope that as your faith grows, we shall be, within our sphere, enlarged even more by you, so as to preach the gospel even to the regions beyond you, and not to boast in what has been accomplished in the sphere of another. (2 Corinthians 10:14–16)

Paul did not overstate or claim credit for what was not his. Nor did he flaunt authority that did not belong to him. He underscored what he had said previously: "I planted, Apollos watered, but God was causing the growth. . . . According to the grace of God which was given to me, as a wise master builder I laid a foundation, and another is building upon it" (1 Cor. 3:6, 10).

Paul was determined to avoid the pride and dishonesty of those who "ministered" in a worldly fashion. He would not go to a place and tell lies about his alleged accomplishments. He would not go into a city and usurp the credit for ministry that belonged to another. Instead, Paul knew that those who truly desired to further God's kingdom would do so through their own virtuous lives.

Romans 15:17–18 summarizes well Paul's attitude about this third aspect of humility: "Therefore in Christ Jesus I have found reason for boasting in things pertaining to God. For I will not presume to speak of anything except what Christ has accomplished through me, resulting in the obedience of the Gentiles by word and deed."

A Willingness to Seek Only the Lord's Glory

A fourth way in which Paul exhibited the true humility of the man of integrity was by a willingness to seek only the Lord's glory. The mere thought of self-glory was utterly repulsive to Paul, whereas those who teach error are willing, for the sake of their own glory and preeminence, to tear up the church and tarnish the glory of Christ.

Paul had already laid out quite plainly in 1 Corinthians his position regarding why Christians should seek only God's glory:

> For consider your calling brethren, that there were not many wise according to the flesh, not many mighty, not many noble; but God has chosen the foolish things of the world to shame the wise, and God has chosen the weak things of the world to shame the things which are strong, and the base things of the world and the despised, God has chosen, the things that are not, that He might nullify the things that are, that no man should boast before God . . . that, just as it is written, "Let him who boasts, boast in the LORD." (1:26–29, 31)

Paul here reminds everyone that if they boast, it must be only in the Lord, and if they seek anyone's glory, it must be only His (cf. Ps. 115:1). That is the essence of humility—the recognition of one's basic unworthiness and the acceptance of no worthiness but God's.

An Unwillingness to Pursue Anything but Eternal Commendation

Authentic biblical humility is also revealed in Paul's unwillingness to pursue anything but eternal commendation. In 2 Corinthians 10:18, he says, "For not he who commends himself is approved, but whom the Lord commends."

False teachers commend themselves. But Paul desired God's approval, and he proved that he did not fabricate his own commendation. The Greek verb that he used for "commends" in verse 18 literally means "to be tested" or "to be approved." That's what Paul meant when he said, "But to me it is a very small thing that I should be examined by you, or by any human court; in fact, I do not even examine myself" (1 Cor. 4:3).

Paul was not concerned about what others thought of him; the only praise and commendation he desired was from the Lord. That is an important reminder for all of us as we pursue integrity: We will receive God's approval, not as a result of our gifts, our skills, our personality, or our popularity, but because of our humility.

In summary, Paul possessed the power of integrity. His motives were pure (1 Cor. 4:5), and he defended them for the right reasons—to glorify

God and promote the truth of the gospel and Christ's church. Paul's humble defense of his integrity is, with the exception of the Lord Jesus Himself, the most outstanding and thoroughly detailed example of Christian integrity found in Scripture. Modeling Paul's integrity should be a goal for us all.

Endnotes

1. Cited in Iain Murray, *The Forgotten Spurgeon,* 2d ed. (Edinburgh: Banner of Truth, 1973), 20.
2. Ibid., 205–6. For a more complete discussion of the Downgrade Controversy and its significance for today's church, see John F. MacArthur Jr., appendix 1 to *Ashamed of the Gospel: When the Church Becomes Like the World* (Wheaton, Ill.: Crossway, 1993), 197–225.

CHAPTER FOUR

Pastoral Ministry in History

James F. Stitzinger

The biblical pattern for pastoral ministry derives from both testaments of the Bible. Deviations from that pattern crept into the church during the second century A.D. and continued, becoming increasingly severe into the medieval period of the church. Nevertheless, certain individuals and isolated groups continued their efforts to follow the biblical pattern, including Chrysostom and Augustine in the early church and the Paulicians, Cathari, Albigenses, and Waldenses during the medieval period. The Reformation witnessed a broader return to the biblical pattern through the magisterial reformation of Luther, Calvin, and others and through the Anabaptist reformation. During the modern period, Puritan leaders such as Baxter, Perkins, and Edwards led a return to biblical principles in pastoral ministry. Bridges, Morgan, and Allen were nineteenth century examples of biblical ministers. The late twentieth century produced others, including Lloyd-Jones, Adams, and MacArthur.

The source of this essay is the volume titled *Rediscovering Pastoral Ministry,* ed. John F. MacArthur Jr. (Dallas: Word, 1995). It is used by permission. Quotations are from the *New American Standard Bible* unless otherwise noted.

* * * * *

In God's gracious sovereignty, He chose to reconcile believers to Himself through Christ. In His marvelous plan, He committed to them the ministry of reconciliation (2 Cor. 5:18), based upon His Word of reconciliation (5:19). The office and function of the pastor has a key role in this ministry of proclaiming the mystery of godliness. His functions have a close association with the church, the pillar and support of the truth (1 Tim. 3:15).

The duty and privilege of pastoral ministry has resulted in the development of the discipline of pastoral theology within the broader framework of practical theology.[1] It has also produced a long procession of individuals who have filled the pages of church history in responding to God's call to be faithful pastors and ministers of the truth. Sadly, traditions[2] not measuring up to the standards of biblical scrutiny have skewed and embellished much of what has been called ministry.

A plethora of mind sets and often conflicting traditions emerge in a study of pastoral ministry in history, although all traditions claim a lineage going back to the apostolic age. In every generation, some people have sought to return to the basic fundamentals of primitive biblical ministry. This pursuit of the "true church," or primitivism, has led Littell and others to speak of the concept of the "Believers' Church."[3] Such a church included people of various ages and regions who followed the same principles of commitment to apostolic truth. These were believers who "gathered and disciplined a 'true church' upon the apostolic pattern as they understood it."[4] For these people, the truth was an ongoing pursuit, not a closed book in a "sectarian" sense. They "wanted fellowship with all who bore the Name and lived the covenant of a good conscience with God."[5]

Other committed believers like these within the wider framework of church history have sought above all else the true, pure, primitive church. They have sought a church and a ministry patterned after the theology and practice of the book of Acts and the NT Epistles. Such individuals and churches have appeared in various forms and have come from various settings, but all displayed a desire to return to a vibrant, biblical church and ministry. Some people have journeyed farther in their plans than in their practice. Some people have advanced farther than others in their quest for biblical ministry.

This chapter focuses on a history of those who have sought to teach and practice biblical pastoral ministry. Examinations of efforts to follow biblical ministry patterns rather than accepted tradition and recurring ministry practices can serve as a helpful guide to a future generation with the same goals. Such historical study provides valuable insights through enabling Christians and churches to learn from the past. Although history is not the unfolding of an unalterable tradition or a hermeneutical principle for interpreting ministry, "the flow of time bears divine sovereignty and providence on its wings and constitutes a general, not special, revelation of God himself."[6] Only the Bible can teach the true theology of pastoral ministry, but the working of the Holy Spirit in the hearts of church leaders through the centuries can flesh out this theology and its practical implementation. The following subsidiary material will provide such information.

The Biblical Period

Many scholars have noted the elusive and complex nature of pastoral theology that makes the discipline hard to define.[7] As Tidball points out, part of this "elusiveness stems from the multitude of labels which exist in this area and which seem to be used without any agreement as to their exact meaning or relationship."[8] As a further reason, he points out that the difficulty "stems from the fact that so many sub-disciplines of practical theology are spoken of as if they are pastoral theology."[9] The historical development of the doctrine of the church generally and of practical theology particularly have no doubt contributed to this elusiveness because tension has surrounded this whole subject from the outset of church history.[10]

Thomas C. Oden, in expanding his definition of pastoral theology, observes the following:

> Pastoral theology is that branch of Christian theology that deals
> with the office, gifts, and functions of the pastor. As theology,
> pastoral theology seeks to reflect upon that self-disclosure of
> God witnessed to by Scripture, mediated through tradition, re-

flected upon by critical reasoning, and embodied in personal and social experience.[11]

Throughout history, it is precisely when the weight of tradition, critical reasoning, and experience have come to bear upon pastoral theology that it has been most likely to drift from its biblical moorings. In reality, it is impossible to say that one has no tradition or critical thinking on this subject. Therefore, one must begin, continue, and end with the Scriptures in a study of true pastoral ministry.

The place to begin is with an investigation of the various aspects of primitive biblical ministry as they relate to the pastoral office and functions. A brief summary of the biblical data can serve as the basis for identifying historic efforts to reproduce that kind of ministry.

Old Testament

A history of pastoral ministry must begin in the OT. The theme "The LORD is my shepherd" (Ps. 23:1) expresses the pastoral role of God with His people. Tidball describes this image as "the underlining paradigm of ministry" and points out that it contains "references to the authority, tender care, specific tasks, courage and sacrifice required of the pastor."[12] Many passages, including Genesis 49:24 and Psalms 78:52–3; 80:1, contribute to the development of this theme. The OT often describes Israel as sheep who need a shepherd (Ps. 100:3; cf. also Pss. 44:22; 119:176; Jer. 23:1; 50:6).

The theme of God's love also contributes to the shepherd theme: "I have loved you with an everlasting love; Therefore I have drawn you with lovingkindness" (Jer. 31:3). God demonstrates His love for Israel in vivid imagery with Hosea's marriage to a harlot (Hos. 1:2). Although Israel spurned His love, God continues loving, as He says in Hosea 11:1: "When Israel was a youth I loved him, And out of Egypt I called My son." In the end, God is there to "heal their apostasy . . . [and] love them freely" (Hos. 14:4). The OT abounds with statements of God's love for His people. Another is in Isaiah 43:4–5: "Since you are precious in My sight, since you are honored and I love you . . . Do not fear, for I am with you."[13]

Associated with the love of God is His disciplining of those whom He loves (Prov. 3:11); His holding accountable of those whom He loves (Ps. 11:7); and His command that men love Him in return (Deut. 6:5). Also associated with the divine pastoral concern are the profound themes of God's mercy (i.e., loyal love, Ps. 62:12; Isa. 54:10; 55:3),[14] God's compassion (Ps. 145:9), and God's delight (1 Sam. 15:22). Combined with them are numerous examples of servant leaders—including Abraham, Joseph, Moses, Samuel, and David—who demonstrated the faithfulness of God as they accomplished His work through faith (Hebrews 11).

Thus, the OT provides an important basis for understanding the office and function of the pastor. The Shepherd Himself displays his fatherly care, love, mercy, discipline, compassion, and delight toward His people, whom He desires to love and fear Him with a pure heart. The image of a shepherd also demonstrates God's authority and faithfulness as well as the necessity and implications of obedience to Him. Servant leaders exemplify both strengths and weaknesses as God uses them to carry out His sovereign plan in human history.

New Testament

The NT builds on this OT foundation as it reveals the Chief Shepherd, Christ, in all of His wisdom, glory, power, and humility (John 10:11, 14; 1 Peter 5:4). The person and work of the Great Shepherd culminates in His death (i.e., the blood of the eternal covenant, Heb. 13:20; 1 Peter 2:25) and resurrection. The Good Shepherd gave His life for His sheep, whom he calls to Himself (John 10:11–16). These "called out" ones are His church. Christ, as head of the church, leads His church (Eph. 1:22; 5:23–25) and shepherds it. He calls pastors as undershepherds to function and give oversight under His authority (1 Peter 5:1–4).

Both as a doctrine (1 Corinthians 12) and through living example, the NT reveals the nature of the church and all of its members and activities. It also furnishes clear teaching about church officers and their functions. The role and duties of a pastor as presented in the NT are the basis of all future biblical ministry in history.

Five distinct terms refer to the pastoral office: (1) elder *(presbyteros)*, a title highlighting the administration and spiritual guidance of the church (Acts 15:6; 1 Tim. 5:17; James 5:14; 1 Peter 5:1–4); (2) bishop or overseer *(episkopos)*, which emphasizes guidance, oversight, and leadership in the church (Acts 20:28; Phil. 1:1; 1 Tim. 3:2–5; Titus 1:7); (3) shepherd or pastor *(poimēn),* a position denoting leadership and authority (Acts 20:28–31; Eph. 4:11) as well as guidance and provision (1 Peter 5:2–3; cf. 2:25); (4) preacher *(kērux),* which points to public proclamation of the gospel and teaching of the flock (Rom. 10:14; 1 Tim. 2:7; 2 Tim. 1:11); and (5) teacher *(didaskalos),* one responsible for instruction and exposition of the Scriptures. Such teaching is both instructive (1 Tim. 2:7) and corrective (1 Cor. 12:28–29).

Scripture is quite clear that these descriptive titles relate to the same pastoral office. The terms *elder* and *bishop* are synonymous in Acts 20:17, 28 and Titus 1:5–7. The terms *elder, bishop,* and *shepherd* are synonymous in 1 Peter 5:1–2. The leadership role of elders is also evident in the shepherdly activity of James 5:14. As Lightfoot clearly noted, in biblical times *elder* and *bishop* were synonymous terms.[15] Not until the rise of sacerdotalism in the second century did bishops take the places of the apostles and preside over groups of elders.[16]

First Timothy 5:17 and Hebrews 13:7 associate the terms *teacher* and *preacher.* Ephesians 4:11 connects shepherds (pastors) with teachers, as do 1 Timothy 5:17 and Hebrews 13:7. These last two passages furnish no exegetical grounds for separating the work of governing from that of teaching.[17] Consequently, the conclusion must be that pastoral leadership in the church included preaching, teaching, oversight, and shepherding. The parity of the titles look to a single role, the office of pastor.

In addition to these five terms, a number of descriptive words shed light on biblical pastoral ministry. These words include *ruler* (1 Thess. 5:12; 1 Tim. 3:4–5; 5:17), *ambassador* (2 Cor. 5:20), *steward* (1 Cor. 4:1), *defender* (Phil. 1:7), *servant* (2 Cor. 4:5), and *example* (1 Tim. 4:12; 1 Peter 5:3). The NT also tells the pastor to preach (1 Cor. 1:17), shepherd (1 Peter 5:2), build up the church (Eph. 4:12), edify (2 Cor. 13:10), pray (Col. 1:9), watch for souls (Heb. 13:17), fight (1 Tim. 1:18), convince (Titus 1:9), comfort (2 Cor. 1:4–6), rebuke (Titus 1:13), warn (Acts 20:31), admonish (2 Thess. 3:15), and exhort (Titus 1:9; 2:15).

So the Scriptures are clear regarding the office and functions of the pastor. The biblical pattern is simple, describing a Spirit-filled man who gives oversight, shepherding, guidance, teaching, and warning—doing all with a heart of love, comfort, and compassion. All of these functions were evident in the first-century church. Purity (including church discipline), primitivism (NT simplicity), voluntarism (no compulsion to join), tolerance (no persecution of those who disagreed), evangelistic zeal (missionary activity), observation of biblical ordinances (baptism and the Lord's Supper), emphasis on the Holy Spirit, and dynamic ministry (involving both pastor and people)—not tradition, hierarchy, and corruption—marked the church at this early stage.

In time, however, a more complex and embellished church doctrine and practice replaced this early church simplicity.[18] This development had direct bearing on the nature of pastoral ministry as it reflected a similar change in scope and complexity of the pastoral role. The remainder of this chapter will identify major examples of those who approached biblical pastoral ministry following the pattern of the first century church.

The Early Christian Church (100–476)

From its earliest days, the Christian church moved from simplicity to complexity as it drifted from a spontaneous living organism to a more settled institution.[19] This ever-dangerous institutionalism arose simultaneously in the second generation of many widely separated churches. No more vivid example exists than that of the second-century church, which developed strong ecclesiastical traditions[20] as it came to view the "bishop" as the successor to the apostle.[21] This trend progressed into the fourth century, causing the church to enter more and more into an era of "speculation on the law and doctrine of the church."[22] The rise and development of sacerdotalism, with its elevation of clergy to the status of priests, in effect, made the minister an instrument of the saving grace of God as he participated with God in the salvation of human beings.[23] This development of the threefold ministry of bishops, elders, and deacons represented a serious departure from simple NT ministry.

In contrast to this general trend, several strong proponents of biblical ministry existed during this period. Polycarp (ca. A.D. 70–155/160) wrote,

And the presbyters also must be compassionate, merciful towards all men, turning back the sheep that are gone astray, visiting all the infirm, not neglecting a widow or an orphan or a poor man: but providing always for that which is honorable in the sight of God and of men. . . . Let us therefore so serve Him with fear and all reverence, as He himself gave commandment and the Apostles who preached the Gospel to us and the prophets who proclaimed beforehand the coming of the Lord.[24]

The spirit here is one of humble and loving service with no seeming regard for the hierarchical relationship of bishops and elders. Clement of Alexandria (ca. A.D. 155–ca. 220) has written in a similar vein, emphasizing that ministers are those who are chosen to serve the Lord, moderate their passions, are obedient to superiors, and teach and care for sheep as a shepherd.[25] He also observed that "bishops, presbyters, deacons . . . are imitations of the angelic glory, and of that economy which, the Scriptures say, awaits those who, follow the footsteps of the apostles, having lived in perfection of righteousness according to the Gospel."[26] Origen (ca. A.D. 185–ca. 254), his pupil, assigned a similar role to the one representing Christ and His house (the church) and teaching others of these truths.[27] This emphasis contrasts sharply with that of Cyprian (ca. A.D. 200–ca. 258), the well known Bishop of Carthage who apparently limited his discussion of pastoral theology to the elevation of the bishop to the level of an apostle.[28]

The powerful pen of John Chrysostom (ca. A.D. 344/354–407) contributed significantly to the early church's understanding of the pastoral position.[29] He developed the role and functions of a pastor both in his commentaries on the Pastoral Epistles and in his Treatises. His statements about the nature of ministry are very biblical:

There is but one method and way of healing appointed, after we have gone wrong, and this is, the powerful application of the Word. This is the one instrument, the finest atmosphere. This takes the place of physic, cautery and cutting, and if it be needful to sear and amputate, this is the means which we must use, and if this be of no avail, all else is wasted: with this we both roust the soul when it sleeps, and reduce it when it is inflamed; with this we cut off excesses, and fill up defects, and perform all manner of other operations which are requisite for the soul's health.[30]

To this Chrysostom adds the necessity of living by example with the ambition that the Word of Christ would dwell in men richly.[31] His statements warm the heart as perhaps the most useful expression of pastoral ministry during the period, but they also reveal signs of the monastic stranglehold that was fast coming upon the organized church of his day.[32] The monastic understanding of pastoral ministry was soon to have a profound effect upon church leadership.

Another important spokesman from this period is Augustine of Hippo (A.D. 354–430). Often best known as a theologian and preacher, Augustine devoted his life to pastoral ministry. Soon after his ordination, he wrote to Valerius, his superior,

> First and foremost, I beg your wise holiness to consider that there is nothing in this life, and especially in our own day, more easy and pleasant and acceptable to men than the office of bishop or priest or deacon, if its duties be discharged in a mechanical or sycophantic way; but nothing more worthless and deplorable and meet for chastisement in the sight of God: and, on the other hand, that there is nothing in this life, and especially in our own day, more difficult, toilsome, and hazardous than the office of bishop or priest or deacon; but nothing more blessed in the sight of God, if our service be in accordance with our Captain's orders.[33]

Augustine's ministry included many well-articulated biblical functions, including those of apologist, administrator, minister to the afflicted, preacher and teacher, judge, and spiritual leader.[34] Much to his credit, he spent considerable time and energy in personal biblical ministry. Pastoral interaction and ministry appear to be at the heart of his book *The City of God,* as he deals with those who challenge God's divine city with an earthly city.[35] At the same time, however, Augustine brought into the church a leprosy of monastic tradition involving both men and women (nunnery), thereby laying the groundwork for the Augustinian Rule.

Independent groups are a final source of biblical ministry patterns during this period. As Gunnar Westin points out, "The process of development which transformed the original Christian congregations to a sacramental, authoritarian Church took place during the latter portion of the second century. . . . This change did not take place without protest."[36] Many church historians have dismissed as "heretics" those churches that opposed the institutionalized church, a campaign often called "The Free Church Movement."[37] Although some of these groups struggled with doctrinal purity, a closer look reveals that the heretical label in most cases was primarily the result of their unwillingness to be loyal to the received tradition of the fathers,[38] not to significant doctrinal weakness.

A thorough investigation of these independents is difficult, because only the works of those who wrote against them have survived, for the most part. So some sensitivity in examining these writings is necessary. Such groups include the Montanists (ca. A.D. 156), Novatians (ca. A.D. 250), and Donatists (ca. A.D. 313), all of whom left the official church of their day to pursue the pure church.[39] An inclusion of these groups in this discussion is not an attempt to demonstrate their consistent soundness of doctrine but to point to their common commitment to the gospel and a primitive church with a primitive biblical ministry.

To explore these groups in depth is beyond the scope of this survey, but the comments of Philip Schaff regarding the Donatists—a group strongly opposed by Constantine after A.D. 325—are noteworthy:

> The Donatist controversy was a conflict between separatism and catholicism; between ecclesiastical purism and ecclesiastical eclecticism; between the idea of the church as an exclusive community of regenerated saints and the idea of the church as the general Christendom of state and people.[40]

The critical issue for the Donatists was the purity of the church and the holiness of its pastors. This resulted in a more biblical ministry.[41]

As the church of the NT passed through its early centuries and became the official or organized church, it frequently departed from simple NT patterns. Nonetheless, strong voices both inside and outside this church called for a biblical ministry.

The Medieval Period (476–1500)

The general structure of the western medieval church focused on the authority and celibacy of its clergy. Many leaders had retreated to the ascetic life of the monastery to escape the worldliness of the Christianity of their day. The pattern of authority centered in Rome with the first pope, Gregory the Great (540–604), who assumed power in 590.

Although Gregory's papacy plunged the church into deeper political involvement and corruption, he also contributed a positive influence on the pastoral ministry of its clergy. In his *Book of Pastoral Rule,* he addressed many issues, including qualifications and duties of ministers as well as listing thirty types of members with rules of admonition for each.[42] He addressed the poor, the sad, the foolish, the sick, the haughty, the fickle, and many others. This monumental work became a textbook of medieval ministry,[43] yet Gregory's own preoccupation with political implications of the papacy caused him to neglect the souls of men while caring for his estates.[44] The rise of the papacy produced complete corruption as popes, in their devotion to an increasingly pagan agenda, resorted to any available means to reach their goals. The monastic church, now fully developed, experienced tremendous corruption as well. In balance, however, Payne points out,

> Though there was widespread spiritual famine in many nominally Christian lands and notorious corruption in high places, the theologians, the mystics and the reformers of the Middle Ages are further evidence of the Holy Spirit within the Church. They came, almost without exception, from the ranks of the clergy.[45]

During the thousand-year period from Nicea to Wycliffe, ministry took place in spite of the church more than because of the official church.

Even more than in the early period, biblical ministry occurred among elements of the Free Church that were and are commonly regarded as heretics.[46] Groups such as the Paulicians (ca. 625), the Cathari (ca. 1050), the Albigenses (1140), and the Waldenses (1180) demonstrated a strong passion for a pure church with biblical ministry. As Bainton notes, these "very definitely were not heretics but only schismatic, and schismatics only because [they were] cast out against their will."[47] The Paulicians, in their important manual *The Key of Truth,* speak of a simple church built on "repentance and faith" and refer to what was "learned from the Lord" about the church. "Good shepherds"—whose responsibilities included ruling, shepherding, preaching, caring, and administration of the sacraments—were its leaders.[48] The following prayer, offered at the time of an elder's election to office, reflects the nature of Paulician ministry:

> Lamb of God, Jesus, help us and especially this thy newly elected servant, whom thou hast joined unto the number of thy loved disciples. Establish him on thy Gospel vouchsafed to thine universal and apostolic Church, the sure and immovable rock at the gate of hell. And bestow on him a goodly pastorship, to tend with great love thy reasonable flock. . . . Keep this thy servant with thine elect; that no unclean spirit of devils may dare to approach him.[49]

The Waldenses, who by 1184 had separated from the Church of Rome and formulated their own church and ministry, exhibit a similar theme of simple biblical ministry. Allix notes that "their ministers exercised these holy functions, extraordinarily to the edification of their people."[50] Their long history of pre-Reformation Christianity in the Piedmont reflects a relatively pure and uncorrupted form of primitive Christianity.[51]

The beliefs and practices of the Albigenses, whose church was in southern France by 1190, also exemplified this theme of purity. They experienced heavy persecution and frequent misunderstanding from others. Commenting on their ministry, Allix writes,

> It appears therefore that the discipline of the Albigenses was the same that had been practiced in the primitive Church: they had their Bishops, their Priests, and their Deacons, whom the Church of Rome at first held for schismatics, and whose ministry she at last absolutely rejected, for the same reasons that made her consider the ministry of the Waldenses as null and void.[52]

Perhaps the greatest voices for biblical ministry were those of the pre-Reformation reformers, who called for true biblical ministry in a day when such convictions often required men to die for their views. John Wycliffe (1324–1384), the leading Oxford scholar of his day, clearly addressed the issue of biblical ministry in his Forty-three Propositions.[53] His writings "restrict the charter of the preacher to the expounding of Scripture," and state that "priests should exercise their primary function, namely, pastoral care. They should not lurk in cloisters."[54] His most powerful statements are in his book *On the Pastoral Office,* where he states,

> There are two things which pertain to the status of pastor: the holiness of the pastor and the wholesomeness of his teaching. He ought to be holy, so strong in every sort of virtue that he would rather desert every kind of human intercourse, all the temporal things of this world, even mortal life itself, before he would sinfully depart from the truth of Christ. . . .

John Huss (1373–1415) followed Wycliffe's rich emphasis on biblical ministry by calling for a pure church and ministry. In his writings are many examples of this teaching. He wrote, "The church shines in its walls, but starves in its poor saints; it clothes its stones with gold, but leaves its children naked."[55] Gillett summarizes his teaching:

> In the early church there were but two grades of office, deacon and presbyter; all beside are of later and human invention. But God can bring back his church to the old pattern, just as the apostles and true priests took oversight of the church in all matters essential to its well-being, before the office of pope was introduced.[56]

He further taught, "Not the office makes the priest, but the priest the office. Not every priest is a saint, but every saint is a priest."[57] Spinka offers his summary of Huss' position: "His reform program may be summarized by defining it as restitutionalism—the return of Christ and His apostles as exhibited in the primitive Church. He contrasts the Church militant with the true spiritual Church—the body of Christ."[58] The writings of William Tyndale (1494–1536) reveal a similar commitment to primitive biblical ministry.[59]

In summary, the Middle Ages, although dominated by a powerful and corrupt institutional church, was a period when many rose up to challenge that body because of their pursuit of the truth. This fact should encourage present-day servants in their quest to rediscover true pastoral ministry. The effort might be extremely difficult in the face of strong traditions, but it is both necessary and possible.

The Reformation Period (1500–1648)

The Protestant Reformation was of great importance in the history of the church and the development of its ministry. Flowing out of late-medieval piety, mysticism, and scholarship,[60] its focus was upon reforming the existing church according to biblical principles. It was more accurately the "Magisterial Reformation" because the reformers retained the mind set of the magistrate who compelled individuals in matters of faith. This state-church concept contrasted sharply with the free-church thinking of true Anabaptists—distinguished from a larger group of Anabaptists—who attempted to build a new church based on the Bible.[61] This important difference has led an increasing number of historians to focus on the "Radical Reformation" as "a major expression of the religious movement of the sixteenth century."[62] Williams identifies this "Radical Reformation" as the "Fourth" Reformation, thereby distinguishing it from Lutheranism, Calvinism, and Anglicanism.[63] Williams acknowledges doctrinal differences within the Fourth Reformation but observes,

> Though Anabaptists, Spiritualists, and Evangelical Rationalists differed among themselves as to what constituted the root of faith and order and the ultimate source of divine authority among them . . . all three groups within the Radical Reformation agreed in cutting back to that root and in freeing church and creed of what they regarded as the suffocating growth of ecclesiastical tradition and magisterial prerogative. Precisely this makes theirs a "Radical Reformation."[64]

In seeking an understanding of the contribution of the Reformation to biblical ministry, one must look to both the magisterial reformers (Luther, Bucer, Calvin, and Knox) and the free church (true Anabaptists). The former worked under the banner of *reformatio* (reformation) whereas the latter had *restitutio* (restitution) as its banner. Both offer important insights.

The Magisterial Reformation

An examination of the reforms implemented by Martin Luther (1483–1546) and John Calvin (1509–1564) reveals that they differed in degrees of progress toward the biblical pattern of church ministry. In the final analysis, both men maintained a magisterial church-state system, believing that any reformation should ultimately result in a Christian state.[65] The two distinguished between the visible and the invisible church, viewing the invisible as the church made up of only the elect.[66] Their view of the visible church, created by a magisterial church-state, precluded a simple doctrine of church and ministry. The difference between the two men was that Luther tended to retain in the church the traditions not specifically condemned in Scripture, and Calvin tended to include only what Scripture taught explicitly about church ministry.[67] This difference is evident in the corresponding traditions of worship emerging from these founders, Lutheran worship being very embellished and incorporating ritual and the Reformed mind set reflecting more simple church settings.

According to general recognition, Luther's doctrine of the church and ministry was complex and changed progressively throughout his life.[68] In his "Open Letter to the Christian Nobility of the German Nation" (1520), Luther called for the pulling down of the three walls of Romanism and popery and offered proposals, including reform to establish a simple national church with parish priests of godly character.[69] The implementation of that church was more complex than Luther first envisioned,[70] but it contained the key elements of the preaching of the Word, the sacraments of baptism and the altar, the keys of Christian discipline and forgiveness, a called and consecrated ministry, public thanksgiving and worship, and suffering, the possession of the holy cross.[71] He stressed ministry of the Word as the duty of pastors and all believers. In particular, the functions of pastors included the ministry the Word, baptizing, administration of the sacred bread and wine, binding and loosing sin, and sacrifice.[72] He put great emphasis on pastoral care, which always related directly to the ministry of the Word.[73]

Martin Bucer (1491–1551), an important disciple of Luther and a teacher of Calvin, had an important ministry in Strasbourg. Tidball rightly calls him the "Pastoral Theologian of the Reformation"[74] because of his extensive work in developing the office and work of the pastor. In his *"De Regno Christi,"* Bucer identified three duties of a pastor: (1) a diligent teacher of the Holy Scriptures, (2) an administrator of the sacraments, and (3) a participant in the discipline of the church. The third duty had three parts: life and manners, penance (involving serious sin), and sacred ceremonies (worship and fasting). A fourth duty was care for the needy.[75] Bucer wrote,

> Those pastors and teachers of the churches who want to fulfill their office and keep themselves clean of the blood of those of their flocks who are perishing should not only publicly administer Christian doctrine, but also announce, teach and entreat repentance toward God and faith in our Lord Jesus Christ, and whatever contributes toward piety, among all who do not reject this doctrine of salvation, even at home and with each one privately. . . . For the faithful ministers of Christ should imitate this their master and chief shepherd of the churches, and seek most lovely themselves whatever has been lost, including the hundredth sheep wandering from the fold, leaving behind the ninety-nine which remain in the Lord's fold (Matt. 18:12).[76]

Calvin's contribution to a biblical understanding of pastoral ministry is tremendous. Although Calvin is often viewed as being primarily a theologian and an exegete, he was also a pastor and churchman.[77] He devotes the fourth book of his *Institutes* to the church, speaking of the necessity of the church's function:

> In order that the preaching of the Gospel might flourish, He deposited this treasure in the church. He instituted "pastors and teachers" [Eph. 4:11] through whose lips He might teach His own; he furnished them with authority; finally, He omitted nothing that might make for holy agreement of faith and for right order.[78]

He used the title "mother" to illustrate the importance and place of the church:

For there is no other way to enter into life unless this mother
conceive us in her womb, give us birth, nourish us at her breast,
and lastly, unless she keep us under her care and guidance until,
putting off mortal flesh, we become like the angels [Matt. 22:30].
Our weakness does not allow us to be dismissed from her school
until we have been pupils all our lives.[79]

Calvin found the duties of a pastor throughout the Bible. Specifically,
he observed that "the teaching and example of the New Testament set
forth the nature and work of the pastorate in the calling and teaching of
the apostles." This, he said, makes a delineation of ministerial work in
the church an important aspect of theology.[80]

Previous writings have described the fourfold office of pastor, teacher,
elder, and deacon in Calvin's Geneva.[81] Calvin placed strong emphasis
on preaching, governing, and pastoring: "A pastor needs two voices, one
for gathering the sheep and the other for driving away wolves and thieves.
The Scripture supplies him with the means for doing both."[82] Furthermore, "Paul assigns to teachers the duty of carving or dividing the Word,
like a father dividing the bread into small pieces to feed his children."[83]
Calvin's concern was the profit and edification of the hearer. To this
responsibility he added the important tasks of administration of the sacraments and visitation of the sick. This philosophy developed in Geneva
into a church polity that was difficult and complex because of Calvin's
understanding of the visible church and a Christian magistracy.[84] In
Geneva, it resulted in a kind of Christian theocracy in Geneva because
of the intersection of religious and civil authorities in implementing the
polity.

The most biblical of the outworkings of Calvin's ecclesiastical and
civil views did not emerge until much later because Calvin never rose
above the magisterial state-church he inherited from Romanism. Woolley
observes, "Calvin was influenced by Rome even while helping to counteract Rome," and "The greater fruitage of Calvin's ideas elsewhere than
in Geneva is due to the fact that in other areas they were not subjected to
implementation by the civil state to the same degree as was true in
Geneva."[85] The issue of civil intolerance, brought about by the state-
church such as existed at Geneva, caused the Anabaptists to seek a more

primitive and biblical church and ministry than what the Magisterial Reformers provided. This result was an unfortunate flaw in the otherwise profound efforts of Calvin to purify, clarify, and systematize the truth of scriptural teaching regarding the ministry and other areas.

One cannot consider the Reformation period without describing the legacy of biblical ministry from John Knox (1514–1572). Following Calvin's lead, Knox developed a manual for the English-speaking church of Geneva, which he pastored from 1556–1559.[86] In addition, his letters and pastoral records reflect a rich understanding of commitment to preach the Word with great passion, deep interest, and care for the spiritual welfare of men.[87]

The Anabaptist Reformation

Anabaptism draws heavily on the work and influence of Luther and Zwingli in its contribution to biblical understanding of the church and its ministry. As was hinted earlier, within the larger number of people known as "Anabaptists" was a smaller group whose root of faith was the Scripture, constituting them as the "true Anabaptists."[88] This group included men such as Conrad Grebel (1495–1526), Michael Sattler (1490–1527), Balthasar Hubmaier (1480–1528), and Menno Simons (1496–1561). Although they were influenced by the theology of the magisterial reformers, these men went further in their efforts to reinstitute a primitive, biblical church and ministry. In describing the nature of their ecclesiology, Bender remarks, "The Anabaptist idea of the church is derivative, based on the deeper idea of discipleship, which of course also implies an active covenanting into a brotherhood, without which discipleship could not be realized."[89]

As a general rule, the Anabaptists rejected the idea of an invisible church, viewing the church as a voluntary association of regenerated saints. They sought to restore the idea of a primitive NT church free from magisterial entanglements. This view allowed the practice of church discipline, but it meant that the church did not have a right to force its views on anyone or to persecute those who opposed it. Friedmann identifies the following characteristics of the Anabaptist church: (1) a visible covenantal community of believers, (2) a shared brotherhood practicing brotherly love, (3) a commitment to exclusion (ban) as an act of brotherly love, (4) a church of order where members submit to authority, (5) a suffering church under the Cross, (6) a church practicing voluntarism or the liberty of conscience, and (7) a church practicing the two ordinances of baptism and the Lord's Supper.[90]

Within this primitive church structure, Anabaptism taught a simple ministry style. Michael Sattler described this ministry as follows:

> This office [of pastor] shall be to read, to admonish and teach, to warn, to discipline, to ban in the church, to lead out in prayer for the advancement of all the brethren and sisters, to lift up the bread when it is broken, and in all things to see to the care of the body of Christ, in order that it may be built up and developed, and the mouth of the slanderer be stopped.[91]

Conrad Grebel held a similar position in his brief but important work,[92] as did Balthasar Hubmaier—the scholar and pastor of Waldshut and Nikolsburg—in his major contribution.[93] The "Discipline of the Church," an Anabaptist document from 1528, summarizes their position:

> The elders and preachers chosen for the brotherhood shall with zeal look after the needs of the poor, and with zeal in the Lord according to the command of the Lord extend what is needed for the sake of and instead of the brotherhood (Gal. 2; II Cor. 8, 9; Rom. 15; Acts 6).[94]

Timothy George reports that Menno Simons[95] said on his deathbed that nothing on earth was as precious to him as the church.[96] This statement well summarizes the Anabaptist commitment to the primitive church and its ministry. Many people paid the ultimate price for this love.[97]

The preceding discussion reveals that the Reformation era refocused the church on a biblical structure for the ministry. The Magisterial Reformers made significant progress in their reformation of the church. Among the radical Reformers are those who carried through this commitment in seeking to reinstitute a consistent biblical ministry.

The Modern Period (1649–Present)

The modern era has many examples of those who have sought a biblical church ministry. Some of them have drawn on the heritage of progress toward a biblical ministry by the Magisterial Reformers. Our survey of this period can cite only a few outstanding examples of biblical ministry. One such pastor was Richard Baxter (1615–1691), the early Puritan divine. He is best known for the book *The Reformed Pastor,* which he wrote in 1656 during a nineteen-year pastorate in Kidderminster, England. The book concentrates on Acts 20:28 in developing his philosophy of ministry. He deals with the pastor's labors, confessions, motives, constraints, and dedication. The work is profoundly deep and intensely spiritual as it flows from the heart of a humble pastor to other pastors:

> I do now, in the behalf of Christ, and for the sake of his Church and the immortal souls of men, beseech all the faithful ministers of Christ, that they will presently and effectually fall upon this work. . . . This duty hath its rise neither from us, but from the Lord, and for my part . . . tread me in the dirt.[98]

The larger Puritan movement advanced the church through its clear focus on the Word of God. Although they never became a distinct and unified denomination, the Puritans nevertheless exerted considerable influence on many others. Anglicanism labeled most English Puritans nonconformists, yet the British Puritans were unable to establish their own churches as American Puritans were able to do. Even in America, though, they identified with various denominations rather than forming their own church. Leland Ryken concludes,

> There was, to be sure, a theoretical Puritan consensus on most issues involving worship and the theory of what a church is. Puritanism also bequeathed at least one permanent legacy, the phenomenon of a "gathered church" separate from the state and with an accompanying proliferation of independent churches.[99]

Ryken identifies several important aspects of the Puritan concept of the church. First, calling the extravagance and elaborate tradition in the church an inadequate authority for religious belief, Puritans reasserted the primacy of the Word, resorting to the "strongest control at their disposal, the Bible. They vowed to limit all church polity and worship practices to what could be directly based on statements or procedures found in the Bible."[100] Second, Puritans viewed the church as a "spiritual reality." "It is not impressive buildings or fancy clerical vestments. It is instead the company of the redeemed," dissociated from any particular place. Certain activities and relationships—including preaching, sacraments, discipline, and prayer—defined the church.[101] Third, the Puritans elevated the lay person's role in the church and participation in worship. Many Puritans gravitated toward either Presbyterian or Congregational polity which provided for lay responsibility within each congregation in choosing ministers.[102] Fourth, the Puritans embraced simplicity in various parts of worship, including orderly and clear organization, curbed ceremony and ritual, simplified church architecture and furnishings, simplified church music, simplification of the sacraments, and a clearly defined goal of worship.[103]

In this very biblical church setting, the teaching and practice of true ministry was commonplace. The Puritan pastor was to preach, minister the sacraments, and pray. Preaching was primary, but closely associated was a godly life.[104] In his "Of the Calling of the Ministry," William Perkins (1558–1602) describes the minister as, first, an "Angel" or "Messenger of God"—that is, the "Messenger of the Lord of Hosts" to the people. He is, second, an "Interpreter"—that is, "one who is able to deliver aright the reconciliation, made betwixt God and man." "Every minister is a double Interpreter, God's to the people and the people's to God."[105] To this he adds the necessity of being a "godly minister" and urges men to dedicate their sons to this, the highest office:

> For the Physician's care for the body, or the Lawyer's care for the cause, are both inferior duties to this of the Minister. A good Lawyer may be one of ten, a good Physician one of twenty, a good man one of 100, but a good Minister is one of 1000. A good Lawyer may declare the true state of thy cause, a Physician may declare the true state of the body: No calling, no man can declare unto thee thy righteousness, but a true minister.[106]

This same pastoral perspective of Perkins characterized many future Puritans after him. "The great names of the Puritan era, John Owen, Thomas Brooks, Richard Sibbes, Robert Bolton, Thomas Manton, Thomas Goodwin and William Gurnal, all adopted this pastoral perspective in their writing of theology."[107] The colorful ministry of William Tennent and his Log College in Neshaminy, Pennsylvania, is also worthy of note.[108]

Jonathan Edwards (1703–1758), known so well as a profound philosopher and theologian, was also a pastor. He wrote,

> More especially is the uniting of a faithful minister with a particular Christian people as their pastor, when done in a due manner, like a young man marrying a virgin. . . . The minister joyfully devoting himself to the service of his Lord in the work of the ministry, as a work that he delights in, and also joyfully uniting himself to the society of the saints that he is set over . . . and they, on the other hand, joyfully receiving him as a precious gift of their ascended Redeemer.[109]

Westra states that Edwards knew that the biblical name *Jonathan* meant "Jehovah's gift" and

> prayerfully dedicated himself to being "Jehovah's gift" to the souls of his care; he did so wholeheartedly convinced that a faithful minister as a means of grace can be "the greatest blessing of anything in the world that ever God bestows on a people."[110]

One needs only to read the Puritans to see that they provide some of the finest pastoral theology of the modern period.

After the Puritan era, Charles Bridges (1794–1869), a pastor in England for fifty-two years, wrote his respected *The Christian Ministry*. He combined a deep and accurate knowledge of Scripture with great spirituality and humility to produce a classic work worthy of careful reading. In a word, he believed that the "sum of our whole labor in this kind is to honor God, and to save men."[111]

Charles Spurgeon (1834–1892), primarily known for his preaching rather than his daily functions in the pastorate, taught his students the principles of preaching;[112] nevertheless, he viewed the ministry as centered on serving the spiritual needs of his people. He wrote, "Ministers are for churches, and not churches for ministers."[113] Significantly, the controversies surrounding Spurgeon's ministry have everything to do with the application of his theology to pastoral duties, such as to evangelism particularly or philosophy of ministry generally.[114]

Nineteenth-century pastors, including G. Campbell Morgan (1863–1945)[115] and missionary Roland Allen (1868–1947), provided other important examples of faithful ministry.[116] The long teaching ministry of Benjamin B. Warfield (1851–1921) at Princeton Theological Seminary (1887–1921) was a great positive influence in promoting biblical ministry.[117]

During the twentieth century, theological liberalism found its way into every major denomination and replaced the passion for biblical ministry in many instances with an agenda of the social gospel.[118] The rise of neo-evangelicalism[119] in 1958, with its intentional accommodation of error and its subsequent tributaries[120] into pragmatic ministry, was another step away from biblical ministry.[121] Much true biblical ministry in recent years has occurred in smaller denominations or churches that have continued the Free Church tradition.[122] The nature of such ministry is obscure and often difficult to identify because of a lack of adequate documentation.

The last half of the twentieth century offered several prominent examples of biblical ministry that are noteworthy. The unusual way that God has used these men is the reason for citing them. It is not that they have been the only ones.

One prime example is D. Martyn Lloyd-Jones (1899–1981). Lloyd-Jones was well respected as an expository preacher, but he was also a devoted and faithful pastor. His biography is full of examples of both preaching and shepherding.[123] He was first a preacher, advocating the irreplaceability of biblical preaching, a right relationship with the congregation (the pew is never to dictate the message, but the preacher must listen to his people), and an adequate preparation of the preacher in all areas.[124] He also had a reputation as a pastoral counselor. Murray records, "Next to the pulpit, Dr. Lloyd-Jones throughout his ministry was constantly engaged in seeking to help individuals."[125] Interestingly, he viewed people as in need of spiritual rather than psychological help.[126] Besides, Lloyd-Jones was a pastor to pastors as he sought to instill in them what God had taught him.[127]

Another example of biblical ministry is that of Jay Adams, a pastor and a long-time professor at Westminster Theological Seminary. Adams has contributed greatly to current understanding of biblical ministry in several areas. In each case, he has built his understanding of pastoral theology firmly on his biblical and exegetical theology. His first major focus was counseling, in which he developed a biblical model of "nouthetic counseling"—note the Greek word *noutheteō*—and emphasizing the need to confront sin with biblical teaching.[128] He has also developed a series of textbooks on pastoral theology, covering pastoral life, pastoral counseling, and pastoral leadership. The foundation of all of these emphases is his firm commitment to sound biblical theology.[129] He has written,

> The directions that one's practical activities take, the norms by which he operates and the motivation behind what he does must emerge from a biblical theological study of the Scriptures. The pursuit of Practical Theology, therefore, must be seen as the study and application of the biblical means of expressing one's theology.[130]

In recent years, Adams has devoted his thinking to biblical preaching and its importance in ministry.[131] All of his teachings have had a profound effect in redirecting ministry toward the biblical pattern.

Another important example of biblical ministry is John MacArthur Jr. MacArthur defines the term *shepherdology* as (1) the study of shepherding, (2) the science of leading a flock, and (3) a method of biblical church leadership.[132] He develops this term by understanding all ministry to flow from the teaching of Scripture.[133] The book *The Anatomy of the Church* represents a significant contribution to a biblical philosophy of ministry in defining the church as (1) the skeletal structure—unalterable doctrines or nonnegotiable truths; (2) the internal systems—proper spiritual attitudes; (3) the muscles—spiritual activities, including preaching and teaching, worship, discipleship, shepherding, and fellowship; and (4) the head—the person and work of Christ.[134] This model has become the basis for biblical ministry in many churches.

MacArthur is continuing to contribute significant works challenging the church not to drift away from the truth. The most significant of these works compares the Downgrade Controversy of Spurgeon's day to the pragmatism of many contemporary evangelical churches.[135]

His contribution is most valuable because he is a committed expositor, a theologian, and a pastor. He has chosen to write and address significant issues in a way that the entire church can understand. God has used him to build a significant church in the Spurgeon tradition, then to start schools for the training of a future generation of servants and preachers and to author significant works dealing with important theological issues facing the church today.

Conclusion

This chapter is but a brief history of biblical pastoral ministry. Such accounts are often based on ministries the records of which remain for future generations to examine. Many faithful ministers have also sought a biblical ministry, and only heaven has recorded their accomplishments. The future examination of each man's ministry (1 Cor. 3:13–15) and the recounting of faithful ministry for God's glory will be a time of great rejoicing in heaven. Today's pastors can find great encouragement and receive great challenges by examining the lives and convictions of faithful ministers of the past. May this generation and future generations of Christ's servants commit themselves to the purest form of primitive, biblical ministry so that when history records their efforts, they may say with Paul, "I *have* fought the good fight, I *have* finished the course, I *have* kept the faith" (2 Tim. 4:7, emphasis added).

Endnotes

1. Thomas C. Oden notes, "Pastoral theology is a special form of practical theology because it focuses on the practice of ministry, with particular attention to the systematic definition of the pastoral office and its function" (*Pastoral Theology: Essentials of Ministry* [San Francisco: Harper, 1982], x).

2. In early church history, Christians understood "tradition" as "revelation made by God and delivered by Him to His faithful people through the mouth of His prophets and apostles." It was something *handed over,* not something *handed down,* and was thus in accord with divine revelation. In the period since the early

church, "tradition means the continuous stream of explanation and elucidation of the primitive faith, illustrating the way in which Christianity has been presented and understood in past ages. It is, that is, the accumulated wisdom of the past" ("Tradition," in *The Oxford Dictionary of the Christian Church,* 2d ed., ed. F. L. Cross and E. A. Livingstone [Oxford: University Press, 1983], 1388). The latter approach to tradition has allowed much deflection from simple, primitive, biblical ministry.

3. Franklin H. Littell, "The Concept of the Believers' Church," in *The Concept of the Believers' Church,* ed. James Leo Garrett Jr. (Scottdale, Pa.: Herald, 1969), 27–32, delineates at least six basic principles or marks of the "Believer's Church" that represent common themes in various churches. They include (1) the Believers' Church, although outwardly constituted by volunteers, is Christ's church and not theirs; (2) membership in the Believers' Church is voluntary and witting (done deliberately); (3) the principle of separation from "the world" is basic, although it has often been misinterpreted; (4) mission and witness are key concepts for the Believers' Church, and all members are involved; (5) internal integrity and church discipline are stressed; and (6) the concept of the secular in relationship to the sacred is interpreted properly. The primary example of an application of this last theme is a state church in which government attempts to control all ideology and thinking, thus limiting human liberty.

4. Franklin Hamlin Littell, *The Origins of Sectarian Protestantism* (New York: Macmillan, 1964), xvii.

5. Littell, "The Concept of the Believers' Church," 25–26.

6. Marc Mueller, "What Is History?" (unpublished chapel lecture, The Master's Seminary, Sun Valley, Calif., 16 February 1989), 5.

7. E.g., Derek J. Tidball, *Skillful Shepherds: An Introduction to Pastoral Theology* (Grand Rapids: Zondervan, 1986), 18.

8. Ibid.

9. Ibid.

10. Note the divergence of views as reflected in Louis Berkhoff's development of the doctrine of the church (*The History of Christian Doctrines* [Edinburgh: Banner of Truth, n.d.], 227–41).

11. Oden, *Pastoral Theology,* 311.

12. Tidball, *Skillful Shepherds,* 54.

13. See Leon Morris, *Testaments of Love: A Study of Love in the Bible* (Grand Rapids: Eerdmans, 1981), 8–100; and Norman Snaith, *The Distinctive Ideas of the Old Testament* (New York: Schocken, 1964), 131–42.

14. The Hebrew word *ḥesed* has been variously translated with meanings such as "mercy, love, loyal love, unfailing love, constant love, strong, faithful love, lovingkindness" (Morris, *Testaments of Love,* 66–67). The *ḥesed* or mercy of God as He covenants with His people to love them and to be faithful to that love always is a rich and profound study that furnishes important insight into true pastoral

activity (see Nelson Glueck, *Hesed in the Bible* [New York: KTAV, 1975]; see also Snaith, *Distinctive Ideas,* 94–130).

15. J. B. Lightfoot, "The Christian Ministry," in *Saint Paul's Epistle to the Philippians* (reprint, Grand Rapids: Zondervan, 1953), 196–201. Although Lightfoot himself became Bishop of Durham in 1879 and remained strongly committed to the Anglican tradition, his work remains of primary significance in understanding primitive church ministry and subsequent embellishments in church history.

16. Ibid., 95–99, 193–96. Both biblical and early patristic data support this conclusion (see John Gill, *Body of Divinity* [1769; reprint, Atlanta: Lassetter, 1965], 863–64; and A. E. Harvey, "Elders," *Journal of Theological Studies* n.s. 25 [1974]: 326.

17. See Lightfoot, *Saint Paul's Epistle to the Philippians,* 195.

18. Adolph Harnack, *History of Dogma* (Boston: Roberts, 1897), 2:77.

19. William A. Clebsch and Charles R. Jaekle, *Pastoral Care in Historical Perspective* (New York: Harper, 1967), 11–31; cf. also Carl A. Volz, "The Pastoral Office in the Early Church," *Word and World* 9 (1989): 359–66; Theron D. Price, "The Emergence of the Christian Ministry," *Review and Expositor* 46 (1949): 216–38; B. H. Streeter, *The Primitive Church* (New York: Macmillan, 1929); and T. W. Manson, *The Church's Ministry* (Philadelphia: Westminster, 1948).

20. Hans Von Campenhausen, *Ecclesiastical Authority and Spiritual Power in the Church of the First Three Centuries* (Stanford: Stanford Press, 1969), 149–77. He describes this process as the apostolic teaching and traditional teaching "taking in more and more material, historical, legal, and dogmatic" (151).

21. The hierarchy of bishop, presbyter, and deacon became known as the "threefold ministry." As an endorsement of the doctrine of "apostolic succession," these layers of authority furnished the groundwork for the papacy (see Dom Gregory Dix, "The Ministry in the Early Church," in *The Apostolic Ministry,* ed. Kenneth E. Kirk [London: Hodder and Stoughton, 1946], 183–304, esp. 186–91).

22. Ibid., 177. See also Fenton John Anthony Hort, *The Christian Ecclesia* (London: Macmillan, 1914), 224.

23. See Benjamin B. Warfield, *The Plan of Salvation* (Grand Rapids: Eerdmans, 1955), 52–68.

24. Polycarp, "Epistle of Polycarp to the Philippians," 6, in J. B. Lightfoot, *The Apostolic Fathers* (London: Macmillan, 1926), 179.

25. Clement of Alexandria, "The Stromata, or Miscellanies," vi:xiii, vii:vii, *The Ante-Nicene Fathers,* ed. Alexander Roberts and James Donaldson (Grand Rapids: Eerdmans, 1983), 2:504, 535.

26. Ibid., vi:xiii, 505. Although Clement mentions the threefold ministry, he does not emphasize it or call attention to a special authority of bishop.

27. "Origen against Celsus," v:xxxiii, *The Ante-Nicene Fathers,* ed. by Alexander Roberts and James Donaldson (Grand Rapids: Eerdmans, 1982), 4:557–58.

28. Cyprian, "The Epistles of Cyprian," Epistle lxviii:8, in *The Ante-Nicene Fathers,* ed. by Alexander Roberts and James Donaldson (Grand Rapids: Eerdmans, 1981),

5:374–75; cf. also Cyprian, "The Treatises of Cyprian," *Treatises,* i:5–6; ibid., 5:5–6.

29. St. Chrysostom, "Treatises Concerning the Christian Priesthood," *A Select Library of the Nicene and Post-Nicene Fathers of the Christian Church,* ed. Philip Schaff (Grand Rapids: Eerdmans, 1983), FS IX:25–83.

30. Ibid., 64.

31. Ibid., 64–65. See Tidball's excellent description of John Chrysostom in *Skillful Shepherds,* 154–63.

32. Ibid., 74–77. Note Chrysostom's statements about reclusion. Monasticism began with Antony of Egypt just before Chrysostom's time.

33. Augustine, "Letters of Saint Augustine," Letter xxi:1, *A Select Library of the Nicene and Post-Nicene Fathers of the Christian Church,* ed. Philip Schaff (Grand Rapids: Eerdmans, 1994), FS 1:237.

34. See Joseph B. Bernardin, "St Augustine the Pastor," in *A Companion to the Study of St. Augustine,* ed. Roy W. Battenhouse (New York: Oxford, 1955), 57–89.

35. Augustine, *The City of God,* bk. 1 of *A Select Library of the Nicene and Post-Nicene Fathers of the Christian Church,* ed. Philip Schaff (Grand Rapids: Eerdmans, 1983), 2:1.

36. Gunnar Westin, *The Free Church Through the Ages* (Nashville: Broadman, 1958), 9.

37. Ibid., 1–8.

38. Jaroslav Pelikan (*The Growth of Medieval Theology [600–1300],* vol. 3 of *The Christian Tradition* [Chicago: University of Chicago Press, 1978], 3:17–18) writes, "The quality that marked Augustine and the other orthodox fathers was their loyalty to the received tradition. The apostolic anathema pronounced against anyone, even 'an angel from heaven,' who preached 'a gospel contrary to that which you have received' by tradition was, as in the East so also in the West, a prohibition of any kind of theological novelty. . . . One definition of heretics could be 'those who now take pleasure in making up new terminology for themselves and who are not content with the dogma of the holy fathers.'"

39. See the discussion by Westin, *Free Church,* 9–23; see also, E. H. Broadbent, *The Pilgrim Church* (London: Pickering and Inglis, 1931), 10–48; and Donald F. Durnbaugh, *The Believers' Church* (New York: Macmillan, 1968), 3–40.

40. Philip Schaff, "Nicene and Post-Nicene Christianity," in *History of the Christian Church* (Grand Rapids: Eerdmans, 1968), 3:365, cf. also 366–70.

41. See W. H. C. Frend, *The Donatist Church, A Movement of Protest in Roman North Africa* (Oxford: Clarendon, 1952), 315–32.

42. Gregory the Great, "The Book of Pastoral Rule," in *A Select Library of Nicene and Post-Nicene Fathers of the Christian Church,* ed. Philip Schaff and Henry Wace (Grand Rapids: Eerdmans, 1983), SS 12.

43. Roland H. Bainton, "The Ministry in the Middle Ages," in *The Ministry in Historical Perspectives,* ed. Richard Niebuhr and Daniel D. Williams (New York: Harper, 1956), 98.

44. Ibid., 86.
45. Ernest A. Payne, "The Ministry in Historical Perspective," *The Baptist Quarterly* 17 (1958): 260–61.
46. Note the easy use of the term *heretic* even by evangelical historians, e.g., J. D. Douglas, *The New International Dictionary of the Christian Church*, rev. ed. (Grand Rapids: Zondervan, 1978). The issue of perspective is always relevant when charging someone with being a heretic.
47. Bainton, "Ministry in the Middle Ages," 108.
48. Fred. C. Conybeare, ed., *The Key of Truth, a Manual of the Paulician Church of Armenia* (Oxford: Clarendon, 1898), 76–77, 106–11.
49. Ibid., 112.
50. Peter Allix, *Some Remarks upon the Ecclesiastical History of the Ancient Churches of Piedmont* (Oxford: Clarendon, 1891), 238f.
51. See John Henry Blunt, ed., "Waldenses," in *Dictionary of Sects, Heresies, Ecclesiastical Parties and Schools of Religious Thought* (London: Longmans, 1891), 616–21; cf. also W. Jones, *The History of the Waldenses* (1816), 2 vols.
52. Peter Allix, *Remarks upon the Ecclesiastical History of the Ancient Churches of the Albigenses,* new ed. (Oxford: Clarendon, 1821), 207.
53. John Wycliffe, cited in *Documents of the Christian Church,* ed. Henry Bettenson (London: Oxford, 1963), 173–75.
54. Herbert E. Winn, ed., *Wyclif: Select English Writings* (London: Oxford, 1929), 41, 68.
55. John Huss, cited by E. H. Gillett, *The Life and Times of John Huss; or the Bohemian Reformation of the Fifteenth Century* (Boston: Gould, 1864), 1:285.
56. Ibid., 1:248.
57. Ibid.
58. Matthew Spinka, *John Hus, A Biography* (Princeton, N.J.: Princeton University Press, 1968), 19. See also Matthew Spinka, *John Hus's Concept of the Church* (Princeton, N.J.: Princeton University Press, 1966). *On Simony* (1413) and *On the Church* (1415) are among Huss's own works.
59. See S. L. Greenslade, *The Works of William Tyndale* (London: Blackie, 1938), 181–96. Tyndale's statements are in sharp contrast to those of his late-medieval contemporaries; see Dennis D. Martin, "Popular and Monastic Pastoral Issues in the Later Middle Ages," *Church History* 56 (1987): 320–32.
60. See Steven Ozment, *The Age of Reform 1250–1550: An Intellectual and Religious History of Late Medieval and Reformation Europe* (New Haven: Yale, 1980), xi–xii, 1–21; Heiko A. Oberman, *The Harvest of Medieval Theology* (Grand Rapids: Eerdmans, 1967); and idem, *The Dawn of the Reformation* (Grand Rapids: Eerdmans, 1992), 1–83.
61. Littel has a good development of this important distinction in *Origins of Sectarian Protestantism,* xvii–xviii, 65–66, 73. Philip Schaff writes, "The Reformers aimed to reform the old Church by the Bible; the Radicals attempted to build a new Church from the Bible. The former maintained the historic continuity; the latter

went directly to the apostolic age, and ignored the intervening centuries as an apostasy. The Reformers founded a popular state-church, including all citizens with their families; the Anabaptists organized on the voluntary principle, select congregations of baptized believers, separated from the world and from the State" (*History of the Christian Church, Modern Christianity, the Swiss Reformation* [reprint, Grand Rapids: Eerdmans, 1969], 8:71).

62. George Huntston Williams, *Spiritual and Anabaptist Writers*, vol. 25 of *The Library of Christian Classics* (London: SCM, 1957), 19.

63. Ibid., 19. This distinguished Harvard scholar further develops the same distinction and the term *Magisterial Reformation* in George H. Williams, *The Radical Reformation* (Philadelphia: Westminster, 1962), xxiii–xxxi. See also, Roland Bainton, "The Left Wing of the Reformation," *Journal of Religion* 21 (1941): 127.

64. Williams, *Spiritual and Anabaptist Writers*, 25:22. See also, Philip Schaff, *History of the Christian Church, Modern Christianity, the German Reformation* (reprint, Grand Rapids: Eerdmans, 1967), 7:607.

65. Williams, *Radical Reformation*, xxiv; cf. also, Timothy George, *Theology of the Reformers* (Nashville: Broadman, 1988), 98.

66. See R. L. Omanson, "The Church," *Evangelical Dictionary of Theology* (Grand Rapids: Baker, 1984), 231.

67. Williams notes this regulatory principle in *Radical Reformation*, xxvii. See also, Francois Wendel, *Calvin* (New York: Harper and Row, 1963), 301–2.

68. Gordon Rupp, *The Righteousness of God, Luther Studies* (London: Hodder, 1953), 310–28.

69. Martin Luther, "An Open Letter to the Christian Nobility of the German Nation Concerning the Reform of the Christian Estate," in *Three Treatises* (Philadelphia: Muhlenberg, 1947), 9–44, 47, 98.

70. George, *Theology of the Reformers*, 86–98.

71. Rupp, *Righteousness of God*, 322.

72. Martin Luther, "Concerning the Ministry" (1523), in *Luther's Works, Church and Ministry*, ed. Conrad Bergendoff and Helmut T. Lehmann (Philadelphia: Fortress, 1958), 40:21–29.

73. Martin Luther, "Instructions for the Visitors of Parish Pastors in Electoral Saxony" (1528), in *Luther's Works, Church and Ministry*, ed. Conrad Bergendoff and Helmut T. Lehmann (Philadelphia: Fortress, 1958), 40:269–320.

74. Tidball, *Skillful Shepherds*, 184.

75. Martin Bucer, *"De Regno Christi," Melanchthon and Bucer*, in *The Library of Christian Classics*, ed. Wilhelm Pauck (London: SCM, 1969), 19:232–59.

76. Ibid., 19:235.

77. For an excellent development of this side of Calvin, see, W. Stanford Reid, "John Calvin, Pastoral Theologian," *The Reformed Theological Review* 42 (1982): 65–73. Cf. also Jim van Zyl, "John Calvin the Pastor," *The Way Ahead* (a paper read to the 1975 Carey Conference, Haywards Heath: Carey, 1975), 69–78.

78. John Calvin, *Institutes of the Christian Religion,* vols. 20–21 of *The Library of Christian Classics,* ed. by John T. McNeill, trans. and indexed by Ford Lewis Battles (Philadelphia: Westminster, 1960), iv:1:1 (21:1011–12).

79. Ibid., iv:1:4 (21:1016).

80. Reid, "John Calvin," 65–66.

81. See George, *Theology of the Reformers,* 235–49; cf. also, John T. McNeill, *The History and Character of Calvinism* (New York: Oxford, 1954), 214–21; and John Calvin, *Calvin's Ecclesiastical Advice,* trans. by Mary Beaty and Benjamin W. Farley (Louisville: Westminster/John Knox, 1991).

82. John Calvin, "The Epistle of Paul to Titus," in *Calvin's New Testament Commentaries,* ed. David W. Torrance (Grand Rapids: Eerdmans, 1964), 361.

83. John Calvin, "The First and Second Epistles of Paul the Apostle to Timothy," in *Calvin's New Testament Commentaries,* ed. David W. Torrance (Grand Rapids: Eerdmans, 1964), 314.

84. Note the excellent work of Harro Hopfl, *The Christian Polity of John Calvin* (Cambridge: Cambridge University Press, 1982).

85. Paul Woolley, "Calvin and Toleration," in *The Heritage of John Calvin* (Grand Rapids: Calvin College and Seminary, 1973), 138, 156.

86. John Knox, "The Form of Prayers and Ministration of the Sacraments, used in the English Congregation at Geneva, 1556," in *The Works of John Knox,* ed. David Laing (Edinburgh: James Thin, 1895), 4:141–216.

87. W. Stanford Reid, "John Knox, Pastor of Souls," *Westminster Theological Journal* 40 (1977): 20–21.

88. Note the classifications of Littell, *Origins of Sectarian Protestantism,* 163; and Williams, *Spiritual and Anabaptist Writers,* 28–31.

89. Harold S. Bender, "The Anabaptist Theology of Discipleship," *Mennonite Quarterly Review* 23 (1950): 26; see also Harold S. Bender, *The Anabaptist Vision* (Scottdale, Pa.: Herald, 1944).

90. Robert Friedmann, *The Theology of Anabaptism* (Scottdale, Pa.: Herald, 1973), 122–43.

91. William Lumpkin, "The Schleitheim Confession, 1527," in *Baptist Confessions of Faith* (Valley Forge: Judson, 1969), 22–30.

92. Harold Bender, *Conrad Grebel c. 1498–1526* (Goshen: Mennonite Historical Society, 1950), 204–8.

93. Balthasar Hubmaier, *Theologian of Anabaptism,* trans. and ed. by H. Wayne Pipkin and John H. Yoder (Scottdale, Pa.: Herald, 1989), 386–425. A careful study of these writings reveals his deep commitment to sound preaching as well as strong pastoral commitment.

94. William R. Estep, ed., "Discipline of the Church: How a Christian Ought to Live (October 1527)," in *Anabaptist Beginnings (1523–1533)* (Nieuwkoop: De Graaf, 1976), 128.

95. In a letter to Gellius Faber on the church and its ministry, Menno Simons offers the

following signs of the church: (1) the unadulterated doctrine of the divine Word, (2) the scriptural use of the sacraments, (3) the obedience to the Word of God, (4) the unfeigned love of one's neighbor, (5) the confident confession of Christ, and (6) the bearing of Christ's testimony in persecution (Menno Simons, "Reply to Gellius Faber," *The Complete Writings of Menno Simons* [Scottdale, Pa.: Herald Press, 1956], 739–41).

96. George, *Theology of the Reformers,* 285.

97. William R. Estep gives a fair account of many Anabaptists' persecutions in *The Anabaptist Story* (Nashville: Broadman, 1963).

98. Richard Baxter, *The Reformed Pastor* (London: Epworth, 1939), 58.

99. Leland Ryken, *Worldly Saints: The Puritans As They Really Were* (Grand Rapids: Zondervan, 1986), 112.

100. Ibid., 112–13.

101. Ibid., 115–16.

102. Ibid., 119, 123–24.

103. Ibid., 121–23.

104. Puritans associated theology with spirituality. See J. I. Packer, *A Quest for Godliness: The Puritan Vision of the Christian Life* (Wheaton: Crossway, 1990), 11–17.

105. William Perkins, *The Works of that Famous and Worthy Minister of Christ in the University of Cambridge,* 3 vols. (Cambridge: 1608–1609), 3:430–31.

106. Ibid., 435–36.

107. Tidball, *Skillful Shepherds,* 200. See also, P. Lewis, *The Genius of Puritanism* (Haywards Heath: Carey, 1975).

108. See Archibald Alexander, *The Log College* (1845; reprint, London: Banner of Truth, 1968); and Archibald Alexander, comp., *Sermons of the Log College* (1855; reprint, Ligonier, Pa.: Soli Deo Gloria, n.d.).

109. Jonathan Edwards, *The Works of Jonathan Edwards,* 2 vols. (1834; reprint, Edinburgh: Banner of Truth, 1974), 2:19–20.

110. Helen Westra, "Jonathan Edwards and the Scope of Gospel Ministry," *Calvin Theological Journal* 22 (1987): 68; cf. also Edwards, *Works of Jonathan Edwards,* 2:960.

111. Charles Bridges, *The Christian Ministry* (1830; reprint, London: Banner of Truth, 1959), 8.

112. Charles Haddon Spurgeon, *Lectures to My Students* (1875–94; reprint, Grand Rapids: Zondervan, 1954).

113. Charles Haddon Spurgeon, *The All-Around Ministry* (1900; reprint, Edinburgh: Banner of Truth, 1960), 256.

114. Iain H. Murray, *The Forgotten Spurgeon* (Edinburgh: Banner of Truth, 1966), 45–46, 99–101, 153–65.

115. G. Campbell Morgan, *The Ministry of the Word* (London: Hodder and Stoughton, 1919), and Jill Morgan, *A Man of the Word: Life of G. Campbell Morgan* (New York: Revell, 1951).

116. He is especially known for his works on indigenization of missions. See Roland

Allen, *The Spontaneous Expansion of the Church* (London: World Dominion, 1960).

117. Benjamin B. Warfield, "The Indispensableness of Systematic Theology to the Preacher," in *Selected Shorter Writings of Benjamin B. Warfield—II,* ed. John E. Meeter (Nutley, N.J.: Presbyterian and Reformed, 1973), 280–88. He writes, "Systematic Theology is, in other words, the preacher's true text-book" (228).

118. See B. J. Longfield, "Liberalism/Modernism, Protestant (c. 1870s–1930s)," in *Dictionary of Christianity in America,* ed. Daniel G. Reid (Downers Grove, Ill.: InterVarsity, 1990), 646–48.

119. Edward John Carnell, *The Case for Orthodox Theology* (Philadelphia: Westminster, 1959), and Roland Nash, *The New Evangelicalism* (Grand Rapids: Zondervan, 1963), 13–17.

120. See Richard Quebedeaux, *The Young Evangelicals, Revolution in Orthodoxy* (New York: Harper and Row, 1973), and Richard Quebedeaux, *The Worldly Evangelicals* (New York: Harper and Row, 1977).

121. See John F. MacArthur Jr., *Ashamed of the Gospel: When the Church Becomes Like the World* (Wheaton: Crossway, 1993). See also, John F. MacArthur Jr., *Our Sufficiency in Christ* (Dallas: Word, 1991).

122. See Ernest A. Payne, *Free Churchmen, Unrepentant and Repentant* (London: Carey, 1965).

123. Iain H. Murray, *David Martyn Lloyd-Jones, The First Forty Years, 1899–1939* (Edinburgh: Banner of Truth, 1982); and idem, *David Martyn Lloyd-Jones: The Fight of Faith, 1939–1981* (Edinburgh: Banner of Truth, 1990).

124. D. Martin Lloyd-Jones, *Preaching and Preachers* (Grand Rapids: Zondervan, 1971), 26, 143, 165.

125. Murray, *Fight of Faith,* 403.

126. Ibid.

127. Ibid., 697–713.

128. Jay Adams, *Competent to Counsel* (Grand Rapids: Baker, 1970), 41–50. Behind this approach is a solid theological foundation, xi–xxii. Adams also draws from the presuppositional apologetics of Cornelius Van Til, *The Defence of the Faith* (Philadelphia: Presbyterian and Reformed, 1955).

129. Jay E. Adams, *Shepherding God's Flock* (Grand Rapids: Zondervan, 1986), 1.

130. Ibid., 2.

131. Jay E. Adams, *Preaching with Purpose* (Grand Rapids: Zondervan, 1982), xiii, 114.

132. John F. MacArthur Jr., *Shepherdology: A Master Plan for Church Leadership* (Panorama City: The Master's Fellowship, 1989), 3. This is now available in a revised edition titled *The Master's Plan for the Church* (Chicago: Moody, 1991).

133. Ibid., 3–5.

134. Ibid., 9–64.

135. MacArthur, *Ashamed of the Gospel,* xi–xx. See also, MacArthur, *Our Sufficiency in Christ,* 25–43.

CHAPTER FIVE

A Biblical Call to Pastoral Vigilance

Richard L. Mayhue

Guarding Christ's flock of believers from spiritual danger remains one of the most neglected pastoral duties in today's church. In addition to commissioning spiritual sentinels to watch over His flock by directing her into truth and righteousness, God has charged these sentinels to protect the flock from doctrinal error and personal sin. Ezekiel 3, 33, and Acts 20 provide clear instruction on the "whys" and "hows" of being a "pastoral watchman." Christ's shepherding example and pastoral exhortations throughout church history urge today's shepherds to undertake their watchman responsibilities faithfully. Undershepherds of the flock will be good servants and obedient imitators of the Chief Shepherd when they regularly watch for and warn of encroaching spiritual dangers.

This essay has been adapted from Richard L. Mayhue's chapter "Watching and Warning" in *Rediscovering Pastoral Ministry,* ed. John F. MacArthur Jr. (Dallas: Word, 1995), 336–50. It is used by permission. Quotations are from the *New American Standard Bible* unless otherwise noted.

* * * * *

"Reengineering the Church" was the theme of a recent pastoral leadership conference on how to prepare the church for the twenty-first century. While reading the conference brochure, I responded, "Why reengineer the church when God designed it perfectly in the beginning? Shouldn't we inspect the church first and demolish only the portions that don't meet God's building code? That way, we can rebuild the defective portions according to the Builder's original plan. Who can improve on God's engineering?"

Obviously, the solution to the problems faced by the church is not *reengineering* but rather *restoration* to the perfect original specifications of the divine designer. The goal of change should be a return to the church's biblical roots in hope that she will regain her former glory.

An inspection of the existing church for possible rebuilding/remodeling should include the following types of questions.

- Have the builders/remodelers consulted the *Owner* (1 Cor. 3:9)?
- Are they dealing with the *original Builder* (Matt. 16:18)?
- Does the church still rest on the *beginning foundation* (1 Cor. 3:11; Eph. 2:20)?
- Is the *first Cornerstone* still in place (Eph. 2:20; 1 Peter 2:4–8)?
- Are the workers using *approved building materials* (1 Peter 2:5; 1 Cor. 3:12)?
- Do they use the right *laborers* (1 Cor. 3:9)?
- Have they used the appropriate *supervisors* (Eph. 4:11–13)?
- Are the initial *standards of quality control* still in place (Eph. 4:13–16)?
- Are the builders continuing to work from the *original blueprint* (2 Tim. 3:16–17)?

The biblical approach to keeping the church from deteriorating during the twenty-first century requires that the role of the *construction supervisors* be one of the first areas for review. With the church pictured as a building, the *supervisors* are none other than the *shepherds* of the flock, according to another biblical metaphor. The rest of this discussion will use the latter terminology.[1]

Paul laid out the basic task of a shepherd with these words:

> And He gave some as apostles, and some as prophets, and some as evangelists, and some as *pastors and teachers,* for the equipping of the saints for the work of service, to the building up of the body of Christ; until we all attain to the unity of the faith, and of the knowledge of the Son of God, to a mature man, to the measure of the stature which belongs to the fulness of Christ. As a result, we are no longer to be children, tossed here and there by waves, and carried about by every wind of doctrine, by the trickery of men, by craftiness in deceitful scheming; but speaking the truth in love, we are to grow up in all aspects into Him, who is the head, even Christ, from whom the whole body, being fitted and held together by that which every joint supplies, according to the proper working of each individual part, causes the growth of the body for the building up of itself in love. (Ephesians 4:11–16, emphasis added)

The True Shepherd

Scripture continually alerts its readers to watch for spiritual counterfeits.[2] Jesus warned of "false prophets, who come to you in sheep's clothing, but inwardly are ravenous wolves" (Matt. 7:15). Elsewhere He characterizes the false shepherd as "a thief and a robber" (John 10:1, 8).

Nowhere in Scripture is this point more apparent than in the OT prophets, who incessantly warned Israel about false prophets, even rebuking the nation when they strayed by following a false leader rather than a true one.[3] Although the NT is not as historically dramatic as the Old, it, too, warns frequently against deceptive and misleading spiritual leaders.[4] Every succeeding generation has proven the need for this caution. It remains a preeminent concern of God that true shepherds lead the church out of danger. One of the authenticating marks of a true shepherd is the ministry of watching and warning.

In the 1891 Lyman Beecher lectures on preaching at Yale, James Stalker insightfully cautioned, "The higher the honor attaching to the ministerial profession, when it is worthily filled, the deeper is the abuse of which it is capable in comparison with other callings. . . ."[5] Unfortunately, the genuine attracts the uninvited clever imitation. Realistically, the true shepherd must protect the flock from the spurious. Shepherds have explicit instructions from Scripture to warn that both overt and covert spiritual dangers continually threaten the pure life of the church because not everyone who claims to be a true shepherd is speaking the truth.

Charles Jefferson, in his classic work *The Minister as Shepherd,* lists seven basic functions of the genuine shepherd:

1. to love the sheep,
2. to feed the sheep,
3. to rescue the sheep,
4. to attend and comfort the sheep,
5. to guide the sheep,
6. to guard and protect the sheep, and
7. to watch over the sheep.[6]

This chapter treats Jefferson's last two categories in particular—guarding and watching over the sheep. No other aspect of contemporary pastoral ministry has fallen into disuse more than the life-saving role of a "watchman." For effective ministry to take place, the recovering of that aspect of shepherdly vigilance that guards and protects the flock from preventable spiritual carnage is vital. The true pastor will make the safety of Christ's flock a top priority. In so doing, he will also help rid the pastoral ranks of pollution caused by unauthorized look-alikes.

Overseeing the Flock

Each of the biblical terms for *pastor, elder,* and *overseer* describes facets of the shepherd's role. All three appear together in Acts 20:17, 28 and 1 Peter 5:1–2. *Elder* and *overseer* link up in Titus 1:5, 7, and both *overseer* and *shepherd* describe Christ in 1 Peter 2:25. Because of its relevance to the current discussion, *overseer* will be the center of attention in the following treatment.

Thomas Oden captures the particular characteristic of "watchfulness" inherent in the term *overseer*:

Bishop translates *episkopos,* which is derived from the family of Greek words referring to guardianship, oversight, inspection—accountably looking after a complex process in a comprehensive sense. *Episkopos* implies vigilance far more than hierarchy.[7]

A shepherd's *oversight* of the flock expresses itself broadly in two ways:[8] first, by providing truthful, positive direction and leadership to the flock, and second, by warning of spiritual dangers such as sin, false teaching, and false teachers, including Satan's assaults against the saints. The warning ministry also entails rescuing stray sheep.

On one hand, the shepherd teaches truth; on the other hand, he warns of sin and refutes doctrinal error. In leading the flock down the path of righteousness, the shepherd also watches for, warns, and even rescues the wandering sheep whom false teaching and alluring sin have enticed. When shepherds exercise their oversight responsibly, they will have both a preventative and a confrontive side to their ministry. One cannot shepherd the flock with credibility in the sight of God unless he provides a corrective oversight of watching and warning.

Spiritual Sentinels

At the end of his ministry, any godly shepherd would like to be able to say with Paul, "I have fought the good fight, I have finished the course, I have kept the faith" (2 Tim. 4:7). Who would not want to hear the Lord's commendation, "Well done, good and faithful servant"?

Paul told the Ephesian elders, "I am innocent of the blood of all men" (Acts 20:26). Using the imagery of Ezekiel 3:18, 20—". . . his blood I will require at your hand"—the apostle testified that he had delivered God's Word to both the lost and the saints. When unbelievers died in their sins, Paul had no pastoral blame because he had fully discharged his duty of preaching the gospel (Acts 20:21). If believers strayed and engaged in prolonged patterns of sin, it was not because Paul failed to communicate the whole purpose of God (v. 27).

If today's shepherds desire to finish their ministry like Paul, then they must not only be *approved workmen* (2 Tim. 2:15) but also *unashamed watchmen.* The theme of "pastoral watchman" strikingly stands out in

Ezekiel 3:16–21; 33:1–9. Later, Paul appropriately employed the same language to describe his ministry (Acts 20:17–31).

Ezekiel 3 and 33

God spoke to Ezekiel, "Son of man, I have appointed you a watchman to the house of Israel; whenever you hear a word from My mouth, warn them from Me" (Ezek. 3:17; cf. 2:7). The prophet then spoke to both the wicked (3:18–19) and the righteous (3:20–21).

Ezekiel 33:1–6 relates the duties of a military watchman to those of a shepherd. Watchmen attentively manned their posts to warn the city of approaching danger and to deliver the citizens from harm. If watchmen diligently discharged their duty, regardless of the outcome, they would be blameless (33:2–5). However, if a watchman failed to alert the city to danger, blame for the resultant destruction fell on him, as if he were the enemy and had personally attacked the city (v. 6).

Twenty-first-century pastoring provides appropriate parallels. The shepherd is to stand watch over the flock as the watchman did over the city. God's warnings apply to both unbelieving sheep outside the flock and believing sheep within the flock. To the degree that pastors faithfully deliver God's Word, regardless of the results, they will receive divine commendation. But where the shepherd neglects the duties of his post, God will hold him accountable for failing to signal coming danger and judgment.

In a life-and-death situation, the pastor must alertly tend the flock like a vigilant watchman protects his city. Oden captures the pastoral analogy thus:

> The image of pastor as watchman, or protective, vigilant all-night guard, was already well developed by the Hebrew prophets. Radical accountability to God was the central feature of this analogy, as dramatically stated by Ezekiel: "The word of the Lord came to me: . . . I have made you a watchman for the Israelites. . . . It may be that a righteous man turns away and does wrong. . . . I will hold you answerable for his death" (Ezek. 3:16–21). Such injunctions for prophetic accountability have often been transferred by analogy to the Christian office of elder.

Listen to the analogy: The watchman over a city is responsible for the whole city, not just one street of it. If the watchman sleeps through an attack, the whole resultant damage is his responsibility. This was the covenantal analogy later applied repeatedly to the pastor, who was charged with nothing less than caring for the souls of an analogous small city, the *ekklēsia.* If the congregation falls prey to seductive teaching or forgetfulness, whose responsibility can it be but that of the *presbuteros,* the guiding elder?[9]

Acts 20:17–31

Paul's address to the elders of the Ephesian church comprises the most explicit and complete instruction on spiritual leadership given to a NT church. He relies heavily on the imagery and ideas of Ezekiel 3 and 33 from which the watchman theme extended itself far beyond Ezekiel's personal ministry.[10] Paul not only served as a vigilant sentinel but also commanded the elders of Ephesus to do likewise.

At least five features attest to the close parallel between Ezekiel 3, 33, and Acts 20. First, both Ezekiel and the Ephesian elders were appointed by God. "I have appointed you a watchman" (Ezek. 3:17). "The Holy Spirit has made you overseers" (Acts 20:28). In both instances, the commission resulted from God's direct call to ministry.

Second, the task assigned to both essentially involved vigilant oversight. The Hebrew *sôpeh,* translated "watchman" in Ezekiel 3:17, is rendered *skopos* in the Greek LXX version.[11] Compare this with *episkopos,* which is translated "overseer" in Acts 20:28.[12] Both prophet and shepherd were accountable to God as a spiritual sentry is responsible to warn of impending danger. Paul warned the Ephesian elders,

Be on guard for yourselves and for all the flock, among which the Holy Spirit has made you overseers, to shepherd the church of God which He purchased with His own blood. I know that after my departure savage wolves will come in among you, not sparing the flock; and from among your own selves men will arise, speaking perverse things, to draw away the disciples after them. Therefore be on the alert, remembering that night and day

for a period of three years I did not cease to admonish each one
with tears. (Acts 20:28–31)

Third, in both passages the watchman is assigned to deliver God's
Word as His warning. What proved true of Ezekiel (2:7; 3:17; 33:7) also
marked Paul's ministry (Acts 20:20–21, 27). They both delivered the
Word of God without compromise. That is why the apostle commended
the elders to the Word of God's grace which would be their message, too
(v. 32).

Fourth, the watchman had a word for both the unrighteous (Ezek.
3:18–19; 33:8–9) and the righteous (Ezek. 3:20–21). Paul preached repentance to both Jew and Gentile (Acts 20:21) and the whole purpose of
God to the church (vv. 20, 27). This twofold responsibility to reach the
lost with the gospel and to watch over the saints continues to the present.

Fifth, both Ezekiel and Paul considered their "watchman oversight"
duties to be issues of highest importance—a matter of life and death.
When Ezekiel carried out his task, regardless of the outcome, he had
delivered himself from any spiritual liability (3:19, 21). On the other
hand, if he failed to sound the warning, God promised, "His blood I will
require at your hand" (vv. 18, 20; 33:8). Paul reported, "I am innocent of
the blood of all men" (Acts 20:26).

The concept of "blood being on your head or hands" originated in
Genesis 9:5–6, a passage that articulates the judicial principle of capital
punishment. This idea finds application in the following three categories
of life:

1. actual death, whether intentional (Josh. 2:19; 1 Kings 2:33; Matt.
   27:25; Acts 5:28) or accidental (Exod. 22:2; Deut. 22:8);
2. heinous crimes not involving death but deserving of death as punishment (Lev. 20:9, 11–13, 16, 27); and
3. spiritual matters of life-and-death proportion (Ezek. 3:18, 20; 33:4,
   6, 8; Acts 18:6; 20:26).

When the shepherd's responsibility as taught in Ezekiel 3, 33, and
Acts 20 arrests a pastor's attention, it will give increased understanding
of why Paul exclaimed, "For woe is me if I do not preach the gospel"

(1 Cor. 9:16). The apostle fully understood the serious responsibility given him by God as a preacher of the gospel. He would incur the displeasure of God if he did anything less. Watching and warning represent required duties in preaching the gospel, not optional tasks or those left to a specialist.

Ezekiel and Paul also shed light on Hebrews 13:17, where the biblical writer succinctly cites the implication of being a faithful overseer, one who watches over the flock and who will one day give an account for his labors: "Obey your leaders, and submit to them; for they keep watch over your souls, as those who will give an account. Let them do this with joy and not with grief, for this would be unprofitable for you." Pastors will stand accountable before God to watch over and warn the flock on spiritual matters. Vigilance plays a vital part in the ministry entrusted by God to His pastoral servants.

The Chief Shepherd's Watchfulness

Nowhere in Scripture is the vigilance of which Ezekiel and Paul teach more evident than in the gospel ministry of the Chief Shepherd—Jesus Christ. Whether one examines the Sermon on the Mount (Matt. 5–7), His discourse on the parables (Matt. 13), or the Olivet Discourse (Matt. 24–25), the fact is indisputable that Jesus continually warned His disciples and the crowds about false teachers, unsound doctrine, and/or ungodly living. Jesus prominently practiced watchfulness in His first-advent ministry.

Christ's postresurrection letters to seven churches illustrate His spiritual concerns most clearly (Rev. 2–3).[13] The certainty that He watched over them becomes evident in the phrase *I know,* which appears in each of the seven letters (cf. 2:2, 9, 13, 19; 3:1, 8, 15). His eyes like a flame of fire (1:14) portray the omniscient vigilance of Christ over His church.

Watchfulness presumes a personal presence, which Christ had promised the disciples. "Lo, I am with you always, even to the end of the age" (Matt. 28:20). Revelation 1:13 pictures Christ standing in the middle of seven golden lampstands, which represent seven churches (cf. 1:20). What was true of Christ and these first-century churches remains true to this very hour. As the Lord of His churches shepherded, so should the present generation of undershepherds.

Christ commented in two different ways on what He observed in the churches: by commendation and by condemnation. Because He watched, He could warn. For example, He warned the Ephesian church that she had lost her first love (Rev. 2:4–5). The church at Pergamum heard about Christ's distaste for compromise, especially as represented by the Balaamites (2:14) and the Nicolaitans (2:15). Jezebel and her consorts in Thyatira did not escape Christ's watchful eye and public rebuke (2:20–23). The Savior put Sardis on notice that she seemed to be a lifeless church (3:1) and confronted Laodicea over her exceeding sinfulness (3:15–18). Just as Christ concluded, "Those whom I love, I reprove and discipline . . ." (3:19), even so contemporary shepherds should follow His lead in watching and warning.

Although the modern shepherd does not possess Christ's divine attribute of omniscience, he has been given the revealed mind of Christ in Scripture (1 Cor. 2:16). Sound doctrine, in regard to both belief and behavior, represents the eyes of Christ through which today's pastors can see and assess the spiritual landscape to watch and warn appropriately and effectively (cf. Gal. 2:11–21; 1 Tim. 4:6; 2 Tim. 1:3; 4:2; Titus 1:9, 2:1).

Christ commanded the disciples to teach obedience to all that He commanded them (Matt. 28:20). Paul ministered to the Ephesian elders by proclaiming the whole will of God (Acts 20:27). The angel commanded the apostles to speak "the full message of this new life" (Acts 5:20 NIV). Paul instructed Timothy to pass the apostolic teachings on to the next generation (2 Tim. 2:2). Christ commended the Ephesian church for taking doctrine seriously (Rev. 2:2, 6). The only adequate approach to biblical truth in these instances is to take seriously the implied responsibility.[14]

Imagine what forsaking divine truth would entail. On what basis would one recognize and reject false teachers (Rom. 16:17; 2 John 9–10) or identify and refute false doctrine (Titus 1:9)? How would believers know what is true and worth holding on to (1 Tim. 3:9; Rev. 2:24)? How would Christians distinguish between right and wrong? How would sin be confronted and corrected?

Obviously, the prevention of this kind of spiritual disaster is the ultimate priority. Twenty-first-century shepherds, like their pastoral predecessors, must watch earnestly over the faith once for all delivered to the saints (Jude 3). Historically, indifference to Christian doctrine has produced heretics, but attention to revealed truth has crowned heroes of the faith and resulted in spiritually healthy flocks such as those at Smyrna (Rev. 2:8–11) and Philadelphia (Rev. 3:7–13).

Several current events such as the "Toronto Experience," for example, illustrate the need for a watching-and-warning ministry. How does one know that the convulsive laughter, hysterics, and other bizarre behavior is actually of God? How can anyone distinguish this conduct from other similar experiences that occur outside of Christianity? Even leaders who are otherwise sympathetic have hesitated to endorse these experiences without a biblical basis for them.[15] Unless a standard of truth exists (i.e., doctrine) to help us discern the authentic from the counterfeit, the evangelical community will be prone to wander like sheep and be easily led astray.

Consider the sixth promise of a prominent ministry to men that encourages "reaching beyond denominational barriers to demonstrate the power of biblical unity." Although the goal of oneness is laudable and the realization of some spiritual good is undisputed, no real unity is worth the sacrificing of biblical truth. This movement brings the barriers down so low and reaches out so far, doctrinally speaking, that Roman Catholic and Mormon officials expressed strong interest in this ministry at a recent Los Angeles rally.[16] When doctrinal barriers become nonapparent, Christians have the right to question, "What makes this ministry uniquely Christian?"

An unofficial document signed by prominent evangelicals and Roman Catholics (Evangelicals and Catholics Together) seemingly distorts the true gospel that salvation is by God's grace alone, through faith alone, in Christ alone without human merit.[17] This accord reportedly seemed to establish common ground for mutual ministry such as opposing abortion, homosexuality, and pornography. But what is the gain in relinquishing the true gospel as provided by Christ and reclaimed by the Reformation? To pay such a great price as possibly compromising the gospel to gain ministry cooperation is unthinkable. "Anathema," shouts Paul who opposed these social/spiritual blights, but he never stopped offering the true gospel and opposing the false (Gal. 1:8–9).

Pastoral Concerns for Vigilance

American patriot Thomas Jefferson observed that "eternal vigilance is the price of victory."[18] Although he spoke of political victory, watchfulness is even more true for the church if she is to win out over false teaching and sin. W. Phillip Keller warned of *Predators in Our Pulpits* through his recent call to restore true, biblical preaching to churches around the world.[19] "Predator" might sound harsh, but it nonetheless follows the example of Christ, who rightfully called the Pharisees blind guides, serpents, and whitewashed tombs (Matthew 23). God's spiritual sentry must be forthright in his challenges and strongly confront those who would maliciously usurp the true shepherd's tasks, thereby leading Christ's flock astray.

The Shepherd of Psalm 23 comforted the sheep with His rod and staff.[20] These implements symbolize not only vigilance but also, in the Shepherd's hand, instruments of protection and direction, which are the fruit of vigilance. The "rod" protected the flock against immediate, encroaching danger. The "staff" served to assemble the sheep, to guide them, and even to rescue them if they wandered away. Likewise, the shepherd of Christ's flock—the church—must be vigilant. The spiritual health and integrity of the flock depend on his devotion to this phase of his responsibility.

In his day, Charles Jefferson memorably captured the protective aspect of an ancient Near Eastern shepherd's duty. The parallels to modern shepherding for pastors are obvious but unfortunately all too often ignored.

> The Eastern shepherd was, first of all, a watchman. He had a watch tower. It was his business to keep a wide-open eye, constantly searching the horizon for the possible approach of foes. He was bound to be circumspect and attentive. Vigilance was a cardinal virtue. An alert wakefulness was for him a necessity. He could not indulge in fits of drowsiness, for the foe was always near. Only by his alertness could the enemy be circumvented. There were many kinds of enemies, all of them terrible, each in a different way. At certain seasons of the year there were floods. Streams became quickly swollen and overflowed their

banks. Swift action was necessary in order to escape destruction. There were enemies of a more subtle kind—animals, rapacious and treacherous: lions, bears, hyenas, jackals, wolves. There were enemies in the air; huge birds of prey were always soaring aloft ready to swoop down upon a lamb or kid. And then, most dangerous of all, were the human birds and beasts of prey—robbers, bandits, men who made a business of robbing sheepfolds and murdering shepherds. That Eastern world was full of perils. It teemed with forces hostile to the shepherd and his flock. When Ezekiel, Jeremiah, Isaiah, and Habakkuk talk about shepherds, they call them watchmen set to warn and save.[21]

Without question, vigilance starts in the pulpit, but it goes far beyond that. Watching over the flock as a body does not preclude watching over the individuals in the congregation. Strong pulpit ministry has always been the backbone of shepherding, but it does not exhaust the shepherd's responsibilities. Consider the persuasion of Charles Bridges:

> Let us not think that all our work is done in the study and in the pulpit. Preaching—the grand lever of the Ministry—derives much of its power from connection with the Pastoral work; and its too frequent disjunction from it is a main cause of our inefficiency. The Pastor and Preacher combine to form the completeness of the sacred office, as expounded in our Ordination services and Scriptural illustrations. How little can a stated appearance in public answer to the lowest sense of such terms as Shepherd, Watchman, Overseer, Steward!—terms, which import not a mere general superintendence over the flock, charge, or household, but an acquaintance with their individual wants, and a distribution suitable to the occasion; without which, instead of "taking heed to the flock, over which the Holy Ghost hath made us overseers," we can scarcely be said to "take the oversight of it" at all.[22]

According to the follow sampling of NT exhortations, pastoral oversight includes a strong emphasis on watching carefully for lurking spiritual danger.

And He was giving orders to them, saying, "Watch out! Beware of the leaven of the Pharisees and the leaven of Herod." (Mark 8:15)

Beware of the scribes, who like to walk around in long robes, and love respectful greetings in the market places, and chief seats in the synagogues, and places of honor at banquets, . . . (Luke 20:46)

Beware of the dogs, beware of the evil workers, beware of the false circumcision; . . . (Philippians 3:2)

Be of sober spirit, be on the alert. Your adversary, the devil, prowls about like a roaring lion, seeking someone to devour. (1 Peter 5:8)

Watch yourselves, that you might not lose what we have accomplished, but that you may receive a full reward. (2 John 8)

The early church took these biblical instructions seriously, as the actions of both the apostle John and his disciple Polycarp confirm:

The same Polycarp, coming to Rome under the episcopate of Anicetus, turned many from the aforesaid heretics to the church of God, proclaiming the one and only true faith, that he had received from the apostles, that, viz., which was delivered by the church. And there are those still living who heard him relate, that John the disciple of the Lord went into a bath at Ephesus, and seeing Cerinthus within, ran out without bathing, and exclaimed, "Let us flee lest the bath should fall in, as long as Cerinthus, that enemy of truth, is within." And the same Polycarp, once coming and meeting Marcion, who said, "acknowledge us," he replied, "I acknowledge the first born of Satan." Such caution did the apostles and their disciples use, so as not even to have any communion, even in word with any of those that thus mutilated the truth, according to the declaration of Paul: "An heretical man after the first and second admonition avoid, knowing that such an one is perverse, and that he sins, bringing condemnation upon himself."[23]

The pattern continued to the fourth generation (Christ, John, and Polycarp being the first three generations) in the ministry of Irenaeus, a disciple of Polycarp.

Inasmuch as certain men have set the truth aside, and bring in lying words and vain genealogies, which, as the apostle says, "minister questions rather than godly edifying which is in faith," and by means of their craftily-constructed plausibilities draw away the minds of the inexperienced and take them captive, [I have felt constrained, my dear friend, to compose the following treatise in order to expose and counteract their machinations.] These men falsify the oracles of God, and prove themselves evil interpreters of the good word of revelation. They also overthrow the faith of many, by drawing them away, under a pretense of [superior] knowledge, from Him who founded and adorned the universe; as if, forsooth, they had something more excellent and sublime to reveal, than that God who created the heaven and the earth, and all things that are therein. By means of specious and plausible words, they cunningly allure the simple-minded to inquire into their system; but they nevertheless clumsily destroy them, while they initiate them into their blasphemous and impious opinions respecting the Demiurge; and these simple ones are unable, even in such a matter, to distinguish falsehood from truth.[24]

In the mid-1960s, Harry Blamires wrote a significant volume warning the British church of its rapid departure from truth. Thereafter, he was associated with the concept of "thinking Christianly" because of his clear call for the restoration of a Christian mind set based on Scripture.

Our culture is bedeviled by the it's-all-a-matter-of-opinion code. In the sphere of religious and moral thinking we are rapidly

heading for a state of intellectual anarchy in which the difference
between truth and falsehood will no longer be recognized. Indeed
it would seem possible that the words *true* and *false* will
eventually (and logically) be replaced by the words *likeable* and
dislikeable. . . .

Christian truth is objective, four-square, unshakable. It is not
built of men's opinions. It is not something fabricated either by
scholars or by men in the street, still less something assembled
from a million answers, Yes, No, and Don't know, obtained from
a cross-section of the human race. Christian truth is something
given, revealed, laid open to the eye of the patient, self-forgetful
inquirer. You do not *make* the truth. You *reside* in the truth. A
suitable image for truth would be that of a lighthouse lashed by
the elemental fury of undisciplined error. Those who have come
to reside in the truth must stay there. It is not their business to go
back into error for the purpose of joining their drowning fellows
with the pretense that, inside or outside, the conditions are pretty
much the same. It is their duty to draw others within the shelter
of the truth. For truth is most certainly a shelter. And it is invio-
lable. If we start to dismantle it and give it away in bits to those
outside, there will be nothing left to protect our own heads—
and no refuge in which to receive the others, should they at length
grow weary of error.[25]

What Blamires wrote to the British church of the 1960s, David Wells
has more recently written to the American church of the 1990s:

The stream of historic orthodoxy that once watered the evangelical soul is now damned by a worldliness that many fail to
recognize as worldliness because of the cultural innocence with
which it presents itself. To be sure, this orthodoxy never was
infallible, nor was it without its blemishes and foibles, but I am
far from persuaded that the emancipation from its theological
core that much of evangelicalism is effecting has resulted in
greater biblical fidelity. In fact, the result is just the opposite.
We now have less biblical fidelity, less interest in truth, less se-

riousness, less depth, and less capacity to speak the Word of God to our own generation in a way that offers an alternative to what it already thinks. The older orthodoxy was driven by a passion for truth, and that was why it could express itself only in theological terms. The newer evangelicalism is not driven by the same passion for truth, and that is why it is often empty of theological interest.[26]

Perhaps no pastor in America has made his point more frequently or forcefully in the past decade than John MacArthur, who warns,

> True discernment has suffered a horrible setback in the past few decades because reason itself has been under attack within the church. As Francis Schaeffer warned nearly thirty years ago in *The God Who Is There,* the church is following the irrationality of secular philosophy. Consequently, reckless faith has overrun the evangelical community. Many are discarding doctrine in favor of personal experience. Others say they are willing to disregard crucial biblical distinctives in order to achieve external unity among all professing Christians. True Christianity marked by intelligent, biblical faith seems to be declining even among the most conservative evangelicals.[27]

Blamires, Wells, and MacArthur stand in the long, unbroken chain of gallant men who have taken seriously the biblical injunctions to watch and warn. They serve as exemplars of shepherdly vigilance in the best tradition of the NT overseer.[28]

Paul wrote Titus that an overseer should hold "fast the faithful word which is in accordance with the teaching, that he may be able both to exhort in sound doctrine and to refute those who contradict" (Titus 1:9). To "exhort" only and not to "refute" amounts to spiritual insubordination, even gross disobedience. Certainly, it is nothing less than dereliction of duty.

John Stott exposed the growing negligence of late twentieth-century shepherds in their failure to watch for and confront doctrinal error.

This emphasis is unpopular today. It is frequently said that pastors must always be positive in their teaching, never negative. But those who say this have either not read the New Testament or, having read it, they disagree with it. For the Lord Jesus and His apostles gave the example and even set forth the obligation to be negative in refuting error. Is it possible that the neglect of this ministry is one of the major causes of theological confusion in the church today? To be sure, theological controversy is distasteful to sensitive spirits and has its spiritual dangers. Woe to those who enjoy it! But it cannot conscientiously be avoided. If, when false teaching arises, Christian leaders sit idly by and do nothing or turn tail and flee, they will earn the terrible epithet "hirelings" who care nothing for Christ's flock. Is it right to abandon His sheep and leave them defenseless against the wolves to be like "sheep without a shepherd"? Is it right to be content to see the flock scattered and individual sheep torn to pieces? Is it to be said of believers today, as it was of Israel, that "they were scattered for lack of a shepherd, and they became food for every beast of the field" (Ezek. 34:5)? Today even some of the fundamental doctrines of historic Christianity are being denied by some church leaders, including the infinite personality of the living God, the eternal deity, virgin birth, atoning death, bodily resurrection of Jesus, the Trinity, and the gospel of justification by grace alone through faith alone without any meritorious works. Pastors are to protect God's flock from error and seek to establish them in the truth.[29]

A Good Servant of Jesus Christ

"In pointing out these things to the brethren, you will be a good servant of Christ Jesus, constantly nourished on the words of the faith and of the sound doctrine which you have been following" (1 Tim. 4:6). For the spiritual good of the Ephesian church, Paul insisted that Timothy point out "these things," referring back to the false doctrine exposed in 4:1–3 and truth taught in 4:4–5. "A good servant of Christ Jesus" points them out to the flock by way of warning and instruction.[30] Failure to warn invites a "spiritual Chernobyl" because real danger still exists even though the sheep are unaware of it. Ultimately, they will suffer harm through the negligence of a shepherd who failed to sound a timely warning.

As a former naval officer, I have stood many four-hour watches on the bridge of a destroyer at sea. During the watch, I had responsibility for the operation and safety of the ship. If a dangerous situation appeared, I had to warn both the captain and the crew. They depended on my alertness in carrying out my assigned task. Failure to function properly according to my charge would have amounted to gross negligence on my part, possible damage to the ship or loss of life, and the dishonorable end of my naval career. Just as "a good naval officer" warns when danger lurks nearby, so must "a good servant of Christ Jesus."

Be assured that it is good and right to protect the flock from false teachers, untrue doctrine, and personal sin, even when it involves exercising church discipline.[31] They will find comfort in your diligent protection (Ps. 23:4). If you begin by preaching the whole of Scripture, then the process of watching and warning will begin to take place in the normal course of ministry because His saints receive warnings through the truth of God's Word (Ps. 19:11).

Although Paul proved to be a courageous shepherd, he still harbored a few fears. One of them he stated thus: "But I am afraid, lest as the serpent deceived Eve by his craftiness, your minds should be led astray from the simplicity and purity of devotion to Christ" (2 Cor. 11:3).

Good servants of Jesus Christ would do well to share Paul's fear, not as a sign of weakness or cowardice but as a significant demonstration of spiritual strength coupled with a clear sense of spiritual reality. To do less would result in hollow ministry, invite Christ's displeasure with their service, and endanger the spiritual health of the flock. The blood of the flock would be on their hands. Because the flock is so susceptible to deception, shepherds must be ever vigilant.

Jesus Christ stands as the ultimate Shepherd and Guardian of people's souls (1 Peter 2:25). Today's undershepherds could do no better than follow His example of watching and warning. Failure to measure up to His pattern would be biblically unthinkable and spiritually unconscionable.

Endnotes

1. See Earl D. Radmacher, *What the Church Is All About: A Biblical and Historical Study* (Chicago: Moody, 1978), 298–307, for a succinct study of the picture of the church as a flock of sheep.

2. The NT frequently exposes the false *(pseudēs)*, including (1) false apostles (2 Cor. 11:13), (2) false brethren (2 Cor. 11:26; Gal. 2:4), (3) false christs (Matt. 24:24), (4) false prophets (Matt. 24:11; 2 Peter 2:1; 1 John 4:1), (5) false teachers (2 Peter 2:1), and (6) false witnesses (Matt. 26:60; Acts 6:13).

3. For example, see Jeremiah 14, 23; Ezekiel 13, 34; Micah 3; and Zechariah 11.

4. For example, see Matthew 23; 2 Corinthians 11; 2 Timothy 3–4; Titus 1; 2 Peter 2; 1 John 4; 2 John 8–11; Jude; and Revelation 2–3.

5. James Stalker, *The Preacher and His Models* (New York: George H. Doran, 1891), 128.

6. Charles Jefferson, *The Minister as Shepherd* (1913; reprint, Hong Kong: Living Books, 1973), 39–66. See also, John F. MacArthur Jr., *The Master's Plan for the Church* (Chicago: Moody, 1991), 169–76.

7. Thomas C. Oden, *Pastoral Theology: Essentials of Ministry* (San Francisco: Harper, 1983), 71.

8. Pastoral oversight of others assumes that the shepherd has first exercised his own "self-watch" of which C. H. Spurgeon writes in *Lectures to My Students,* 1st series (1875–94; reprint, Grand Rapids: Baker, 1977), 1–17. More recently, John Stott observed, "Only if pastors first guard themselves, will they be able to guard the sheep. Only if pastors first tend their own spiritual life, will they be able to tend the flock of God" ("Ideals of Pastoral Ministry," *Bibliotheca Sacra* 146, no. 581 (January–March 1989): 11.

9. Oden, *Pastoral Theology,* 70. Great church reformers of the past such as John Knox ("The First Blast of the Trumpet," in *On Rebellion,* ed. Roger A. Mason [Cambridge: Cambridge University Press, 1994], 7–8); and Martin Luther (*Luther's Works,* vol. 39, ed. Eric W. Gritch [Philadelphia: Fortress, 1957], 249–50) clearly sensed the watchman analogy in Ezekiel 3 and 33, a factor that strongly influenced their ministries.

10. See F. F. Bruce, *The Book of Acts, New International Commentary on the New Testament* (Grand Rapids: Eerdmans, 1980), 415; Charles Lee Feinberg, *The Prophecy of Ezekiel* (Chicago: Moody, 1969), 29; Everett F. Harrison, *Acts* (Chicago: Moody, 1975), 315; Evald Lövestam, "Paul's Address at Miletus," *Studia Theologica* 41 (1987): 1–10; Walter R. Roehrs, "Watchmen in Israel: Pastoral Guidelines from Ezekiel 1–3," *Concordia Journal* 16, no. 1 (January 1990): 6–17; and Stott, "Ideals of Pastoral Ministry," 6–7.

11. A watchman is "fully aware of a situation in order to gain some advantage or keep from being surprised by the enemy" (R. Laird Harris et al., ed., *The Wordbook of the Old Testament,* vol. 2 [Chicago: Moody, 1980], 773). *Watchman* is used in a true military sense in 1 Samuel 14:16; 2 Samuel 18:24; 2 Kings 9:17–20; and

Isaiah 21:6. Watching in a spiritual sense also appears in Jeremiah 6:17 and Habakkuk 2:1.

12. John Calvin, *Commentaries on Ezekiel,* vol. 1 (reprint, Grand Rapids: Eerdmans, n.d.), 148–49, commented, "For we know that the word Bishop means the same as watchman." The related verb *skopeō* ("watch over") is used in the NT of watching both for the positive (Phil. 3:17) and for the dangerous (Rom. 16:17).

13. For a fuller discussion consult Richard Mayhue, *What Would Jesus Say About Your Church?* (Ross-shire, Scotland: Christian Focus Publications, 1995); cf. also, Steven J. Lawson, *Final Call* (Wheaton: Crossway, 1994).

14. See Richard Mayhue, "Why We Need Doctrine," *Moody Monthly* 96, no. 5 (January–February 1996): 16–17, for a more complete discussion of "sound doctrine."

15. See James A. Beverly, "Vineyard Severs Ties with 'Toronto Blessing' Church," *Christianity Today* 40, no. 1 (8 January 1996): 66, who reported that John Wimber of the Vineyard Association of Churches is ". . . unable because of my own scriptural and theological convictions to any longer give an answer for, or defend the way, this particular move is being pastored and/or explained."

16. As reported by John Dart, "'Promise Keepers,' a Message to L.A. Men," *Los Angeles Times* (6 May 1995): B12–13.

17. For a lucid analysis of this document, see John F. MacArthur Jr., *Reckless Faith* (Wheaton: Crossway, 1994), 119–52.

18. John Bartlett, *Familiar Quotations* (1855; reprint, Boston: Little, Brown and Co., 1982), 397.

19. W. Phillip Keller, *Predators in Our Pulpits* (Eugene, Ore.: Harvest House, 1988).

20. For a vivid description of the shepherds' rod and staff, see W. Phillip Keller, *A Shepherd Looks at Psalm 23* (Grand Rapids: Zondervan, 1970), 92–103.

21. Jefferson, *The Minister As Shepherd,* 41–42.

22. Charles Bridges, *The Christian Ministry* (1830; reprint, Edinburgh: Banner of Truth, 1980), 343.

23. Eusebius Pamphilus, *Eusebius' Ecclesiastical History* (ca. A.D. 325; reprint, Grand Rapids: Guardian, 1955), 141–42.

24. Irenaeus, *Against Heresies,* vol. 2 of *The Ante-Nicene Fathers,* ed. A. Roberts and J. Donaldson (ca. A.D. 178; reprint, Grand Rapids: Eerdmans, 1956), 315.

25. Harry Blamires, *The Christian Mind* (1963; reprint, Ann Arbor, Mich.: Servant, 1978), 112–14.

26. David F. Wells, *No Place for Truth or Whatever Happened to Evangelical Theology* (Grand Rapids: Eerdmans, 1993), 11–12.

27. MacArthur, *Reckless Faith,* 19; cf. also John F. MacArthur Jr., *Ashamed of the Gospel: When the Church Becomes Like the World* (Wheaton: Crossway, 1993); and idem., *The Vanishing Conscience* (Dallas: Word, 1994).

28. Doctrinal error does not always appear in its most obvious or despicable form. "Error, indeed, is never set forth in its naked deformity, lest, being thus exposed, it

should at once be detected. But it is craftily decked out in an attractive dress, so as, by its outward form, to make it appear to the inexperienced (ridiculous as the expression may seem) more true than the truth itself" (Irenaeus, *Against Heresies,* 315).

29. Stott, "Ideals of Pastoral Ministry," 8.

30. Charles Haddon Spurgeon proved to be a classic watchman in the nineteenth century, as is illustrated in such writings as "How to Meet the Evils of the Age" and "The Evils of the Present Time" (in *An All-Round Ministry* [1900; reprint, Pasadena, Tex.: Pilgrim, 1983], 89–127, 282–314).

31. For helpful material on "church discipline" as a means of dealing with and prayerfully restoring a sinning believer, see J. Carl Laney, *A Guide to Church Discipline* (Minneapolis: Bethany, 1985); and John MacArthur Jr., *Matthew 16–23* (Chicago: Moody, 1988), 123–39.

CHAPTER SIX

The Only Sure Word

John Sherwood

In the face of challengers, the apostle Peter makes clear in 2 Peter 1:16–21 that God's Word is his source of authority and spiritual knowledge. In doing so, he shows that the knowledge in God's written revelation prevails over that gained anywhere else. Because of its superiority, Scripture deserves concentrated attention. All other conceivable sources of knowledge must bow the knee to God's Word.

This article appeared in *TMSJ* 7, no. 1 (spring 1996): 53–74. John Sherwood is an Associate Director of UFM, International. Originally from Atlanta, Georgia, he earned a B.A. degree in History from Georgia State University, a Th.M. degree from Grace Theological Seminary, and a D.Min. degree in Pastoral Counseling from Westminster Theological Seminary. Before assuming his present position with UFM, he served with the same mission doing church planting in the Philippines for nine years.

* * * * *

We were robbed! A Roman Catholic charismatic group snatched some key businessmen who had been studying the Bible with us for several months, and it hurt. In contrast to our steady work in God's Word, they could offer fantastic charismatic experiences such as being slain spiritually and speaking in tongues without stepping outside the bounds of tradition and the Mother Church. How could we compete?

We often have faced this type of question. A member of one of our Bible studies asks what I think about the recent apparitions of the Virgin Mary on a neighboring island of the Philippines. An estimated one million people were expected to visit it, hoping to hear Mary's voice with a new message for the nation. How can we convince these new Bible students, coming as they do from an experience-oriented culture, that any search for spiritual knowledge outside of God's Word amounts to a rejection of God and His Word?

The advantages of ministering in the Philippines, the "only Christian nation in Asia"[1] (i.e., 85 percent Roman Catholic), include the assumption of the vast majority of people that the Bible is the Word of God. For example, missionaries to the Philippines rarely face inerrancy as an issue. However, the superiority of Scripture to all other sources of knowledge is constantly under challenge. Direct apparitions, other "miraculous" happenings, signs and omens, superstition, various prophets receiving new revelation, and the more subtle traditions, teachings, and experiences of men all vie for equal status and even superiority to written revelation.

Peter evidently faced a similar challenge from foes of a pre-Gnostic variety, as noted in his second letter.[2] Consequently, in 2 Peter 1:16–21, he answers their challenge with a *comparison of four different sources of knowledge.* He moves through the passage from the least authoritative source to the source with the most authority.

For both Peter's readers and modern readers, it is not enough merely to recognize God's written revelation as being without error; it must also be recognized as being *superior* to all other sources of knowledge and *sufficient* for "everything that relates to life and godliness" (1:3). An understanding of Peter's progress of thought in these verses, together with their context, will correct a wrong understanding of the passage perpetuated by most of the current English translations. (See the comments on v. 19 under the discussion of the third source.)

Peter wrote, "For we did not follow cleverly devised tales when we made known to you the power and coming of our Lord Jesus Christ" (2 Peter 1:16).[3]

As Peter neared the end of his life, he wanted to remind his readers of the most important truths (1:12–15).[4] Yet, even as he wrote, he remained mindful of attacks upon his authority and therefore identified his sources of knowledge about these vital truths. His teaching is only as valuable as the source on which he bases it.

First Source: Illegitimate Myths

For we did not follow cleverly devised tales when we made known to you the power and coming of our Lord Jesus Christ. (2 Peter 1:16a)

The first possible source—an illegitimate one—Peter calls *mythos* ("myth"), from which the English word *myth* with the same meaning comes.[5] The adjectival participle used to describe these myths as "cleverly devised" comes from *sophizō* ("I become wise, skilled"). This word also took on a sarcastic meaning as early as Plato and Demosthenes (*Rep,* 496a; Demos. 25:18), possibly in relation to those clever Greek sophists who could invent ingenious arguments for any side of an issue. "Cleverly concocted" and "artfully spun" (NEB) both adroitly convey the idea.[6] Peter uses an instrumental participle of *exakoloutheō* ("I follow, depend on") to introduce this first source: "Not by means of following cleverly concocted tales. . . ."

One of the vital truths that Peter emphasized in his first letter and about which someone may have accused him of concocting tales is Christ's "power and coming" (1 Peter 1:5, 7, 11, 13; 2:12; 4:5–7, 13; 5:4; cf. 2 Peter 2:9; 3:4, 7, 9–12).[7] As here, normally it is Jesus' return rather than His incarnation that Scripture associates with power (e.g., see the previous references in Peter's letters). In addition, "coming," *parousia* ("arrival, presence"), when used in relation to Christ in the NT, describes only His second coming. This point agrees with its Koine use for a hidden divinity making his presence felt by a revelation of his power or, in a secular sense, for the visit of a high-ranking person.[8]

The mystery religions that surged in popularity in the Greek and Roman worlds around the beginning of the first millennium developed elaborate schemes of the supernatural to which only the initiated were privy. Peter had nothing to do with those schemes.

This first source of knowledge, being manmade, encompasses a large number of ancient as well as modern claims of knowledge.[9] This very passage shows the deficiency of Catholic tradition and religious experience as potential guides to Christian experience.

Second Source: Legitimate Personal Perception

> But we were eyewitnesses of His majesty. For when He received honor and glory from God the Father, such an utterance as this was made to Him by the Majestic Glory, "This is My beloved Son with whom I am well-pleased"—and we ourselves heard this utterance made from heaven when we were with Him on the holy mountain. (2 Peter 1:16b–18)

Next, Peter mentions the second source of knowledge, one on which he did rely and that he considered valuable. If the earlier participle, *exakolouthēsantes* ("following," v. 16a), is instrumental, the parallel participle, *genēthentes* ("becoming," v. 16b), probably is, too: "not by (means of) following cleverly concocted myths did we make known to you . . . , but *(all')* by (means of) being (becoming) eyewitnesses. . . ."[10]

Peter flings a verbal dart at his pre-Gnostic adversaries with his use of *epoptai* ("eyewitnesses"). A NT *hapax legomenon* (i.e., used only this once in the NT), *epoptēs* had become by NT times a technical term used in mystery sects to designate people who were initiated into a higher knowledge. If Peter intended this cultic sense, he did so to reverse their snobbish use of the word by excluding the false teachers from his circle of true eyewitnesses.

Peter, with John and James, had personally witnessed Christ revealed in glory on the mountain of Matthew 17:1–8.[11] Clearly, he considered this mountain experience to be a basis for belief in the second coming of Christ. That sanctified mountain[12] episode foreshadowed the glory and power in which Christ will return. All three of the Synoptic Gospels record that Jesus also understood an intended connection between the Transfiguration and "the Son of Man coming in His kingdom" (Matt. 16:28; cf. Mark 9:1; Luke 9:27).[13]

Perhaps this connection in Peter's mind is also visible when he records the messianic proclamation announced[14] by the Magnificent[15] Father (cf. Ps. 2:7; Isa. 5:1; 42:1).[16] Unfortunately, this title remains rather hidden in the KJV, NASB, RSV, and NIV renderings, all of which render "beloved" as adjectivally modifying "Son." More accurate are the NEB and RSV footnotes which translate the two articular phrases separately—"this is My Son, my Beloved"—because Peter adds a second pronoun, *mou* ("my"), that none of the gospel accounts includes.

Verse 17 poses the interesting syntactical challenge of identifying which independent verb the participle *labōn* ("having received") modifies. Kistemaker, with others, explains it as an incomplete sentence, broken by verse 18 and continued in verse 19.[17] An ellipsis is possible here such as "[the prophetic word was established] when . . . ," but it is much simpler to understand the participle as temporally modifying the finite verb in verse 18, *ēkousamen* ("we heard"): for example, "When He received honor and glory . . . *we* also heard this voice."[18]

In short, Peter considers his eyewitness experience as valid and even powerful for corroborating truth. Experience is not reliable as a final arbitrator of truth because the interpretation of experience apart from divine revelation is subjective. The next step in Peter's sequence demonstrates this fact. Nevertheless, experience is not without value.[19] Accordingly, believers receive encouragement and an expansion of their faith when they see the truth of God's promises confirmed by some incident in their lives. We Western missionaries, in our desire to elevate objective truth, must not be too hasty to demean experience in its valid role of fleshing out truth. The sad result will be an elevation of biblical truth out of the realm of practice and into the realm of theory.[20]

Third Source: Superior Scripture

And so we have the prophetic word *made* more sure, to which you do well to pay attention as to a lamp shining in a dark place, . . . (2 Peter 1:19a, emphasis added)

Verse 19 introduces one of the two major interpretive problems of this passage, both of which have theological importance. Green summarizes this first problem with the following questions: "Does [the verse] mean that the Scriptures confirm the apostolic witness (AV)? Or does it mean that the apostolic witness [eyewitness experience] fulfills, and thus authenticates, Scriptures . . . ?"[21] Almost all of the modern English translations reflect this second sense (including NASB, NIV, NKJV, JB, RSV, and NEB).

An examination of the NASB clarifies the issue: "And *so* we have the prophetic word *made* more sure. . . ." In this translation, Peter's experience on the mountain confirms the prophetic or written Word. In other words, Scripture would have lacked some of its authority had apostolic experience not authenticated it. Objective truth would thus be dependent upon subjective truth; signs and wonders would continue to confirm the canon; this fact might lead to reliance on philosophies and theories of men to complement the inadequacies of the Bible.

The translation choice revolves around the use of *kai* ("even" or "and") and of *bebaioteron* ("sure").

Kai: Epexegetical or Simple Conjunction?

By adding the word *so*, the NASB has supported the idea that verse 19 gives a *result* of the previous verses. In that case, written revelation receives its confirmation and is "made more sure" by the visual revelation of the Transfiguration. Similarly, Strachan suggests that the transfiguration experience made the OT "prophetic Word" more certain, even though it was already certain before Peter's time. Therefore, he translates, "Thus we have still further confirmation of the words of the prophets."[22]

Kai can sometimes contain that type of epexegetical or inferential sense (i.e., thus, so), but only rarely. Much more plausible, rather, is the simple *kai* copula introducing an *additional* source for the truths that Peter is bringing to their memories as he continues to ascend, as it were, through his four-part sequence.

The Meaning of *Bebaios*

Bebaios ("reliable, firm") and its cognates, used nineteen times in the NT, originally described something firm, fit to tread on; it "is concerned with that which is based, or still to be fixed or anchored to a foundation, assumed to be unshakable."[23] In secular Greek, it was often a legal term used of an unassailable position or guarantee. Good translations include "permanent, firm, reliable, dependable, certain." In a significant parallel usage of the cognate verb, Mark wrote that Jesus "*confirmed* the word by the signs that followed" (16:20, emphasis added).

A verbal interpretation of *bebaios* in the present verse, "*made* more sure," seen in many versions including the NASB, is unlikely for two reasons.

1. *Bebaios* is clearly an adjective, and it seems tenuous to translate it verbally, "made more sure," as if it were *bebaiothenta.* In fact, Peter does use this adjective with a verbal sense only a few verses earlier in this very letter, *but only* with the complementary *poieisthai* ("do, make"), "to make certain" (1:10). (Incidentally, the reduplicated stem adds no more of a perfective or verbal sense than in *bebēlos* ["worldly"] or *pepoithēsis* ["confidence"].)
2. A different approach translates *bebaios* elatively so that the comparative adjective implies no comparison: "We also have the *very* certain prophetic Word." However, of the seven other times Peter uses a comparative adjective, he always uses it comparatively instead of elatively, sometimes with an expressed object of comparison (1 Peter 1:7; 3:17; 2 Peter 2:20, 21), sometimes without (1 Peter 3:7; 5:5; 2 Peter 2:11). (First Peter 5:5 is a possible exception in using a comparative adjective substantively if translated "young men.") If the present verse follows that norm, he must be comparing the prophetic word to something. Since the following verses make clear that he is speaking of the written Word, he has now advanced to present the written Word as superior to the audio/visual experiences of verses 17–18.[24]

Hence, *bebaios* is an adjective (as in all of its nine uses in the NT), moved forward in its clause for emphasis.[25] Almost alone, the AV correctly translates, "We have also a more sure word of prophecy."[26] Barbieri paraphrases, "If you don't believe what I have said, then believe what is written in the Word of God."[27] In good presuppositional form, Peter asserts that the written Word needs no authentication from religious experience or otherwise.

Theologically, such an interpretation makes especially good sense coming from a Jew whose heritage traditionally favored written revelation over oral revelation.[28] Furthermore, in the larger context of the NT, support from the OT was the irrefutable source of apostolic authority, the "final word" as it were.[29]

Kistemaker takes yet another approach and writes,

> This wording [the common translation in which the transfiguration serves to confirm written revelation] does justice to the sequence of the apostolic message confirmed by the transfiguration and by the Old Testament Scripture.[30]

In this case, he confines "the prophetic Word" to the OT Scriptures and chronologically juxtaposes it with the apostolic witness in the NT, which confirms the former.

But Peter does not seem to be confining himself to the OT. Rather, he equates this "prophetic Word" *(ton prophētikon logon)* with the "prophecy of Scripture" *(prophēteia graphēs)* in verse 20. With the reuse of that same term, *graphē* ("writing"), he equates "prophecy of Scripture" with other writings of Scripture, including Paul's mentioned in 2 Peter 3:15–16. Furthermore, *prophētikos* ("prophetic") appears again only in Romans 16:26, where it refers specifically to the NT. Finally, a study of Peter's use of the word *logos* ("word") suggests no restriction to the OT.[31] Kistemaker's limitation to the OT fails here.

Because written revelation remains the highest authority for truth during the present age, Peter commends his readers for focusing on it.[32] *Prosechō* ("pay attention") usually pairs with a dative to define its focus, what occupies attention. When used positively, the word speaks of deliberate concentration on something (e.g., Heb. 2:1).

Moulton and Milligan point out that *eu* ("well") or *kalōs* ("well") with the future tense *poiēseis* ("will do, make") and a following participle, can suggest an imperative similar to "please" or "kindly"[33] (e.g., 3 John 6). However, in this clause *poieite* is a present indicative, so Peter is commending them for something that they were already doing (e.g.,

James 2:8, 19). Of course, a commendation can have the same practical force as a mandate. Peter knew that this focus on the written Word would protect them from false teachers who relied on man-made tales.

Peter's comparison of God's Word to a lamp suggests several OT passages (2 Sam. 22:29; Pss. 18:28; 119:105; Prov. 6:23). The word for "dark" *(auchmērǭ)* only here in the NT, also connotes a dry place, or even murky and filthy.[34] The light from Scripture shows the dirt of people's lives and the filth of false teaching, cleaning them out and providing guidance for a straight walk. God's Word alone provides everything needed pertaining to life and godliness (2 Peter 1:3) so that believers can grow in Christlikeness (1:4).

When more than a million people flock to a small Philippine town and claim to hear Mary's voice commanding them to pray the rosary and to see Mary cry tears of blood, we can only point back to the unchanging Word for protection. Subjective experiences are subject to man's misuse whereas God's unchanging Word explains itself.[35]

Fourth Source: Face to Face with Christ

Until the day dawns and the morning star arises in your hearts.
(2 Peter 1:19b)

Several different interpretations of 2 Peter 1:19b are possible, none of which is without difficulty.

1. Some people, pointing at the final phrase, "in your hearts," suggest that *until* refers to a time when a higher level of divine insight in a Christian's life will supersede a lower level of faith in the written Word.[36] This view smacks of the very Gnostic elitism that Peter is confronting. Paul clearly refutes the notion of perfectionism in Philippians 3:12–14.

2. Kistemaker[37] and Hiebert[38] think that this time alludes to a subjective response ("in your hearts") of those awaiting Christ's return. Yet, *heōs* ("until") introduces a terminal point, whether related to location, quantity, some activity, or time, as in this case. In what sense would that positive attitude toward Christ's return provide an end to the need to concentrate on Scripture?

3. A more novel approach would have this final part of verse 19 providing the terminal point for neither the reliable Word,[39] nor for the time of focusing on that Word, but modifying the immediately preceding clause, "as to a lamp shining in a dark place" (v. 19a). Accordingly, the lamp of God's Word shines in a dark heart until the day of salvation faith dawns. This view finds support in 2 Corinthians 4:6: "God . . . is the One who has shone in our hearts to give the light of the knowledge of the glory of God in the face of Christ." This interpretation is unlikely because of the following preferred view.

4. The most common explanation emphasizes the need to concentrate on God's Word until the time that Christ returns and believers receive fuller light in heaven directly from Him.[40] Scripture frequently compares Messiah Jesus to a star or light (Num. 24:17; Mal. 4:2; Luke 1:78; 2 Cor. 4:6; Eph. 5:14), even a Morning Star (Rev. 2:28; 22:16).[41] Moreover, the day of Christ's return relates to an ending of darkness for believers when they stand in the complete light of God's presence (Rom. 13:12; Rev. 21:23–25). Many people understand 1 Corinthians 13:9–12, "when the perfect comes . . . ," to speak of this superseding of written revelation by Christ's presence. Presence with God, then, would be the fourth source of spiritual knowledge but one not yet available to the believer.

This preferred view prompts some interesting questions: Will written revelation be of no more relevance at the revelation of Christ? Or will it rather be replaced by something superior such as "adult" things inevitably replace C. S. Lewis's child's sandbox? Will Christians know all in heaven, or will heaven be a place of eternal learning?

The only obstacle to this view lies in the final phrase, "in your hearts," which does not seem to fit an eschatological interpretation. Several scholars suggest that this phrase refers to the final transformation of the believer's heart connected with Jesus' return (1 John 3:2),[42] but this is a weak rejoinder.

A convenient and preferable solution to the problem lies in beginning a new sentence with the problematic phrase and continuing into verse 20: "Since you know this first of all in your hearts. . . ."[43] En ("in") prepositional phrases do sometimes introduce nominative participial clauses, even starting new sentences on rare occasions.[44] Furthermore, in an idea parallel to knowing something in one's heart, Ephesians 1:18 explains that when the heart is enlightened, one *knows* the hope to which God has called believers.[45]

This explanation of the prepositional phrase has it introducing 2 Peter 1:20–21, where a second major interpretive problem exists.

Third Source Revisited

But know this first of all, that no prophecy of Scripture is a *matter* of one's own interpretation, for no prophecy was ever made by an act of human will, but men moved by the Holy Spirit spoke from God. (2 Peter 1:20–21, emphasis added)

Divine Origin of Written Revelation

After his brief look at the ultimate, face-to-face exposure to knowledge still to come, Peter returns to the present and written revelation. Strachan takes *ginōskontes* ("knowing") *temporally*—"while realizing this"—and Green renders it as an *imperative*—"Recognize this truth to be of utmost importance"[46]—but it suits the context better to see a *causal* force, giving the reason why believers should concentrate on Scripture, "Since you know this above all."[47] Thus, Peter returns to the earlier emphasis, reminding them of the most important truths.[48]

Verse 20 gives one of the reasons why written revelation is superior to subjective experiential knowledge.[49] The final clause of verse 20 includes the second major syntactical problem of the passage. The problem revolves around the word *epiluseōs* (literally "loosen, untie"). The NT uses the noun only here, but Mark 4:34 uses the verb to speak of interpreting a parable, and Acts 19:39 uses the verb for unraveling and settling a dispute. Although the semantic connotation is clear, the object of the interpretation remains unclear. Four potential meanings are worthy of discussion.

1. Individual interpretation must yield to corporate interpretation.

It is primarily the Roman Catholic tradition that understands Peter to be discouraging individuals from trying to interpret Scripture apart from the authoritative aid of the church (i.e., that he forbids private interpretation by individual readers).[50]

Idias ("one's own") can mean "private" in contrast to "corporate" (e.g., Mark 4:34; Gal. 2:2). However, this view is contextually difficult because it renders verse 21 useless, although the verse's clear function is to support what verse 20 expresses.[51] Moreover, this meaning contradicts other Scriptures that recommend that the individual approach Scripture to understand it for himself (Acts 17:11; 2 Tim. 2:15; 1 Peter 2:2; 1 John 2:27). Calvin asks how Scripture can be called "light" if it is not clear to the individual Christian. He writes bluntly, "Execrable, therefore, is the blasphemy of the Papists, who pretend that the light of Scripture does nothing but dazzle the eyes, in order to keep the simple from reading it."[52]

2. Verses must be interpreted in light of other Scriptures.

Here, *idias* would mean "its own" (as in Luke 6:44; John 15:19; 1 Cor. 15:38; 1 Tim. 5:8), emphasizing the solidarity of God's Word. Indeed, extraction of verses from their nearby and greater contexts leads to error. This view certainly harmonizes with biblical truth but is an unlikely meaning here. Aside from leaving verse 21 hanging, it does not properly handle the very unusual clause "is *a matter* of one's own interpretation" (NASB, RSV, *idias epiluseōs ou ginetai*). A fuller discussion of this clause relates more closely to the next view.

3. Meaning is not dependent on the individual reader's interpretation.

This view—held by Barbieri, Kistemaker, and Green—invalidates all arbitrary exegesis, denying that any one verse can have multiple meanings for different individuals.[53] Rather, as verse 21 explains, because God Himself wrote Scripture, it is sure that a single, objective meaning exists for any passage and the interpreter must strive to discover it. Divine origin (v. 21) implies a divine and immutable meaning.

This view fits nicely into the context by showing why objective written revelation is superior to the subjective, visual revelation of verses 16–18, the latter of which lends itself to various interpretations by various witnesses.[54] Peter may be offering this as a corrective to the false teachers who were twisting Scripture to support their myths and stories (3:16).

The use of *idias* in this instance is impersonal, referring to any reader, one's own (novel) interpretation. The other eight times that Peter uses this pronoun, its antecedent is always clear. Yet, the only possible antecedent here is the plural *your* in verse 19b. But it cannot be the antecedent because the subject of verse 19b is not interpretation. It is necessary to infer an antecedent. The impersonal translation is possible but unlikely because it is uncommon in the NT. This is the only time that the NASB translates *idios* by "one's own."

The meaning of the genitive *idias epiluseōs* with *ginetai* poses a more perplexing problem. This coupling of *ginomai* ("I become") with a genitive in the predicate is very rare.[55] If *ginetai* were translated as the simple copula, "is," the genitive would then carry a loose descriptive meaning, such as "a matter of," "related to," or "dependent on."[56] It is also possible to perceive direction or purpose in the genitive: "no prophecy . . . is for one's own interpretation, or designed for a personal interpretation."[57]

4. Scripture did not originate in the human author's interpretation of what he saw.[58]

In this instance, *idias* refers to the writer of Scripture rather than to the reader. Human authors and prophets did not receive visions and have permission to explain personally those visions resulting in Scripture. Nor in foretelling did they personally decipher the meaning of current events to forecast what was to come. Instead, as verse 21 clarifies, their prophecies came from God. Both Hiebert and Calvin, together with the NIV, hold this final view, which describes the inspiration process.[59]

In this case, the focus is not interpretation of Scripture itself but interpretation of history or visions to write Scripture. Like the two previous views, this one does find support in other Scripture (Dan. 12:8–9; 1 Peter 1:10–12) and in verse 21, which parallels and expands the idea. Furthermore, this fourth view receives its strongest recommendation from *ginetai* plus the genitive to describe Scripture's origin. *Ginomai* often carries the meaning "come about" or "arose," describing the origin of something (e.g., 1 Tim. 6:4; 1 Peter 4:12; 2 Peter 2:1). This semantic connotation pairs nicely with a genitive (or ablative) of source—"comes about *from* the author's own interpretation"—or of means—"comes about *by means of* the author's own interpretation."[60]

The fourth interpretation that refers verse 20 to the divine origin of written revelation is preferable, but the third interpretation is a definite possibility.

The Method of Divine Inspiration

In what amounts to an example of synthetic parallelism, Peter restates in verse 21 the essence of verse 20 with further details on inspiration's mechanics. He adds emphasis to his first statement by moving *thelēmati anthrōpou* ("will of man") forward to its beginning and by the addition of *pote* ("formerly, ever") to the negative *ou* ("not"): "for *never* by means of human will was prophecy uttered."[61] This reference to human will is reminiscent of John 1:13, which describes mistaken sources of regeneration.

Peter gives the most detailed description of the inspiration process by any biblical writer. Evidently, a cooperation took place by which the human author, while normally not losing self-control or bypassing himself, received guidance from God to write God's words. Although the nominative participle, *pheromenoi* ("being carried along"), can be either adjectival or adverbial,[62] an adverbial participle is more enlightening. Whether it be a participle of means—"men by means of being carried along by the Holy Spirit spoke from God"—or cause—"men because they were carried along by the Holy Spirit spoke from God"—the participle clarifies *how* men spoke from God. The same passive participle describes the powerful sound of blowing wind when the Spirit came to control the apostles at Pentecost (Acts 2:2). Perhaps more descriptive is the same word used of a ship that is uncontrollably driven by storm wind (Acts 27:15, 17). Green brings out the idea of cooperation with these appropriate comments: "The prophets raised their sails, so to speak (they were obedient and receptive), and the Holy Spirit filled them and carried their craft along in the direction He wished."[63]

The preposition *hypo* ("by") indicates the Spirit's role as agent of God's revelation. Second Samuel 23:2, Acts 1:16, and 1 Corinthians 2:10 indicate the same, as do John 14:26 and 16:13–15. God's work *through* a man, while not forcing his will or skirting his personality and yet totally controlling the outcome, surely magnifies His power. Indeed, God's Word is one of His greatest miracles![64] Fully appreciated, it certainly surpasses being slain in the Spirit or a crying, dancing image of Mary.

A Suggested Translation of 2 Peter 1:16–21

[16]For it was not by means of following cleverly concocted tales that we made known to you the power and coming of our Lord Jesus Christ, but because we were eyewitnesses of his majesty. [17]For at the time that He received honor and glory from God the Father when such an announcement was uttered by the Magnificent Glory, "This is My Son, My Beloved in Whom I am well pleased," [18]we also heard this voice uttered from heaven when we were with Him on the holy mountain. [19]In addition, we have the more dependable prophetic word, to which you are doing well to devote yourself as to a lamp shining in a dark place, until the day dawns and the Morning Star rises, [20]since you know this above all in your hearts, that no prophecy of Scripture comes from an author's own interpretation; [21]for prophecy was never uttered by means of human will, but men, by being carried along by the Holy Spirit, spoke from God.

Conclusion

In our age, enemies of Christianity disbelieve God's Word, but even some professing Christians belittle Scripture by adding to it. Added to Scripture are myths and miracles of still quasi-pagan religious, fabulous experiences eagerly sought by people looking for excitement instead of truth, and sophisticated psychotherapies and theories grounded in godless presumptions. These "prophets of addition" demean Scripture's sufficiency by suggesting alternate sources of spiritual knowledge and solutions. Peter responds to them with his message of Scripture's superiority. God uttered this same message to them more than seven centuries before Peter when He said of those who advised Isaiah to look elsewhere for answers,

> And when they say to you, "Consult the mediums and the wizards who whisper and mutter," should not a people consult their God? Should they consult the dead on behalf of the living? To the law and to the testimony! If they do not speak according to this word, it is because they have no dawn. (Isaiah 8:19–20)

Endnotes

1. David B. Barrett, ed., *World Christian Encyclopedia* (Oxford: Oxford University Press, 1982), 562.

2. Michael Green (*Second Peter and Jude,* Tyndale New Testament Commentary [Grand Rapids: Eerdmans, 1968], 81; cf. also comments on v. 16b) believes that these false teachers are not pre-Gnostics because Peter is here answering their accusation that he was using fables, when they themselves used the same. This assertion requires too much consistency on the part of false teachers, however, that they would not accuse Peter of doing the very thing of which they were guilty. Moreover, it could be that Peter contrasts his method of not relying on legends with theirs to show the superiority of his authority.

3. All Scripture quotations are from the *New American Standard Bible* unless otherwise specified.

4. Note the phrases "remind you of these things" (v. 12), "stir you up by way of reminder" (v. 13), and "call these things to mind" (v. 15).

5. It is unlikely that Peter had seen Paul's use of this word for fanciful Jewish genealogies in 1 Timothy 1:4; 2 Timothy 4:4; and Titus 1:14 because those letters originated at approximately the same time as 2 Peter. Peter refers to this kind of error as "heresies" (2 Peter 2:1) and "false words" (2 Peter 2:3).

6. John Calvin uses some adroitness himself when he writes that Peter is explaining that he is not like the teachers "who presumptuously mount the pulpit to prattle of speculation unknown to themselves," in *Calvin: Commentaries* in *Library of Christian Classics* (Philadelphia: Westminster, 1958), 23:383.

7. This could possibly be an occurrence of *hendiadys* to avoid a long string of genitives in which case *dynamin kai parousian* ("power and coming") would stand for *dynamin parousiou* ("power of [His] coming"). Thus, the Twentieth Century NT translates it "the Coming in power."

8. Calvin (*Library of Christian Classics,* 23:382) understood this as referring to the first appearance of Christ. In addition, John Owen, in a footnote in his translation of Calvin, writes, "The whole passage refers only and expressly to his first coming." This leads him to understand that it is the believer's own experience with the gospel ("star arise in your hearts") that renders the written prophecies more sure to him personally (ibid., 386).

9. Such man-made guides addressed include religious leaders, modern counseling and psychology, new revelation in the signs-and-wonders movement, popular techniques of spiritual warfare, philosophy and rational thinking, science, tradition, and even personal experience and emotion. Several books have recently addressed this very topic from the point of view of the sufficiency of God's Word, including *Power Religion,* ed. Michael Horton (Chicago: Moody, 1992); Thomas Ice and Robert Dean Jr., *Overrun by Demons* (Eugene, Ore.: Harvest House, 1990); and John F. MacArthur Jr., *Our Sufficiency in Christ* (Dallas: Word, 1991). We laughingly remember the occasion when I shared this passage in a devotional medita-

tion before leaving from the mission field for a furlough. After the meditation, a woman approached my wife and remarked with emotion as she patted her heart, "I just *feel it in my heart* that you will return."

10. One may take both participles to be causal without a change of meaning: "not because we followed . . . but because we were eyewitnesses. . . ."

11. This reference to the Transfiguration experience confirms Peter as the author of this epistle, liberal scholarship notwithstanding. Peter even uses the emphatic pronoun *hēmeis* ("we") and refers both to being an eyewitness (v. 16) and to hearing (v. 18). Many people dismiss this as secondhand mention by someone who had heard of the Transfiguration from Peter or another apostle (e.g., Bo Reike, *The Epistles of James, Peter, and Jude,* vol. 37 of *The Anchor Bible* [Garden City, N.J.: Doubleday, 1964], 142, 144).

12. The mountain became "holy" because of what took place there. Similarly, Jerusalem was the "holy city" (Matt. 4:5; Rev. 11:2).

13. Although Green (*Second Peter and Jude,* 82) says that mention of the Transfiguration is rare in early Christian literature, in the Apocalypse of Peter someone familiar with 2 Peter also mentions it in connection with Christ's return (in the *Akhmim* and *Ethipoic* fragments, *The Apocryphal New Testament,* trans. J. K. Elliot [Oxford: Clarendon, 1993], 609–12). This view may reflect the early church's interpretation of the verse.

14. "Announced" (*enechtheisēs,* lit. "was brought," v. 17). The word also depicts God's utterance of a word or an announcement in verses 18, 21. Could this be the origin of the southern expression, "Preacher sure brought a good message this morning"?

15. *Megaloprepous* is probably a euphemism for God.

16. *Toiasde* ("of such kind") evidently introduces the following announcement in much the same way as *toioutos* does in Classical Greek (F. Blass, A. Debrunner, and R. W. Funk, *A Greek Grammar of the New Testament and Other Early Christian Literature* [Chicago: University of Chicago Press, 1961], par. 289). Joseph Henry Thayer adds that it suggests something excellent or admirable (*A Greek-English Lexicon of the New Testament,* trans. and rev. Joseph Henry Thayer [1889; reprint, Edinburgh: T. & T. Clark, 1958], 627).

17. Simon Kistemaker, *First and Second Peter and Jude* (Grand Rapids: Baker, 1987), 267.

18. Both the NASB and the RSV seem to handle the syntax this way.

19. Biblical signs and wonders provided testimony to the truth for those who witnessed them. Yet, they are clearly inferior in the witness of written revelation and point to further revelation that interprets them (cf. Luke 16:29–31; John 20:29).

20. Rodney Henry (*Filipino Spirit World* [Manila: OMF Publishers, 1971]) discusses this separation in the realm of the spirit world.

21. Green, *Second Peter and Jude,* 86.

22. R. H. Strachan, "The Second Epistle General of Peter," *The Expositor's Greek*

Testament (Grand Rapids: Eerdmans, 1961), 5:131. Likewise, Moffatt translates, "gained fresh confirmation of the prophetic word."

23. H. Schönweiss, "Firm, Foundation, Certainty, Confirm," in *New International Dictionary of New Testament Theology,* ed. C. Brown (Grand Rapids: Zondervan, 1971), 1:658.

24. Comparatives can sometimes be used for superlatives. Thus Bo Reicke (*Epistles of James, Peter, and Jude,* 158) translates, "And we regard the prophetic word as most reliable." This would fit well if Peter is comparing three different sources of knowledge, namely, myths, direct revelation, and written revelation. The preceding suggestion is preferable.

25. Interestingly, this construction, verb-adjective-article-adjective, is quite uncommon. A study of its occurrences is inconclusive as to whether the adjective, in this case *bebaios,* is used attributively or predicatively. Apart from its idiomatic uses with *pas* ("all, every") and *holos* ("whole, complete"), the construction appears only a few times. Luke 5:7 has the adjective *amphotera* ("both") used attributively in this construction. Particularly parallel to 2 Peter 1:19 is Acts 17:16, which describes Athens as "the full-of-idols city." (Or is it "that the city was full of idols"?) Hebrews 11:23 can be understood as either attributive, "they saw the beautiful child," or predicate, "they saw that the child was beautiful." Cf. also Romans 4:16, with *einai* ("to be").

26. The presence of the article would be better translated as "the more sure word. . . ."

27. Louis Barbieri, *First and Second Peter,* Everyman's Bible Commentary (Chicago: Moody, 1977), 105.

28. Unfortunately, this preference for written revelation was not applied to a preference for the OT. In fact, the rabbis seemed to favor the *Mishnah* and *Gemara* to the OT. Edersheim, citing the Talmud tractate Baba Met 33a, writes, "The Talmud has it, that he who busies himself with Scripture only (i.e., without either the *Mishnah* or *Gemara*) has merit, and yet no merit" (Alfred Edersheim, *The Life and Times of Jesus the Messiah* [1883; reprint, Peabody, Mass.: Hendrickson, 1993], 75). However, concerning the value of oral revelation, the rabbis had developed the concept of the *bat qôl,* literally the "daughter of a voice," "an echo of a heavenly voice that was audible on earth and proclaimed some divine oracle or judgment" (M. J. Harris, "Quiet, Rest, Silence, etc.," in *New International Dictionary of New Testament Theology,* ed. C. Brown [Grand Rapids: Zondervan, 1971], 3:113).

29. Especially prominent in Matthew, the apostles' sermons in Acts, Romans 9–15, Hebrews, and 1 Peter 2.

30. Kistemaker, *First and Second Peter and Jude,* 269.

31. A study of Peter's fourteen uses of *logos* (including those in Acts) reveals a wide variety of meanings, most often referring to the gospel. It never refers to only the OT.

32. Strachan ("Second Epistle General," 131f.) suggests that the pronoun *hō* refers not to the preceding noun but to the whole preceding clause. In that case, the "lamp

shining" would refer to the Transfiguration as an especially crucial sign of Christ's return, substantiating the prophecies. Conversely, of the forty-nine times that *hō* appears in the NT without a preposition, it *always* refers to a noun or pronoun, usually expressed and rarely implied, but never to a clause. In addition, the Transfiguration has not, in fact, served such a significant role historically.

33. J. H. Moulton and G. Milligan, *The Vocabulary of the Greek Testament* (1930; reprint, Peabody, Mass.: Hendrickson, 1997), 95.

34. One Koine epitaph reads, "May there be many blossoms upon the newly built tomb, not *parched [aumēros]* bramble, not worthless goat-weed." It is also used to describe the dark and dry sleeping place called Hades (ibid., 95).

35. Experiences that were valid and legitimate in the time of Peter, such as witnessing the Transfiguration, no longer continue in the same way in this time following the completion of the NT canon.

36. Henry Alford, *The Greek Testament*, 4 vols., 4th ed. (London: Longmans, Green, and Co., 1903), 4:400.

37. Kistemaker, *First and Second Peter and Jude*, 271.

38. D. Edmond Hiebert, "The Prophetic Foundation for the Christian Life: An Exposition of 2 Peter 1:19–21," *Bibliotheca Sacra* 141, no. 562 (April–June 1984): 158–68.

39. Both the NASB and Nestle's 26th edition of the Greek NT suggest this with their punctuation.

40. Green, *Second Peter and Jude*, 89. This interpretation would be even more obvious if one follows the textual variant that places the article before *hēmera* ("*the* day"), but the textual support for the article is weak.

41. Although Revelation uses a different term, *ho astēr ho prōinos* ("morning star"), rather than *phōsphoros* ("morning star") used here, the terms are synonymous.

42. Calvin, *Library of Christian Classics*, 23:381ff.

43. Green (*Second Peter and Jude*, 89) does not allude to this possibility.

44. Cf. Matthew 11:25; 13:1; Ephesians 3:17; Philippians 2:7; Colossians 1:10–11; 3:16, 22; 1 Timothy 5:10; Titus 3:3; Hebrews 4:7; 10:10; Jude 20. The first two begin even a new sentence in the Nestle 26th ed. Greek text.

45. Many other activities take place within believers' hearts, including sin (Matt. 5:28; 9:4; Acts 7:39; James 3:14), thinking and remembering (Matt. 24:48; Mark 2:6; Luke 2:19, 51; 3:15; 9:47), doubt (Mark 11:23; Luke 24:38), God's love (Rom. 5:5), and belief (Rom. 10:9). Furthermore, the Holy Spirit and Christ dwell there (2 Cor. 1:22; Eph. 3:17).

46. Strachan, "Second Epistle General," 132; Green, *Second Peter and Jude*, 89. Although the simple temporal participle is very often possible, it is often best to resort to it only when no other interpretive possibilities fit (Dan Wallace, "Selected Notes" [unpublished syllabus, Grace Theological Seminary, circa 1981]). The NASB and the NIV understand an imperatival participle in both 1:20 and 3:3. This is possible, but the rarity of this use of a participle makes it unlikely. In contrast, of the

twenty-two times that the nominative participle of *ginōskō* used adverbially appears in the NT, nineteen either clearly or probably express the cause for an associated action (Matt. 12:15; 16:8; 22:18; 26:10; Mark 6:38; 8:17; 15:45; Luke 9:11; John 5:6; 6:15; Acts 23:6; Rom. 1:21; 6:6; Gal. 2:9; 4:9; Eph. 5:5; Phil. 2:19; Heb. 10:34; James 1:3; 2 Peter 1:20; 3:3).

47. *Touto prōton* ("this first") occurs only here in the NT, but it appears with the same meaning of "above all" in the LXX of Isa. 9:1, stressing urgency of action.

48. This verse is grammatically similar to 3:2–3, where Peter gives the reason for his readers to remember the words of the prophets.

49. Although Peter might view prophecy in its narrow sense—those truths and events *foretold* by the prophets—he probably sees it in the broader sense of all Scripture. The same word in the following verse has its wider sense because of its similarity to 2 Timothy 3:16.

50. The *Jerome Biblical Commentary* explains, "This is to be found in the apostolic tradition handed on in the Church" (Raymond E. Brown, Joseph A. Fitzmeyer, and Roland E. Murphy, eds., *Jerome Biblical Commentary* [Englewood Cliffs, N.J.: Prentice-Hall, 1968], 496). The Jerusalem Bible translates, "Interpretation of scriptural prophecy is never a matter for the individual." In our own setting in the Philippines, one particular lay organization of the Roman Catholic Church advised members to read the Bible devotionally and meditatively but to depend on the Church and its clergy for deeper interpretation.

51. Although *gar* ("for," v. 21) can sometimes function in ways other than expressing cause or providing an explanation, of the twenty-five times that Peter uses the conjunction, an overwhelming majority give a supporting reason for a previous statement.

52. Calvin, *Library of Christian Classics,* 23:389.

53. It is important to distinguish between meaning, which is singular for any passage, and application, which can be multiple.

54. Thayer suggests that the point is the believer's need of the Holy Spirit to understand what he reads, "an interpretation which one thinks out for himself, opp. to that which the Holy Spirit teaches" (*Greek-English Lexicon,* 296). Just as the Spirit is the source of the writing, verse 21, so He also is the source of interpretation or understanding.

55. Of the three other possible occurrences of this combination of *ginomai* and a genitive in the predicate, Mark 13:18 uses a genitive of description, "happen in the winter"; Revelation 11:15 uses the genitive possessively; and Acts 20:3 remains enigmatic.

56. In Romans 9:16, the genitive has the idea of dependence: "so then it *does* not *depend* on the man who wills. . . ." A. T. Robertson admits that the genitive had become very broad by Koine times, often overlapping with the accusative (*A Grammar of the Greek New Testament in the Light of Historical Research* [Nashville: Broadman, 1934], 506).

57. For other genitives of direction/purpose in Peter, cf. 1 Peter 2:16, "as a covering

for evil"; 3:21, "an appeal to God *for* a good conscience"; 5:2, "exercising oversight . . . not *for* sordid gain."

58. The Living Bible paraphrases, "was ever thought up by the prophet himself."

59. Hiebert, "Prophetic Foundation," 165. In a similar vein, Strachan ("Second Epistle General," 131ff.) understands it to mean that the prophet, when he described a revelation applied to his own generations' historical situation, did not give the only application, but other historical applications were possible: "The prophets . . . saw clearly only the contemporary political or moral situation, and the principles involved and illustrated therein."

60. Admittedly, both genitives (or ablatives) of source and means are rare, but 1 Peter 3:21 may be an example of the former, "dirt *from* the flesh," and the participle in 1 Peter 2:15 is certainly an example of genitive (or ablative) of means, "*by* doing right you may silence the ignorance. . . ." In addition, a genitive of means would parallel the dative of means, *thelēmati* ("through the will") in verse 21.

61. For *pote* with the negative, cf. also Ephesians 5:29; 2 Peter 1:10.

62. Of the approximate 134 times that Peter uses the anarthrous, nominative participle (the articular participle is uncommon), both adjectival and adverbial are very common.

63. Green, *Second Peter and Jude,* 91.

64. Several important texts add *hagioi* instead of *apo,* resulting in the translation "holy men of God spoke" (cf. KJV, RSV n.). Mss. supporting the alternative include the Majority text, uncials *aleph* A 33 C, and Vulgate. But the reading with *apo* found in p[72] and in B P and numerous other manuscripts is stronger.

CHAPTER SEVEN

The Mandate of Biblical Inerrancy: Expository Preaching

John F. MacArthur Jr.

The special attention that evangelicalism has given to the inerrancy of Scripture in recent years carries with it a mandate to emphasize the expository method of preaching the Scriptures. The existence of God and His nature requires the conclusion that He has communicated accurately and that an adequate exegetical process is required to determine His meaning. The Christian commission to preach God's Word involves the transmitting of that meaning to an audience, a weighty responsibility. A belief in inerrancy thus requires, most importantly, exegetical preaching and does not have to do primarily with the homiletical form of the message. In this regard, it differs from a view of limited inerrancy.

This essay was initially given as a response at the International Council on Biblical Inerrancy, Summit II (November 1982). It was subsequently published under the title "Inerrancy and Preaching: Where Exposition and Exegesis Come Together," in *Hermeneutics, Inerrancy, and the Bible,* ed. Earl Radmacher and Robert Preus (Grand Rapids: Zondervan, 1984), 801–31. It was updated to serve as the foundational article for the inaugural issue of *The Master's Seminary Journal* and also appeared as chapter 2 in *Rediscovering Expository Preaching,* ed. Richard L. Mayhue and Robert L. Thomas (Dallas: Word, 1992), 22–35.

* * * * *

The theological highlight of recent years has, without question, been evangelicalism's intense focus on biblical inerrancy.[1] Much of what has been written defending inerrancy[2] represents the most acute theological reasoning our generation has produced.

Yet, our commitment to inerrancy seems to be somewhat lacking in the way it fleshes out in practical ministry. Specifically, evangelical preaching ought to reflect our conviction that God's Word is infallible and inerrant. Too often, it does not. In fact, a discernable trend exists in contemporary evangelicalism *away* from biblical preaching and *toward* a pragmatic, topical, and experience-centered approach in the pulpit.

Should not our preaching be biblical exposition, reflecting our conviction that the Bible is the inspired, inerrant Word of God? If we believe that "all Scripture is inspired by God" and inerrant, must we not be equally committed to the reality that it is "profitable for teaching, for reproof, for correction, for training in righteousness; that the man of God may be adequate, equipped for every good work"?[3] Should not that magnificent truth determine how we preach?

Paul gave this mandate to Timothy: "I solemnly charge you in the presence of God and of Christ Jesus, who is to judge the living and the dead, and by His appearing and His kingdom: *preach the word;* be ready in season and out of season; reprove, rebuke, exhort, with great patience and instruction."[4] Any form of preaching that ignores that intended purpose and design of God falls short of the divine plan. J. I. Packer eloquently captured the pursuit of preaching thus:

> Preaching appears in the Bible as a relaying of what God has said about Himself and His doings, and about men in relation to Him, plus a pressing of His commands, promises, warnings, and assurances, with a view to winning the hearer or hearers . . . to a positive response.[5]

The only logical response to inerrant Scripture, then, is to preach it expositionally. By *expositionally,* I mean preaching in such a way that the meaning of the Bible passage is presented *entirely* and *exactly* as it was intended by God. Expository preaching is the proclamation of the truth of God as mediated through the preacher.[6]

Admittedly, not all expositors have an inerrant view. (See William Barclay's treatment of Mark 5 or John 6 in *The Daily Study Bible Series*.) It is also true that not everyone who holds to inerrancy practices expository preaching. These positions, however, are inconsistencies because an inerrantist perspective demands expository preaching, and a noninerrantist perspective makes it unnecessary.

To put it another way, what does it matter that we have an inerrant text if we do not deal with the basic phenomena of communication (e.g., words, sentences, grammar, morphology, syntax, etc.)? And if we do not, why bother preaching it?

In his much-needed volume on exegetical theology, Walter Kaiser pointedly analyzes the current anemic state of the church as a result of flock-feeding being rendered inadequate because of the absence of expository preaching:

> It is no secret that Christ's Church is not at all in good health in many places of the world. She has been languishing because she has been fed, as the current line has it, "junk food"; all kinds of artificial preservatives and all sorts of unnatural substitutes have been served up to her. As a result, theological and Biblical malnutrition has afflicted the very generation that has taken such giant steps to make sure its physical health is not damaged by using foods or products that are carcinogenic or otherwise harmful to their physical bodies. Simultaneously a worldwide spiritual famine resulting from the absence of any genuine publication of the Word of God (Amos 8:11) continues to run wild and almost unabated in most quarters of the Church.[7]

The cure is expository preaching.

The mandate, then, is clear. Expository preaching is the declarative genre in which inerrancy finds its logical expression and the church has its life and power. Stated simply, inerrancy demands exposition as the only method of preaching that preserves the purity of Scripture and accomplishes the purpose for which God gave us His Word.

R. B. Kuiper reinforces this mandate when he writes, "The principle that Christian preaching is proclamation of the Word must obviously be determinative of the content of the sermon."[8]

Inerrancy, Exegesis, and Exposition

Postulates and Propositions

I would like to begin the main discussion with the following logically sequential postulates that introduce and undergird my propositions (as well as form a true basis for inerrancy).[9]

1. God is (Gen. 1:1; Pss. 14; 53; Heb. 11:6).
2. God is true (Exod. 34:6; Num. 23:19; Deut. 32:4; Pss. 25:10; 31:6; Isa. 65:16; Jer. 10:10; 10:11; John 14:6; 17:3; Titus 1:2; Heb. 6:18; 1 John 5:20).
3. God speaks in harmony with His nature (Num. 23:19; 1 Sam. 15:29; Rom. 3:4; 2 Tim. 2:13; Titus 1:2; Heb. 6:18).
4. God speaks only truth (Pss. 31:5; 119:43, 142, 151, 160; Prov. 30:5; Isa. 65:16; John 17:17; James 1:18).
5. God spoke His true Word as consistent with His true Nature to be communicated to people (a self-evident truth that is illustrated at 2 Tim. 3:16–17; Heb. 1:1).

Therefore, we must consider the following propositions.

1. God gave His true Word to be communicated *entirely* as He gave it, that is, the whole counsel of God is to be preached (Matt. 28:20; Acts 5:20; 20:27). Correspondingly, every portion of the Word of God must be considered in the light of its whole.
2. God gave His true Word to be communicated *exactly* as He gave it. It is to be dispensed precisely as it was delivered without altering the message.
3. Only the exegetical process that yields expository proclamation will accomplish propositions 1 and 2.

Inerrancy's Link to Expository Preaching

Now, let me substantiate these propositions with answers to a series of questions. They will channel our thinking from the headwaters of God's revelation to its intended destination.

1. Why preach?

Very simply, God so commanded (2 Tim. 4:2), and the apostles so responded (Acts 6:4).

2. What should we preach?

The Word of God, that is, *Scriptura sola* and *Scriptura tota* (1 Tim. 4:13; 2 Tim. 4:2).

3. Who preaches?

Holy men of God (Luke 1:15-17; Acts 3:21; Eph. 3:5; 2 Peter 1:21). Only after God had purified Isaiah's lips was he ordained to preach (Isa. 6:6–13).

4. What is the preacher's responsibility?

First, the preacher must realize that God's Word is not the preacher's word. Rather, the following points are true.

- He is a messenger, not an originator *(euangelizō).*
- He is a sower, not the source (Matt. 13:3, 19).
- He is a herald, not the authority *(kērussō).*
- He is a steward, not the owner (Col. 1:25).
- He is the guide, not the author (Acts 8:31).
- He is the server of spiritual food, not the chef (John 21:15, 17).

Second, the preacher must reckon that Scripture is *ho logos tou theou* ("the Word of God"). When he is committed to this awesome truth and responsibility,

His aim, rather, will be to stand under Scripture, not over it, and to allow it, so to speak, to talk through him, delivering what is not so much his message as its. In our preaching, that is what should always be happening. In his obituary of the great German conductor, Otto Klemperer, Neville Cardus spoke of the way in which Klemperer "set the music in motion," maintaining throughout a deliberately anonymous, self-effacing style in order that the musical notes might articulate themselves in their own integrity through him. So it must be in preaching; Scripture itself must do all the talking, and the preacher's task is simply to "set the Bible in motion."[10]

A careful study of the phrase *logos theou* ("the Word of God") reveals more than forty uses in the New Testament. It is equated with the Old Testament (Mark 7:13). It is what Jesus preached (Luke 5:1). It was the message that the apostles taught (Acts 4:31; 6:2). It was the word that the Samaritans received (Acts 8:14) as given by the apostles (Acts 8:25). It was the message that the Gentiles received as preached by Peter (Acts 11:1). It was the word that Paul preached on his first missionary journey (Acts 13:5, 7, 44, 48, 49; 15:35–36), and on his second missionary journey (Acts 16:32; 17:13; 18:11), and on his third missionary journey (Acts 19:10). It was the focus of Luke in the book of Acts in that it spread rapidly and widely (Acts 6:7; 12:24; 19:20). Paul was careful to tell the Corinthians that he spoke the Word as it was given from God, that it had not been adulterated and that it was a manifestation of truth (2 Cor. 2:17; 4:2). Paul acknowledged that it was the source of his preaching (Col. 1:25; 1 Thess. 2:13).

As it was with Christ and the apostles, so Scripture is also to be delivered by preachers today in such a way that they can say, "Thus saith the Lord." Their responsibility is to deliver it as it was originally given and intended.

5. How did the preacher's message begin?

The message began as a true word from God and was given as truth because God's purpose was to transmit truth. It was ordered by God as truth and was delivered by God's Spirit in cooperation with holy men who received it with exactly the pure quality that God intended (2 Peter 1:20–21). It was received as *Scriptura inerrantis* by the prophets and apostles (i.e., without wandering from Scripture's original formulation in the mind of God). Inerrancy, then, expresses the quality with which the writers of our canon received the text that we call Scripture.

6. How is God's message to continue in its original true state?

If God's message began true, and if it is to be delivered as received, what interpretive processes necessitated by changes of language, culture, and time will ensure its purity when it is preached now? The answer is that only an exegetical approach is acceptable for accurate exposition.

Having established the essential need for exegesis, the most logical question is, "How is interpretation/exegesis linked with preaching?" Packer answers best:

> The Bible being what it is, all true interpretation of it must take the form of preaching. With this goes an equally important converse: that, preaching being what it is, all true preaching must take the form of biblical interpretation.[11]

7. Now, pulling our thinking all together in a practical way, "what is the final step that links inerrancy to preaching?"

First, the true text must be used. We are indebted to those select scholars who labor tediously in the field of textual criticism. Their studies recover the original text of Scripture from the large volume of extant manuscript copies that are flawed by textual variants. This is the starting point. Without the text as God gave it, the preacher would be helpless to deliver it as God intended.

Second, having begun with a true text, we must interpret the text accurately. The science of hermeneutics is in view.

> As a theological discipline hermeneutics is the science of the correct interpretation of the Bible. It is a special application of the general science of linguistics and meaning. It seeks to formulate those particular rules which pertain to the special factors connected with the Bible. . . . Hermeneutics is a science in that it can determine certain principles for discovering the meaning of a document, and in that these principles are not a

mere list of rules but bear organic connection to each other. It is also an art as we previously indicated because principles or rules can never be applied mechanically but involve the skill *(technē)* of the interpreter.[12]

Third, our exegesis must flow from a proper hermeneutic. Of this relationship, Bernard Ramm observes that hermeneutics

> . . . stands in the same relationship to exegesis that a rule-book stands to a game. The rule-book is written in terms of reflection, analysis, and experience. The game is played by concrete actualization of the rules. The rules are not the game, and the game is meaningless without the rules. Hermeneutics proper is not exegesis, but exegesis is applied hermeneutics.[13]

Exegesis can now be defined as the skillful application of sound hermeneutical principles to the biblical text in the original language with a view to understanding and declaring the author's intended meaning to both the immediate and subsequent audiences. In tandem, hermeneutics and exegesis focus on the biblical text to determine what it said and what it meant originally.[14] Thus, exegesis in its broadest sense will include the various disciplines of literary criticism, historical studies, grammatical exegesis, historical theology, biblical theology, and systematic theology. Proper exegesis will tell the student what the text says and what the text means, guiding him to make a proper personal application of it.

> Interpretation of Scripture is the cornerstone not only of the entire sermon preparation process, but also of the preacher's life. A faithful student of Scripture will seek to be as certain as possible that the interpretation is biblically accurate.[15]

Fourth, we are now ready for a true exposition. Based on the flow of thinking through which we have just come, I assert that expository preaching is really exegetical preaching and not so much the homiletical form of the message. Merrill Unger appropriately noted,

It is not the length of the portion treated, whether a single verse or a larger unit, but the manner of treatment. No matter what the length of the portion explained may be, if it is handled in such a way that its real and essential meaning as it existed in the light of the overall context of Scripture is made plain and applied to the present-day needs of the hearers, it may properly be said to be expository preaching.[16]

As a result of this exegetical process that began with a commitment to inerrancy, the expositor is equipped with a true message, true intent, and true application. It gives his preaching perspective historically, theologically, contextually, literarily, synoptically, and culturally. His message is God's intended message.

Now, because this all seems so patently obvious, we might ask, "How did the church ever lose sight of inerrancy's relationship to preaching?" Let me suggest that in the main it was through the "legacy of liberalism."

The Legacy of Liberalism

An Example

Robert Bratcher is the translator of the American Bible Society's (ABS) *Good News for Modern Man,* a former research assistant with ABS, and an ordained Southern Baptist pastor. As one of the invited speakers to a Christian Life Commission of the Southern Baptist Convention, he addressed the topic "Biblical Authority for the Church Today." Bratcher was quoted as saying,

Only willful ignorance or intellectual dishonesty can account for the claim that the Bible is inerrant and infallible. No truth-loving, God-respecting, Christ-honoring believer should be guilty of such heresy. To invest the Bible with the qualities of inerrancy and infallibility is to idolatrize [sic] it, to transform it into a false god.[17]

This thinking is typical of the legacy of liberalism that has robbed preachers of true preaching dynamics. I ask, "Why be careful with content that does not reflect the nature of God or with content the truthfulness of which is uncertain?"

False Notions

Bratcher and others who would subscribe to "limited" or "partial" inerrancy are guilty of error along several lines of reasoning.[18] *First,* they have not really come to grips with that which Scripture teaches about itself.

Benjamin Warfield focused on the heart of the issue with this inquiry: "The really decisive question among Christian scholars . . . is thus seen to be, 'What does an exact and scientific exegesis determine to be the Biblical doctrine of inspiration?'"[19]

The answer is that nowhere do the Scriptures teach that there is a dichotomy of truth and error nor do the writers ever give the slightest hint that they were aware of this alleged phenomenon as they wrote. The human writers of Scripture unanimously concur that it is God's Word; therefore, it must be true.

Second, limited or partial inerrancy assumes that an authority higher than God's revelation in the Scriptures exists to establish the reliability of Scripture. They err by *a priori* giving the critic a place of authority over the Scriptures. This view assumes that the critic himself is inerrant.

Third, if limited inerrancy is true, then its promoters err in assuming that any part of the Scriptures is a trustworthy communicator of God's truth. An errant Scripture would definitely disqualify the Bible as a reliable source of truth.

Presuppositions are involved either way. Will men place their faith in the Scriptures or the critics? They cannot have their cake (trustworthy Scripture) and eat it too (limited inerrancy). Pinnock aptly noted, "The attempt to narrow down the integrity of the Bible to matters of 'faith' and its historical reliability is an unwarranted and foolish procedure."[20]

If the Bible is unable to produce a sound doctrine of Scripture, then it is thus incapable of producing, with any degree of credibility, a doctrine about any other matter. If the human writers of Scripture have erred in their understanding of Holy Writ's purity, then they have disqualified themselves as writers for any other area of God's revealed truth. If they are so disqualified in all areas, then every preacher is thoroughly robbed of any confidence and conviction concerning the alleged true message that he would be relaying for God.

The Bottom Line

G. Campbell Morgan, hailed as the twentieth century's "prince of expositors," was a messenger whom God used widely. For a time in his life, however, he wrestled with the very issue that we now discuss. He concluded that if the biblical message contained errors, it could not be proclaimed honestly in public. Following is the account of young Campbell Morgan's struggle to know if the Bible was surely God's Word:

> For three years this young man, seriously contemplating a future of teaching and ultimately of preaching, felt the troubled waters of the stream of religious controversy carrying him beyond his depth. He read the new books which debated such questions as, "Is God Knowable?" and found that the authors' concerted decision was, "He is not knowable." He became confused and perplexed. No longer was he sure of that which his father proclaimed in public, and had taught him in the home.
>
> Other books appeared, seeking to defend the Bible from the attacks which were being made upon it. The more he read, the more unanswerable became the questions which filled his mind. One who has never suffered it cannot appreciate the anguish of spirit young Campbell Morgan endured during this crucial period of his life. Through all the after years it gave him the greatest sympathy with young people passing through similar experiences at college—experiences which he likened to "passing through a trackless desert." At last the crisis came when he admitted to himself his total lack of assurance that the Bible was the authoritative Word of God to man. He immediately cancelled all preaching engagements. Then, taking all his books, both those attacking and those defending the Bible, he put them all in a corner cupboard. Relating this afterwards, as he did many times in preaching, he told of turning the key in the lock of the door. "I can hear the click of that lock now," he used to say. He went out of the house, and down the street to a bookshop. He

bought a new Bible and, returning to his room with it, he said to himself: "I am no longer sure that this is what my father claims it to be—the Word of God. But of this I am sure. If it be the Word of God, and if I come to it with an unprejudiced and open mind, it will bring assurance to my soul of itself." "That Bible found me," he said, "I began to read and study it then, in 1883. I have been a student ever since, and I still am (in 1938)."

At the end of two years Campbell Morgan emerged from that eclipse of faith absolutely sure that the Bible was, in very deed and truth, none other than the Word of the living God. Quoting again from his account of the incident: ". . . This experience is what, at last, took me back into the work of preaching, and into the work of the ministry. I soon found foothold enough to begin to preach, and from that time I went on."

With this crisis behind him and this new certainty thrilling his soul, there came a compelling conviction. This Book, being what it was, merited all that a man could give to its study, not merely for the sake of the personal joy of delving deeply into the heart and mind and will of God, but also in order that those truths discovered by such searching of the Scriptures should be made known to a world of men groping for light, and perishing in the darkness with no clear knowledge of that Will.[21]

May God be pleased to multiply the tribe of men called "preachers" who, being convinced of the Bible's inerrant nature, will diligently apply themselves to understand and to proclaim its message as those commissioned of God to deliver it in His stead.

Our Challenge

One of the most godly preachers ever to live was Scotland's Robert Murray McCheyne. In the memoirs of McCheyne's life, Andrew Bonar writes,

It was his wish to arrive nearer at the primitive mode of expounding Scripture in his sermons. Hence when one asked him, if he was ever afraid of running short of sermons some day, he replied—"No; I am just an interpreter of Scripture in my sermons; and when the Bible runs dry, then I shall." And in the same spirit he carefully avoided the too common mode of accommodating texts—fastening a doctrine on the words, not drawing it from the obvious connection of the passage. He endeavoured at all times to preach the mind of the Spirit in a passage; for he feared that to do otherwise would be to grieve the Spirit who had written it. Interpretation was thus a solemn matter to him. And yet, adhering scrupulously to this sure principle, he felt himself in no way restrained from using, for every day's necessities, all parts of the Old Testament as much as the New. His manner was first to ascertain the primary sense and application, and so proceed to handle it for present use.[22]

The expositor's task is to preach the mind of God as he finds it in the inerrant Word of God. He understands it through the disciplines of hermeneutics and exegesis. He then declares it expositorily as the message that God spoke and commissioned him to deliver.

John Stott deftly sketched the relationship of the exegetical process to expository preaching thus:

Expository preaching is a most exacting discipline. Perhaps that is why it is so rare. Only those will undertake it who are prepared to follow the example of the apostles and say, "It is not right that we should give up preaching the Word of God to serve tables. . . . We will devote ourselves to prayer and to the ministry of the Word" (Acts 6:2, 4). The systematic preaching of the Word is impossible without the systematic study of it. It will not be enough to skim through a few verses in daily Bible reading, nor to study a passage only when we have to preach from it. No. We must daily soak ourselves in the Scriptures. We must not just study, as through a microscope, the linguistic minutiae of a few verses, but take our telescope and scan the wide expanses of God's Word, assimilating its grand theme of divine sovereignty in the redemption of mankind. "It is blessed," wrote C. H. Spurgeon, "to eat into the very soul of the Bible until, at last, you come to talk in Scriptural language, and your spirit is flavoured with the words of the Lord, so that your blood is Bibline and the very essence of the Bible flows from you."[23]

Inerrancy demands an exegetical process and an expository proclamation. Only the exegetical process preserves God's Word entirely, guarding the treasure of revelation, and declaring its meaning exactly as He intended it to be proclaimed.[24] Expository preaching is the result of the exegetical process. Thus, it is the essential link between inerrancy and proclamation. It is mandated to preserve the purity of God's originally given inerrant Word and to proclaim the whole counsel of God's redemptive truth.[25]

Endnotes

1. Over a ten-year period (1977–1987), the International Council on Biblical Inerrancy held three summits for scholars (in 1978, 1982, and 1986) and two congresses for the Christian community-at-large (in 1982 and 1987) the purposes of which were to formulate and disseminate the biblical truth about inerrancy.

2. Paul D. Feinberg, "Infallibility and Inerrancy," *Trinity Journal* 6, no. 2 (fall 1977): 120, crisply articulates critical inerrancy as "the claim that when all facts are known, the scriptures in their original autographs and properly interpreted will be shown to be without error in all that they affirm to the degree of precision intended, whether that affirmation relates to doctrine, history, science, geography, geology, etc."

3. Second Timothy 3:16–17. Scripture quotations in this essay are taken from the *New American Standard Bible* (La Habra, Calif.: Foundation Press, 1971) unless otherwise noted.

4. Second Timothy 4:1–2 (emphasis added).

5. James I. Packer, "Preaching as Biblical Interpretation," *Inerrancy and Common Sense,* ed. Roger R. Nicole and J. Ramsey Michaels (Grand Rapids: Baker, 1980), 189.

6. D. Martyn Lloyd-Jones, *Preaching and Preachers* (Grand Rapids: Zondervan, 1971), 222.

7. Walter C. Kaiser Jr., *Toward an Exegetical Theology* (Grand Rapids: Baker, 1981), 7–8.

8. R. B. Kuiper, "Scriptural Preaching," *The Infallible Word,* 3d rev. ed., ed. Paul Woolley (Philadelphia: Presbyterian and Reformed, 1967), 217.

9. See Norman Geisler, "Inerrancy Leaders: Apply the Bible," *Eternity* 38, no. 1 (January 1987): 25, for this compact syllogism:

God cannot err;

The Bible is the Word of God;

Therefore, the Bible cannot err.

10. Packer, "Preaching as Biblical Interpretation," 203.

11. Ibid., 187.

12. Bernard Ramm, *Protestant Biblical Interpretation* (3d rev. ed.; Grand Rapids: Baker, 1970), 11.

13. Ibid. See also, Jerry Vines and David Allen, "Hermeneutics, Exegesis and Proclamation," *Criswell Theological Review* 1, no. 2 (spring 1987): 309–34.

14. This definition has been adapted from John D. Grassmick, *Principles and Practice of Greek Exegesis* (Dallas: Dallas Theological Seminary, 1974), 7.

15. Al Fasol, *Essentials for Biblical Preaching* (Grand Rapids: Baker, 1989), 41.

16. Merrill F. Unger, *Principles of Expository Preaching* (Grand Rapids: Zondervan, 1955), 33.

17. "Inerrancy: Clearing Away Confusion," *Christianity Today* 25, no. 10 (29 May 1981): 12.

18. These arguments have been adapted from Richard L. Mayhue, "Biblical Inerrancy in the Gospels" (unpublished paper; Winona Lake, Ind.: Grace Theological Seminary, 1977), 12–15.

19. Benjamin Breckinridge Warfield, *The Inspiration and Authority of the Bible* (1948; reprint, Philadelphia: Presbyterian and Reformed, 1948), 175.

20. Clark H. Pinnock, "Our Source of Authority: The Bible," *Bibliotheca Sacra* 124, no. 494 (April–June 1967): 154.

21. Jill Morgan, *A Man of the Word: Life of G. Campbell Morgan* (Grand Rapids: Baker, 1978), 39–40.

22. Andrew A. Bonar, *Memoir and Remains of Robert Murray McCheyne* (Grand Rapids: Baker, 1978), 94.

23. John R. W. Stott, *The Preacher's Portrait* (Grand Rapids: Eerdmans, 1961), 30–31.

24. See 1 Timothy 6:20–21 and 2 Timothy 2:15.

25. These central truths about the inerrant Bible, hermeneutics, exegesis, and preaching reflect the heart of The Master's Seminary curriculum and the faculty's commitment to prepare faithful expositors of God's Word for the twenty-first century.

CHAPTER EIGHT

The Priority of Prayer in Preaching

James E. Rosscup

*Prayer is not an elective feature but the principal element in the kaleido-
scope of spiritual characteristics that mark a preacher. These multiple
traits unite into a powerful spiritual force. They build a spokesman for
God. Jesus, the finest model, and other effective spokesmen for God have
been mighty in prayer coupled with the virtues of godliness and dependence on God. The composite of qualities that centers in prayer is conspicuous in God's long line of proclaimers in the OT, NT, and church
history, even to the present day. Some books on essentials for preaching
slight prayer, but others acknowledge its invaluable role. Preachers who
follow the biblical model of preaching take prayer very seriously. In
sermon preparation, they steep themselves in prayer.*

This article appeared as a chapter in *Rediscovering Expository Preaching,* ed.
Richard L. Mayhue and Robert L. Thomas (Dallas: Word, 1992), 63–84. It is used by
permission. Quotations are from the *New American Standard Bible* unless
otherwise noted.

* * * * *

The preacher who follows the biblical way finds prayer to be a superb weapon. Prayer, blending in composite harmony with other spiritual priorities, is evident in biblical preaching throughout history as an essential quality for the proclaimer through whom God displays His power.

The Necessity of Prayer for Spirituality

If the preacher is to deliver God's message with power, prayer must permeate his life and furnish a life-long environment for the fruit of the Spirit (Gal. 5:22–23). His spiritual example causes others to take his message seriously. As a follower of God, his spiritual credibility forcefully attracts others to follow himself because, as a trail-blazer, he practices single-minded devotion to God. He humbly renders all glory to God and submits to His Word. He demonstrates honesty and discipline of the tongue, time, mind, and body along with fervent resourcefulness. As he calls others to obedience, God uses his trail-blazing leadership to mark the way. All desirable spiritual qualities, particularly godliness and dependence on God, are basic ingredients in the experience of a praying preacher.

Godliness

A noble man of God, a man of prayer, is passionate in pursuing God and His values (Ps. 42:1–2). He runs hard after God in a life shaped by the godliness that he recommends for others. He is deeply serious about God's principle of following righteousness and wants God to show him His salvation (Ps. 50:23). God's light shines ever more brightly in him, compelling his hearers to seek the beauties of God.

The preacher's greatest example is Jesus. From boyhood, the heart of the Savior was fixed on "the things of My Father" (Luke 2:49 NASB margin). His passion as He entered public ministry was "to fulfill all righteousness" (Matt. 3:15 KJV). Taking His resolute stand for God against the devil, He experienced severe testing and made godly value choices based on the Word of God (Matt. 4:1–11). Near the end of His life, He celebrated it as having been godly: "I have glorified Thee on the earth, having accomplished the work which Thou has given Me to do" (John 17:4 KJV).

A further example is Paul. He had been crucified with Christ (Gal. 2:20). In light of this fact, he lived in godliness that consistently reflected his death with Christ. His empowering secret was the statement "not I, but Christ liveth in me" (KJV). Paul was an example of Christ in godly values and service (1 Cor. 11:1). He did not take the easy way but faced the hardships entailed in a godly pursuit (1 Cor. 4:8ff.; 2 Cor. 6:3–10).

A modern example. Phillips Brooks (1835–1893) had power in heralding God's Word at the Church of the Holy Trinity, Philadelphia, and Trinity Church, Boston. Piety was of utmost importance in his sermon preparation.

> Nothing but fire kindles fire. To know in one's whole nature what it is to live by Christ; to be His, not our own; to be so occupied with gratitude for what He did for us and for what He continually is to us that His will and His glory shall be the sole desires of our life . . . that is the first necessity of the preacher. . . .[1]

Godliness does not stand alone. It includes dependence, its inseparable companion.

Dependence on the Power of God

Jesus covered His territory like a flame, preaching God's Word in the Spirit's power (Luke 4:14). "The Spirit of the Lord is upon Me," He said, "because He anointed Me to preach the gospel . . ." (Luke 4:18 NKJV). Through the Spirit's enablement, He proclaimed release to the captives and recovery of sight to the blind. "The Father abiding in Me does His works," He acknowledged (John 14:10). If Jesus the man depended on divine power, how much more other preachers need to do the same.

Paul relied on the Spirit (Rom. 15:19). He thus counseled other believers (Gal. 5:16–18). To the Corinthians, he spoke "in demonstration of the Spirit and of power" (1 Cor. 2:1–5). God was his sufficiency (2 Cor. 3:5–6; 4:7). In preaching, he took to heart the principle of Christ, "Without Me, you can do nothing" (John 15:5 NKJV).[2]

Prayer, with its composite of spiritual virtues, is indispensable in

biblical preaching. It saturates the preacher and godly preaching, fulfills
the preacher's dependence on God, and is authentically biblical.

The Necessity of Prayer in Sermons of the Bible

In ministries during Bible times, prayer perpetually played a major
role. Since biblical days, prayer remains a top priority for preachers.

Books That Slight Prayer's Importance

It is puzzling that books on essentials of sermon preparation frequently
do *not* discuss prayer. This is the more perplexing when their authors
claim to teach the *biblical* pattern. Prayer is not prominent among their
essentials. They discuss what they consider to be important, as though
prayer has no vital part.[3] Neglect of prayer casts it in a minor role. A
sense of fairness gives these writers the benefit of the doubt and questions whether they intended such an impression. Yet, when little or nothing is said about prayer and much is made of human craft and polish,
only one conclusion is possible.[4]

Some books require a long search to find any idea, however brief, of
the importance of private prayer. The reader does not see it in chapter
titles, subheadings, or topical indices.[5] It might appear at the end of a
book or in a short discussion as an afterthought. Happily, some authors
who at times write little about prayer grant it a crucial place in other
books.[6] How can a writer ever give prayer so little attention if Scripture
makes it of such urgent consequence in preparation to preach?

Books That Emphasize Prayer's Importance

Other books on preaching, or biographies of preachers, assign much
space to prayer. They refer to it often,[7] or put it first,[8] or state strong
convictions about its cruciality in preparing messages.[9] Some entire books
are devoted to the significance of prayer in preaching.[10]

The truth is that many things are important in preaching. No consci-
entious herald of God will choose consciously to neglect any of them.
He will labor hard on the exegesis of his text, use reliable sources,
stimulate his mind from a breadth of reading, take pains to be accurate, and develop a clear outline. He will search for vivid analogy,
memorize Scripture, nourish an evangelistic and edifying aim, and al-

ways be looking to God. He may write out his message entirely or preach it from notes. He will integrate details and form clear transitions. He will know the people to whom he speaks. He will pay attention to earnestness, enthusiasm, artistic touches, forcefulness, grace, and tasteful humor. He will be concerned about enunciation, gestures, courage, posture, timing, eye contact, and other matters, and he will guard against hurtful remarks.

The emphasis on prayer need not undercut any of these other aspects, but *these others should not remove the spotlight from the necessity of prayer.* Unfortunately preachers get unbalanced in several ways.

1. They emphasize prayer alone and lazily shirk the responsibility to be God's workmen through faithful study.
2. They emphasize solely the human aspects of sermon preparation and have no pervasive dependence on God in prayer. God can, in spite of this, bless, but the preacher serves up only a product of human craft. Its fine technique is impressive, but it lacks vital forcefulness.
3. They emphasize homiletical ingenuity but offer only a shallow exposure to God's Word through neglect of diligent labor in study and prayer. They have little to feed the hungry and reflect little dependence on God.

But there is good news! Preachers can be balanced. They emphasize a prayerful choice of a text and prayerful diligence studying the passage and books that clarify its meaning. They search diligently for relevant illustrations, labor earnestly to organize their material well, and build good transitions. They pray the whole time. Then they deliver their messages, fortified by a godly life and a spirit that relies on God. This is the preferred way. Prayer is a major force, but the other essentials are not taken lightly.

Proclamation in Old Testament Times

What role has prayer played during Bible times and since? An examination of prayerful preaching by men with a great impact for God is very informative.

Moses. The lawgiver Moses had a ministry similar to that of today's preacher. He spoke God's Word and made it relevant to the needs of his day. Prayer figured heavily in his ministry.[11]

One example is Moses' pleading with God to spare Israel after their idolatrous worship of the golden calf. He interceded with God to retain His purpose in *redemption* of Israel from Egypt. Second, he was zealous that God preserve His *reputation* from all taint of dishonor before the ungodly. He also implored God to furnish a *remembrance* of His own covenant pledge (Exod. 32:11–13). He begged God to forgive His people (Exod. 32:32).

Samuel. To encourage his people, Samuel, a priest and a prophet, used God's loyalty to His covenant aim for Israel's good (1 Sam. 12:22). He saw the Lord's steadfastness as consistent with His reputation. For God to renege on His promise would make Him unfaithful to His Word and character, sacrificing His very honor. Samuel knew God's covenant purpose to possess Israel and submitted his will to God's purpose. Walking in step with God, he told his hearers, "Far be it from me that I should sin against the Lord by ceasing to pray for you" (1 Sam. 12:23).

The link between *preaching* God's Word to them and *praying* for them is evident. Prayer harmonizes with God's will. The preacher Samuel, rather than sinning by failing to pray, took the God-honoring way: "I will instruct you in the good and right way" (1 Sam. 12:23). He set an example for every preacher in his *perception* of the will that God's Word articulated, *prayer* for the people to relate to that will, and *proclamation* of that will. All three elements, including prayer, were crucial.

Daniel. Daniel was the human channel whom God used to record His prophetic plan for centuries to come. Daniel's preparation for this task revolved around prayer. He made it paramount in receiving God's *information* about Nebuchadnezzar's dream. He also sought the *interpretation* by prayer (Daniel 2). Later, he meditated on Jeremiah 25 and 29 about the seventy years that God had set for Israel to be in Babylonian exile (Daniel 9) and made three requests for his people: the restoration of Jerusalem (Dan. 9:16), the rebuilding of the temple (Dan. 9:17), and the return of the people (Dan. 9:18–19). God's answer was His plan to grant all three requests in His time (Dan. 9:24–27). In Daniel 10, Daniel humbled himself for three weeks of fasting and prayer (Dan. 10:2–3).

He prayed (Dan. 10:12) and received God's Word about developments in Persia, Greece, and later powers (Daniel 10–12).

Proclamation in New Testament Times

Jesus. The Savior used prayer to prepare Himself for ministry.[12] Luke refers to His prayer more often than do the other gospel writers. This fact fits Luke's emphasis on Jesus' humanity. Jesus is king (Matthew), servant (Mark), and God (John), but He is also man and prays as a man.

Prayer was of overwhelming importance in the preaching of Jesus. The Son of man commenced and consummated His ministry on earth in prayer (Luke 3:21–22; 24:49–51). He saw prayer as vital when people were thronging to hear Him preach. Differing from some of today's preachers, Jesus took the awesome demand on His time as a call to keep prayer as a priority. He ". . . would often slip away to the wilderness and pray" (Luke 5:16). The desert solitude with God was an essential before serving a multitude that gathered to hear. For preachers sensitive to God's heartbeat, bent knees are as crucial to the kingdom as opened lexicons. Jesus' vigil before God reflected His value system; Jesus depended on God even though He was Himself God in the flesh!

Back from such a rendezvous in prayer (Luke 5:16), Jesus was ready to preach and confound antagonistic religious experts (Luke 5:17). One wonders what the lips of the preacher had prayed. Was it for wisdom to meet trials or for the crowds to have their blinders removed to see their desperate spiritual need (Luke 5:15, 26)? One thing is certain: Whatever He prayed, the Jesus who preached was the Jesus who prayed.

Before appointing the twelve disciples, Jesus "went off to the mountain to pray" (Luke 6:12). Exhibiting His dependence on and submission to God by an all-night session in prayer, Jesus later preached the Sermon on the Plain (Luke 6:20–49). Still later, one of the twelve requested, "Lord, teach us to pray" (Luke 11:1). In response, the praying preacher taught "The Disciples' Prayer" (Luke 11:2–4) and other matters related to prayer (Luke 11:5–13).

Prayer preceded Jesus' announcements about the church and the keys of the kingdom and about His death, resurrection, a man's losing his soul, men being ashamed of Him, and His future coming (Matt.

16:18–29; Luke 9:18, 29–35). It also prefaced His transfiguration (Luke 9:18, 29–35).

Jesus urged His disciples to pray. He dealt with men whom He was molding into preachers. "Beseech the Lord of the harvest to send out workers into His harvest" (Matt. 9:38). Observing that priority could keep the preachers praying all of their lives.

Early Christians. An urgency to pray gripped early Christians. In Acts, they prayed in many circumstances.[13] Luke continued his emphasis on prayer in this, his second volume. The prayers of these early saints are a great stimulant to others who want to please God.

The Christians in Acts prayed, awaiting the Spirit's coming with power at Pentecost (Acts 1:14; cf. 1:5–7; 2:33), an important preparation for Peter's potent message of Acts 2. Their prayers also sought God's choice in replacing Judas among the Twelve (Acts 1:15–26).

Prayer was one of four Christian essentials (Acts 2:42). If it was that important then, how crucial it must be for preachers today. Believers prayed on a regular schedule (Acts 3:1; 10:9) as well as at any moment of urgency. Peter and John furnish an example. They were God's channels for His miraculous healing of the lame man (Acts 3:7–10). Later, they and others prayed for boldness in witnessing (Acts 4:29–31), a prayer that God answered by enabling them to face enemies. They were empowered, unified, and selfless. Later, the apostles revealed the importance of prayer in preaching: "We will devote ourselves to prayer, and to the ministry of the Word" (Acts 6:4). The order is interesting.[14] Even if the mention of prayer first is not significant, prayer is certainly just as primary for preachers as the Word.

Paul. Paul prayed that God would help new converts grow (Acts 14:23). Apparently, he viewed prayer as being inseparable from preaching, as did his predecessors (cf. Acts 6:4). Behind the prayer of Acts 14:23 and the appointment of elders lies the reminder of God's concern for new believers. Their spiritual growth depended on the appointment of elders who could exhort them and feed them from the Word of God (cf. Acts 14:22). Prayer was needed to undergird this process.

Paul and his associates prayed when they preached God's Word in Europe (Acts 16:13). They penetrated the heavenly curtain before they penetrated the human curtain (Acts 16:14). God used prayer to prosper their ministry, which was also *His* ministry.

Paul's dependence on prayer in preaching is synonymous with his dependence on God rather than human ability (cf. 1 Cor. 2:1–5). This dependence, however, did not rule out his skillful use of effective techniques of communication. Just as Jesus adopted good methods, such as parables, so did Paul.[15] Paul, however, depended ultimately on the cross-centered content of God's Word and the power of God's Spirit for effectiveness in preaching, a dependence that was exhibited in prayer.

Paul's dependence on God also surfaces in appeals for others to pray for him. An example is Ephesians 6:18–20. As a part of his call for Christians to don God's armor, he describes that armor in detail and bids them pray "all-out" for him (note the fourfold use of *all*).

1. *All situations.* Pray "through (*dia*) all prayer and petition." Engage in every form of prayer. The word *proseuchēs* can mean prayer in general, in all its expressions,[16] such as praise/thanks, confession, petition, and intercession. "Petition" *(deēseōs)* specifies each request.[17]

2. *All seasons.* "At every time" takes in all of the opportunities when believers pray. Pray "in the Spirit" for the success of the preacher and the preached Word. Ask in submission to the Spirit's will and wisdom, with reliance on His power and motives keyed to His values.

3. *All steadfastness.* Paul wants them "alert with all perseverance and petition." "Keep alert" *(agrupneō)* refers to staying awake to carry out a task. Alert prayer is with "all perseverance" *(proskarterēsis).* The related verb means "to hold fast to."[18] The same word is used for the early Christians who *clung* to the Word (Acts 2:42). Paul wants alert, tenacious people praying for him in every specific request *(deēsis).*

4. *All subjects.* Paul wants prayer warriors to intercede for "all the saints," including himself: "pray on my behalf" (Eph. 6:19). Pray for what? Paul mentions "boldness" twice. He wants to wield the sword of the Spirit, preaching "as I ought to speak." Speaking with boldness suits the fact that if "filled with the Spirit" (Eph. 5:18), Paul would speak "in the strength of His might" (Eph. 6:10). Boldness is necessary if the preacher is to triumph over fear and

the forces pitted against his success (Eph. 6:12). It also matches a
message that provides every spiritual blessing (Eph. 1:3) and an
inheritance with God (Eph. 1:11, 14). The preacher should not
voice such truths in a vague, weak, or confusing way.

The prayer that drenched Paul's sermons is also suggested in
Philippians 4:6. "In everything" includes more than sermons as objects
of prayer, but it certainly includes every aspect of sermon preparation
too. "By prayer" uses the word *proseuchē,* a general word for prayer,
again.[19] Paul continues, "with supplication" *(deēsis),* a "special petition
[request] for the supply of wants. . . ."[20] Paul exhorts, "Let your requests
be made known." These requests *(aitēmata),* as Lightfoot supposes, are
"the several objects of *deēsis.*"[21]

Such praying is "with thanksgiving." Why? The praying person wants
to show gratitude for past answers that sweetened life. Thanks is also
apropos for God's present bounty in granting His audience and action.
Thanksgiving is due the Spirit for His help (Rom. 8:26–27; Eph. 6:18–
20; Phil. 1:19). These illustrate the many reasons for gratitude.

Prayer continues through the centuries of church history since the NT
era.

The Necessity of Prayer for Power in Preaching Today

The clarion call for prayer as preparation for preaching resounds in
preachers of relatively modern times up to the present. Preachers pray
and solicit others to pray for their messages, and God's power in preaching is the result.

Power Through Preachers' Prayers

R. Kent Hughes, currently the senior pastor of the College Church of
Wheaton, assessed scores of books on preaching, and was frequently
disappointed that authors said little or nothing about prayer. This led
him to comment,

> This, and what experience God so far has given me in preaching
> and prayer, has brought a conviction. Should I ever write a book
> on essentials for preaching, I know now that I would devote at

least a *third* of it to spiritual preparation in matters such as prayer. This would be the *first* third.[22]

E. M. Bounds (1835–1913) served as a Civil War chaplain for the Confederacy. He later pastored several churches and became a man driven by prayer. His morning habit was to pray from 4:00 to 7:00. His listeners commented on his powerful public prayers and his messages. At least eight of his manuscripts on prayer have been published,[23] and a biography is soon to appear.[24] Bounds's books have aroused many people to greater fervor in prayer. He wrote,

> The young preacher has been taught to lay out all his strength on the form, taste, and beauty of his sermon as a mechanical and intellectual product. We have thereby cultivated a vicious taste among the people and raised the clamor for talent instead of grace, eloquence instead of piety, rhetoric instead of revelation, reputation and brilliancy instead of holiness.[25]

Much in this statement is true, but it is not an "either-or" situation. The combination of homiletical skill *and* much prayer is the answer. Bounds also wrote, "Light praying will make light preaching. Prayer makes preaching strong [the God who answers prayer does this] . . . and makes it stick."[26]

David Larsen, Professor of Homiletics at Trinity Evangelical Divinity School, has emphasized prayer:

> Strange it is that any discussion of preaching should take place outside the context of believing prayer. We have not prepared until we have prayed. . . .
>
> We cannot represent God if we have not stood before God. It is more important for me therefore to teach a student to pray than to preach. . . .[27]

After a powerful message by Alexander Whyte (1836–1921), pastor of Free Saint George's West in Edinburgh, Scotland, a listener exulted, "Dr. Whyte, you preached today like you had just emerged from the throne chamber of the Almighty." The preacher replied, "In point of fact, I have."[28]

At an ordination of a man preparing to preach, Whyte advised, "Be up earlier than usual to meditate and pray over it. Steep every sentence of it in the Spirit. . . . And pray after it."[29]

A biographer says that as much as Whyte valued public worship and prepared diligently for it, secret prayer was more important to him. The "master notes of his preaching"[30] were discipline, prayer, inner motive, humility before God and men, and purity attained through suffering. The same writer notes that Whyte's secret prayer led to public prayer that had a powerful impact on people. One of Whyte's students spoke of the days when "every sermon in Free St. George's was a volcano, and every opening prayer a revelation."[31] Whyte "never grew weary of emphasizing the need of prayer and of discipline in the Christian life—the need of humility and of 'ever-new beginnings.'"[32]

A "morning watch" was almost as regular as the sun rising for H. A. Ironside (1876–1951). This expositor meditated in his Bible and prayed for an hour[33] and afterward gave himself to more intensive study and further prayer. Rivers of living water overflowed from his times with God to crowds who heard him. He insisted, "If we would prevail with men in public, we must prevail with God in secret."[34]

Worshipers at Trinity Chapel in Brighton, England, heard searching messages by Frederick W. Robertson (1816–1853). Some have called him the greatest of the English preachers. In early years, he concentrated on reading about David Brainerd and Henry Martyn.[35] He bathed his life in communion with God, longing to be conformed to the image of Christ and adjusting his values to His ideals.[36] He prayed without ceasing, different concerns drawing his attention each day: Sunday, parish and outpouring of the Spirit; Monday, special devotion; Tuesday, spread of the gospel; Wednesday, kingdom of Christ; Thursday, self-denial; Friday, special examination and confession; Saturday, intercession.[37]

Charles Finney (1792–1875), evangelistic in focus, lived like Jesus, slipping away to engage in special vigils of prayer and fasting. Speaking after much prayer, he saw God bring great blessing on his ministry.[38] He was convinced about the importance of prayer:

Without this you are as weak as weakness itself. If you lose your spirit of prayer, you will do nothing, or next to nothing, though you had the intellectual endowment of an angel. . . . The blessed Lord deliver, and preserve His dead church from the guidance and influence of men who know not what it is to pray.[39]

Finney said, "I would say that unless I had the spirit of prayer I could do nothing."[40] If even for a moment he lost the sense of the spirit of grace and prayer, he could not preach with power and was impotent in personal witness.

William Sangster (1900–1960), a famous Methodist preacher of England, believed closeness to God to be of utmost importance in preparing a message, because after prayerful study,

. . . the preacher seems to fade out and leave the hearers face to face with God. . . . If we are driven to make comparisons, we must insist that grace-gifts are more important than natural gifts. It is true that the Holy Spirit can work on very little, and if *effectiveness* is borne in mind rather than popularity, the unction of the Spirit is the greatest gift of all.[41]

For more than forty-six years, George W. Truett (1867–1944) pastored the First Baptist Church, Dallas, Texas. After time with his family each evening, he went to his library to study and pray from 7 P.M. until midnight.[42] He also prepared at other hours. Once he was aboard a ship tossed by heavy winds and waves. The distress prompted a request for Truett to preach. He went alone with God, seeking a fitting message. After prayer, he found the message in Hebrews, "Ye have need of patience." When he announced his subject, the storm-weary people smiled their approval.[43]

Truett had a passion that people be saved. He said that the person who will win others to Christ must pray much for himself and for them.[44] Requests came from all over the world for Truett to pray. On a Dallas street, he met a noted elderly criminal lawyer.

"Dr. Truett," the man said, "I was at your church Sunday and heard what you said about prayer. I don't suppose you ever pray for a sinner like me."

Truett responded, "I have prayed for you, by name, daily, for years," and he produced a notebook with the lawyer's name in it to prove it.

The lawyer's lips trembled and his eyes grew moist. "Thank you, Doctor, thank you for remembering a hardened old sinner."[45]

Thomas Armitage paints the following picture of prayer:

> A sermon steeped in prayer on the study floor, like Gideon's fleece saturated with dew, will not lose its moisture between that and the pulpit. The first step towards doing anything in the pulpit as a thorough workman must be to kiss the feet of the Crucified, as a worshipper, in the study.[46]

Whitesell, a teacher of preaching, bears down on prayer:

> The preacher must be a man of prayer. . . . He should pray for his messages . . . soak them in prayer, . . . pray as he goes into the pulpit, pray as he preaches insofar as that is possible, and follow up his sermons with prayer. . . .[47]

Also in support of this point is Sinclair Ferguson, a Scottish pastor who since 1982 has been Professor of Systematic Theology at Westminster Theological Seminary and now pastors in Edinburgh:

> For me, it is of primary importance that all my preparation be done in the context of a praying spirit . . . looking to the Lord and depending on the grace of His illuminating and enlivening Spirit. This is punctuated by specific ejaculations and periods of petition for both exposition and application. . . .
>
> To use a picture from John Owen, I think of the Spirit moving among the people, giving to each a parcel of identical shape, size, and wrapping (the sermon); but . . . the gift inside is specially appropriate to each. My prayer, therefore, is that my material may be in harmony with His purpose and my spirit sensitive to His gracious character, so that I may not distort Him in my words or by my spirit.[48]

An expositor at many Plymouth Brethren conferences, Henry Holloman, Professor of Systematic Theology at Talbot School of Theology, has said,

> Behind every good biblical preacher is much hard labor in preparation (1 Tim. 5:17; 2 Tim. 2:15). However, only prayer can assure that his work is not wasted and that his message will spiritually impact the hearers. As the biblical preacher interweaves prayer with his preparation, he should focus on certain petitions: (1) that he will receive God's message . . . in spiritual as well as mental *comprehension,* 1 Cor. 2:9–16; (2) that God's message will first grip his own heart in strong *conviction,* 1 Thess. 1:5; (3) that he will clearly and correctly convey God's message in the power of the Spirit in effective *communication,* . . . 1 Thess. 1:5; (4) that the Spirit will use the message to produce proper response and change, . . . spiritual *transformation,* 2 Cor. 3:18 . . . and (5) that the whole process and finished product will accomplish God's purpose in *glorification* of God through Christ, 1 Cor. 10:31; 1 Peter 4:11.[49]

Holloman clarifies that "knowledge and organization is what we must do, but prayer gives us what only God can do."

John MacArthur, pastor-teacher of Grace Community Church, Sun Valley, California, sees prayer as inseparable from preparing and preaching.

> During the week . . . locked up with my books, . . . study and . . . communion mingle as I apply the tools of exegesis and exposition in . . . open communion with the Lord. I seek His direction, thank Him for what I discover, plead for wisdom and insight, and desire that He enable me to live what I learn and preach.
>
> A special burden for prayer begins to grip my heart on Saturday evening. Before I go to sleep, I . . . spend one final time going over my notes. That involves an open line of communication with God as I meditatively and consciously offer my notes up to the Lord for approval, refinement and clarity.

I awake Sunday morning in the same spirit of prayer. Arriving at the church early, I spend time . . . in prayer, then join elders who pray with me for the messages. On Sunday afternoon, I go through a similar time of reviewing my evening message prayerfully. . . .[50]

John Stott says that a preacher, like a father (1 Thess. 2:11), should pray for his church family. Preachers will make time for this hard and secret work only if they love people enough. "Because it is secret and therefore unrewarded by men, we shall only undertake it if we long for their spiritual welfare more than for their thanks. . . ."[51]

Robert Murray McCheyne (1813–1842) pastored St. Peter's Church in Dundee, Scotland. References to prayers sprinkle his journal almost as thickly as heather blooms on a Scottish meadow. He wrote to Dan Edwards on October 2, 1840, after Dan had been ordained for missionary service to the Jews and for study in Germany:

I know you will apply hard to German; but do not forget the culture of the inner man. . . . How diligently the cavalry officer keeps his sabre clean and sharp; . . . Remember you are God's sword, His instrument. . . . In great measure, according to the purity and perfections of the instrument, will be the success. It is not great talents God blesses [He does bless, using gifts He gave as they are given back to Him] so much as great likeness to Jesus. A holy minister is an awful weapon in the hand of God.[52]

Andrew Blackwood, long-time Professor of Homiletics at Princeton Theological Seminary, counsels the preacher to lay down one rule and never make an exception: Start, continue, and end with prayer.[53] A biblical sermon, he says, will likely be worth whatever the preacher invests in it, the time he devotes, the thought he gives, and the prayer. For

. . . in his study the prophet can build his altar and on it lay the wood. There he can lovingly place his sacrifice . . . sermon . . . but still he knows that the fire must come down from God. Come it will, if he prays before he works, and if he works in the spirit of prayer.[54]

Edward Payson (1783–1827) exemplified sermon preparation by diligent study infused with hours of prayer. He pastored the Second Congregational Church, Portland, Maine. His reading rapidity, sharpness in assimilating details, and good scholarship were notable.[55] He studied the writings of Jonathan Edwards and others,[56] but his greatest zeal was in studying the Bible and praying for God's help interpreting and applying it.[57] Prayer was "the most noticeable fact in his history. . . ."[58] He ". . . studied theology on his knees. Much of his time he spent literally prostrated with the Bible open before him, pleading the promises."[59]

Payson's discipline led him to guard his time. His usual schedule was twelve hours a day for study, two for devotion, two for relaxing, two for meals and family devotions, and six for sleep.[60] In his diary and letters, comments such as the following recur: "Was much assisted in my studies . . . enabled to write twelve pages of my sermon. It was the more precious, because it seemed to be in answer to prayer."[61] He wrote on March 17, 1806, that since beginning to plead God's blessing on his preparation, "I have done more in one week than in the whole year before. . . ."[62]

Even in cases when Payson felt that he had been weak in preaching, his people were refreshed. When lifeless in devotions, he often prayed on to victory.[63] God greatly enlivened this preacher as He quickened the psalmist.[64] Payson prayed for hours for the lost and often witnessed to them. He saw many saved and added to the church.

A brother told Payson he felt discouraged about preaching because of inexperience and ignorance. Payson wrote to him, admitting that he himself always felt inadequate:

This led me to pray almost incessantly. . . . He who has thus guided me, and thousands of others equally foolish will, I trust, guide you. . . . If we would do much for God, we must ask much of God; . . . I cannot insist on this too much. Prayer is the first thing, the second thing, and the third thing necessary for a minister, especially in seasons of revival. . . . Pray, then, my dear brother, pray, pray, pray. . . .[65]

The greatly used preacher Charles Spurgeon (1834–1892) put heavy emphasis on prayer. He believed that ministers ought to pray without ceasing (1 Thess. 5:17). "All our libraries and studies are mere emptiness compared with our closets. We grow, we wax mighty, we prevail in private prayer,"[66] he wrote. He prayed in choosing a topic, getting into the spirit of a text, seeing God's deep truths, lifting those truths out, receiving fresh streams of thought, and for delivery. For

> . . . nothing can so gloriously fit you to preach as descending fresh from the mount of communion with God to speak with men. None are so able to plead with men as those who have been wrestling with God on their behalf.[67]

Spurgeon studied hard, but he got some of his best thoughts while preaching.[68] Or, feeling fettered, he secretly groaned to God and received unusual liberty. "But how dare we pray in the battle if we have never cried to the Lord while buckling on the harness!"[69]

After preaching, Spurgeon found prayer strategic. "If we cannot prevail with men for God, we will, at least, endeavor to prevail with God for men."[70]

So, the preacher who does his work God's way prays, but he also enlists others to pray for the success of the Word.

Power Through Others' Prayers

Early in this century, John Hyde prayed for speakers at conferences in India. He and R. M'Cheyne Paterson prayed for a month for a conference in 1904. George Turner joined them for three of those weeks.[71] God saved hundreds of people and renewed believers. Hyde knelt for hours in his room, or was prostrate on the floor, or sat in on a message while interceding for the speaker and the hearers.

Dwight L. Moody (1837–1899), founder of the Moody Bible Institute, often saw God work in power when others prayed for his meetings in America and abroad. He often wired R. A. Torrey at the school, urging prayer. Faculty and students prayed all evening or into the early morning or all night.[72]

After Moody's death, Torrey (1856–1928) preached in many countries. He, too, had prayer backing. In Australia, 2,100 home prayer groups met for two weeks before he arrived. God turned many lives around.[73] After Torrey died, Mrs. Torrey said, "My husband was a man of much prayer and Bible study. He denied himself social intercourse with even his best friends, in order that he might have time for prayer, study, and the preparation for his work."[74]

Torrey said, "Pray for great things, expect great things, work for great things, but above all pray."[75] He told church members, "Do you want a new minister? I can tell you how to get one. Pray for the one you have till God makes him over."[76] He believed, "Prayer is the key that unlocks all the storehouses of God's infinite grace and power."[77] He was for many years pastor of the Chicago Avenue Church, later called Moody Memorial Church. Much of the growth there resulted from prayer by Torrey and his praying people, who met on Saturday nights and Sunday mornings.[78]

Payson, already mentioned, rallied people to meet for prayer in "Aaron and Hur Societies" in fours and fives for an hour. They prayed before Payson preached.[79] A preacher needs to lead in prayer and also to get the church

> excited to pray for the influences of the divine Spirit; and that they should frequently meet for this purpose. . . . In that duty we explicitly acknowledge, not only to Him, but to our fellow-creatures, that nothing but the influences of His Spirit can render any means effectual, and that we are entirely dependent . . . on His sovereign will.[80]

Payson depended on others' prayers. His speaking schedule was often heavy. He prepared four sermons a week and sometimes sermons for the press. Within a two-month period, he also had three ordination messages, two messages for missions societies, and one for a women's asylum.[81] No matter how busy, he kept his own prayer vigils. His biographer says that "prayer . . . was eminently the business of his life . . . through which he derived inexhaustible supplies." He adds that "his conversation was in heaven." [82]

Spurgeon said much about others praying. The preacher, no matter how brilliant, godly, or eloquent, has no power without the Spirit's help:

The bell in the steeple may be well hung, fairly fashioned, and of soundest metal, but it is dumb until the ringer makes it speak. And . . . the preacher has no voice of quickening for the dead in sin, or of comfort for living saints unless the divine spirit [Spirit] gives him a gracious pull, and begs him speak with power. Hence the need of prayer for both preacher and hearers.[83]

Spurgeon said he would plead even with tears for others' prayers.[84] Only by abundant intercession could the church prosper or even continue. He saw the Monday night prayer meeting at London's Metropolitan Tabernacle as "the thermometer of the church."[85] A large part of the main auditorium and first gallery were filled at this meeting for years.[86] In Spurgeon's mind, the prayer meeting was "the most important meeting of the week."[87]

Conclusion

Prayer reigns supreme along with the Word of God in ministries of the Old Testament, New Testament, and since then. The preacher today, as always, needs a wise balance between the different aspects of sermon preparation that depend on human skill and the facets that call on God for His almighty power. The man who represents God in the pulpit should cultivate an ever-growing passion to be the most prayerful and diligent channel he can be for broadcasting the greatest message of all time.

Endnotes

1. Phillips Brooks, *The Joy of Preaching* (1895; reprint, Grand Rapids: Kregel, 1989), 47.

2. *Nothing* defined by its context is the opposite of *fruit*. The person who is abiding in Christ bears *some* fruit (John 15:2b) and can bear *more* fruit (John 15:2b) and *much* fruit (John 15:5, 8).

3. E.g., Don M. Wardlaw, *Preaching Biblically* (Philadelphia: Westminster, 1983); and John E. Baird, *Preparing for Platform and Pulpit* (New York: Abingdon, 1968). Wardlaw focuses on good things such as learning biblical structure, style, content, and imagery as crafted and managed by the preacher. Prayer and dependence on the Spirit are not integrated in any way to show the whole picture. Baird correctly refutes the logic that the Spirit prepares a man such that he needs no study (*Preparing for Platform and Pulpit,* 8). Yet, he offers no balance when emphasizing a one-sided picture, preparation by human skills alone.

4. Cf. R. E. O. White, *A Guide to Preaching* (Grand Rapids: Eerdmans, 1973). He covers preaching as worship, values of biblical preaching, hermeneutics, technique, gathering and shaping materials, aids to style, zeal, etc., but prayer is given little place. "Of the preacher's private preparation for the pulpit little need be said. [Why?] Most men find they must have opportunity before every service for quiet prayer, recollection, and mental rehearsal . . ." (152). White surely must not have intended it, but the weight of details suggests dependence on what the *preacher* can do. More attention to what only *God* can do (cf. Acts 6:4) would give a better perspective.

5. E.g., Dwight Stevenson and Charles Diehl, *Reaching People from the Pulpit: A Guide to Effective Sermon Delivery* (New York: Harper and Brothers, 1958). The book says that it covers all topics essential to effective oral communication (81), but prayer is not in the table of contents, subheadings, or index. A vague reference to prayer may be found in the statement that the preacher can help others because he has found a power not of himself to give him sobriety (81). An opportunity to include prayer comes in "Preparing the Man" (100–102), but the focus on full sleep, good health, full vigor, freedom from distractions, and bringing "all his powers to bear" (99) crowd out prayer. Among these excellent suggestions, one wonders why prayer was not added to balance the preacher's power with that of God.

6. Cf. two books by Andrew W. Blackwood. In *Preaching from the Bible* (New York: Abingdon-Cokesbury, 1941), he gives no arresting focus to the Holy Spirit, power, holiness, or prayer. A terse comment at the end of the Foreword says that the Holy Spirit should be our teacher (9). The statement that the preaching in the apostolic church was in a spirit of prayer (18) is rather buried in other emphases. Prayer gets brief mention in the last paragraph of chapter 11 (196), and brief words about prayer are elsewhere (207–8, 218, 222). More is made of prayer in *The Preparation of Sermons* (New York: Abingdon, 1948), e.g., 36, 208, and in the statement that "the Scriptures and prayer go together as inseparably as the light and heat of the sun . . ." (45).

7. E.g., Asa Cummings, *A Memoir of the Rev. Edward Payson* (New York: American Tract Society, 1830); and Andrew Bonar, ed., *Memoirs of McCheyne* (Chicago: Moody, 1947).

8. E.g., R. A. Bodey, ed., *Inside the Sermon: Thirteen Preachers Discuss Their Methods of Preparing Messages* (Grand Rapids: Baker, 1990), 28–35. Bodey says "faithful, earnest prayer and long hours of diligent, believing study of the Word of God" are more necessary than anything else (28).

9. Roger Martin, *R. A. Torrey: Apostle of Certainty* (Murfreesboro, Tenn.: Sword of the Lord, 1976). J. I. Packer rightly applauds Richard Baxter's words: "Prayer must carry on our work as well as preaching: he preacheth not heartily to his people, that prayeth not earnestly for them. If we prevail not with God to give them faith and repentance we shall never prevail with them to believe and repent" (Richard Baxter, *The Reformed Pastor* [London: Banner of Truth, 1974], 120–23;

cited by J. I. Packer, *A Quest for Holiness: The Puritan Vision of the Christian Life* [Wheaton: Crossway, 1990], 289).

10. Gardiner Spring, *The Power of the Pulpit* (1948; reprint, Carlisle, Pa.: Banner of Truth, 1986), esp. "Ministers Must Be Men of Prayer," 137–44; and W. E. Sangster, *Power in Preaching* (1958; reprint, Grand Rapids: Baker, 1976), esp. chap. 7, "Steep It in Prayer," 96–107.

11. Prayer is frequent in Moses' life. Some instances are Exodus 3:1–4:17; 5:22–23; 6:12, 30; 8:12, 30; 9:33; 15:1–18, 25; 17:8–13; 19:23; 32:7–14, 30–34; 33:18; Numbers 11:2, 11–15, 21–22; 12:13; 14:13–19; 16:15, 22; 27:15–17; Deuteronomy 3:23–28; 9:26–29; 32:1–43.

12. Cf. Charles E. Hoekstra, "An Examination of the Prayer Life of Jesus to Ascertain the Relation of Prayer to the Pastor's Work" (D.Min. dissertation, Covenant Theological Seminary, St. Louis, Mo., 1987). Besides surveying instances of prayer in Jesus' ministry, Hoekstra relates prayer to pastoral work and suggests applications.

13. Cf. Hermann Wang, "The Prayers of Acts" (unpublished Th.M. thesis, Talbot School of Theology, La Mirada, Calif., 1988), a treatment of most of the prayers in Acts; and Warren Wiersbe, *Something Happens When Churches Pray* (Wheaton: Victor Books, 1984). Wiersbe sees God's Word as the source of wisdom in prayer, successful efforts stemming from prayer, the Spirit's power through prayer, etc.

14. Sinclair Ferguson wonders about the significance of the mention of prayer before preaching in Acts 6:4, without drawing a conclusion (Bodey, *Inside the Sermon,* 82).

15. Jesus and Paul used introductory devices, good organization, vivid examples, appeals for a verdict, etc.

16. J. B. Lightfoot, *Saint Paul's Epistle to the Philippians* (1868; reprint, Grand Rapids: Zondervan, 1953), 160.

17. Ibid.

18. W. F. Arndt and F. W. Gingrich, *A Greek-English Lexicon of the New Testament and Other Early Christian Literature* (Cambridge: University Press, 1979), 715.

19. Lightfoot, *Philippians,* 160.

20. Ibid.

21. Ibid.

22. R. Kent Hughes, personal conversation, 21 December 1990; cf. Kent and Barbara Hughes, *Liberating Ministers from the Success Syndrome* (Wheaton: Tyndale, 1987). The chapter "Success Is Prayer," 71–81, esp. 77, emphasizes the primacy of prayer; cf. also R. Kent Hughes, *Ephesians: The Mystery of the Body of Christ* (Wheaton: Crossway, 1990), in which he discusses Ephesians 6:18–20.

23. All published in recent editions by Baker Book House. Cf. E. M. Bounds, *Purpose in Prayer* (Grand Rapids: Baker, n.d.). A biographical sketch of Bounds is given on pp. 5–7 and the back cover.

24. Lyle W. Dorsett, *E. M. Bounds: Man of Prayer* (Grand Rapids: Zondervan, 1991). The second part of Dorsett's book has selections from Bounds' writings, espe-

cially some long-lost essays in Christian papers. He includes data, including pictures, from Bounds's descendants.

25. E. M. Bounds, *Power Through Prayer* (Grand Rapids: Baker, n.d.), 74.

26. Ibid., 31.

27. David Larsen, *The Anatomy of Preaching: Identifying the Issues in Preaching Today* (Grand Rapids: Baker, 1989), 53–54. Chapter 4 is helpful on spiritual preparation, stressing identity in Christ, the Word, prayer, the Spirit's power, and personal holiness.

28. Ibid., 55.

29. G. F. Barbour, *The Life of Alexander Whyte* (New York: George H. Doran, 1923), 296–97.

30. Ibid., 307.

31. Ibid., 309.

32. Ibid., 388–89.

33. E. S. English, *H. A. Ironside, Ordained of the Lord* (Grand Rapids: Zondervan, 1946), 176.

34. H. A. Ironside, *Praying in the Holy Spirit* (New York: Loizeaux Brothers, n.d.), 59.

35. Stopford A. Brooke, *Life and Letters of Fredk. W. Robertson, M.A.* (New York: Harper & Brothers, 1865), 60.

36. Ibid.

37. Ibid., 60–61.

38. L. G. Parkhurst, *Charles G. Finney's Answers to Prayer* (Minneapolis: Bethany House, 1983). See, for example, chapter 25.

39. Ibid., 126–27.

40. Ibid., 59; cf. John 15:5, inability without Christ to do anything that will bear fruit. Bearing fruit (doing what counts as success before God) is related closely to prayer (John 15:7–8).

41. William Sangster, *The Approach to Preaching* (London: Epworth, 1951), 18; cf. also n. 10 in this article.

42. Joe W. Burton, *Prince of the Pulpit* (Grand Rapids: Zondervan, 1946), 26.

43. Ibid., 27.

44. Ibid., 65.

45. P. W. James, *George W. Truett: A Biography* (New York: Macmillan, 1945), 267–68.

46. Thomas Armitage, *Preaching: Its Ideals and Inner Life* (Philadelphia: American Baptist Publication Society, 1880), 170.

47. Faris D. Whitesell, *The Art of Biblical Preaching* (Grand Rapids: Zondervan, 1950), 86; cf. the essentials of preaching in chapter 3.

48. Sinclair B. Ferguson, cited by Bodey, *Inside the Sermon,* 82–83.

49. Henry Holloman, letter to author, 14 January 1991.

50. John MacArthur, letter to author, "Expository Preaching," 16 January 1991.

51. John R. W. Stott, *The Preacher's Portrait* (Grand Rapids: Eerdmans, 1961), 98–99.

52. Bonar, *Memoirs of McCheyne,* 95.

53. Andrew W. Blackwood, *The Preparation of Sermons* (New York: Abingdon Press, 1948), 36.

54. Blackwood, *Preaching from the Bible,* 196.

55. Cummings, *Memoir of the Rev. Edward Payson,* 13–14.

56. Ibid., 65.

57. Ibid., 71.

58. Ibid., 242.

59. Ibid., 74.

60. Ibid., 75.

61. Ibid., 81.

62. Ibid., 59.

63. Ibid., 106.

64. Cf. Psalm 119:25b, 37, 88.

65. Cummings, *Memoir of the Rev. Edward Payson,* 255–56.

66. Helmut Thielicke, *Encounter with Spurgeon* (Philadelphia: Fortress, 1963), 117.

67. Ibid., 118.

68. Ibid., 119.

69. Ibid.

70. Ibid.

71. E. G. Carre, ed., *Praying Hyde* (South Plainfield, N.J.: Bridge, 1982), 13–14.

72. R. A. Torrey, *Why God Used D. L. Moody* (Chicago: Moody, 1923), 16–17.

73. Martin, *R. A. Torrey,* 139; for the impact after people prayed, see 110, 131–32, 134, 144, 169–70, 173, 186.

74. Ibid., 279.

75. Ibid., 166.

76. R. A. Torrey, *The Prayer of Power* (New York: Revell, 1924), 35.

77. Ibid., 17.

78. Martin, *R. A. Torrey,* 110.

79. Cummings, *Memoir of the Rev. Edward Payson,* 180.

80. Ibid., 256.

81. Ibid., 260–61.

82. Ibid., 122.

83. Charles H. Spurgeon, *The Quotable Spurgeon* (Wheaton: Harold Shaw, 1990), 207.

84. Charles H. Spurgeon, *Metropolitan Tabernacle Pulpit* (1974; reprint, Pasadena, Tex.: Pilgrim, 1971), 19 (1873): 169.

85. Susannah Spurgeon and Joseph Harrald, *The Full Harvest, 1860–1892,* vol. 2 of *C. H. Spurgeon Autobiography,* rev. ed. (Carlisle, Pa.: Banner of Truth, 1987), 321.

86. Ibid.

87. Ibid., 322.

CHAPTER NINE

The Sufficiency of Scripture in Counseling

Wayne A. Mack

A belief in biblical inerrancy entails an affirmation of Scripture's suffi-ciency for understanding and resolving the non-physical problems of man. Counseling that is truly Christian must be Christ-centered, church-centered, and Bible-based counseling. Various contemporary approaches to counseling question the sufficiency of Scripture, namely, the two-book, the no-book, and the filtering device approaches. All three views join in affirming that the traditional biblical resources for dealing with man's problems are not enough. They fail to take into account, however, the finiteness of man's knowledge, the depravity of human nature, and the sufficiency of Scripture. Psalm 19:7–11; 2 Timothy 3:15–17; and 2 Pe-ter 1:2–8 affirm clearly the sufficiency of Scripture and Christ in deal-ing with man's problems. Secular psychological principles are unnecessary and may even be harmful in trying to understand and help people.

This essay is adapted from the chapter "What Is Biblical Counseling?" *Totally Sufficient,* ed. Ed Hinson and Howard Eyrich (Eugene, Ore.: Harvest House, 1997). It is used by permission. Quotations are from the *New American Standard Bible* unless otherwise noted.

* * * * *

The Chicago Statement on biblical inerrancy declares that "the authority of Scripture is a key issue for the Christian Church in this and every age. Those who profess faith in Jesus Christ as Lord and Savior are called to show the reality of their discipleship by humbly and faithfully obeying God's written Word. To stray from Scripture in faith and conduct is disloyalty to our Master. Recognition of the total truth and trustworthiness of Holy Scripture is essential to a full grasp and adequate confession of its authority."

As a Christian, I wholeheartedly agree with every aspect of this general statement on biblical inerrancy and authority. For me, the inerrancy of Scripture and the authority of Scripture are like Siamese twins—they are inseparably joined to each other. Holy Scripture, being God's law and testimony, is true and should therefore serve as our standard for all matters of faith and practice (Isa. 8:19–20). God's Word being both truthful (John 17:17) and authoritative, it calls us to humble and faithful obedience in every area of which it speaks. No authority is higher than that in Scripture. Wherever and on whatever subject the Scriptures speak, one must regard them as both inerrant and authoritative.

Because I, as a Christian, affirm the preceding convictions, I believe in the sufficiency of Scripture in the area of counseling. Scripture is not silent about its own sufficiency both for understanding man and his nonphysical problems and for resolving those problems. To me, those issues are crystal clear. And because this is what I understand Scripture to be teaching about itself, my profession of faith in Jesus Christ as Lord and Savior compels me to submit to this sufficiency teaching. As I see it, doing anything less would make me disloyal to my Master.

Many people, both in our day and before, have affirmed the inerrancy and authority of Scripture in matters of faith and practice, but they have not always affirmed the sufficiency of Scripture for understanding and resolving the spiritual (nonphysical) problems of man. They believe that we need the insights of psychology to understand and help people. In essence, they believe that when it comes to these matters, the Bible is fundamentally deficient. They believe that God did not design the Bible for this purpose, so we must rely on extrabiblical, psychological theories and insights. For many Christians, the Bible has titular (i.e., given a title and respected in name) rather than functional (i.e., actual, practical, real, and respected in practice) authority in the area of counseling. They acknowledge it to be the Word of God and therefore worthy of our respect, but when it comes to understanding and resolving many of the real issues of life, they give it limited value.

A Definition of Christian Counseling

Christian Counseling Is Christ-Centered

The attitude that many Christians have toward the Scriptures was vividly illustrated by a person who came to interview me about the kind of counseling I did. This person was traveling around the United States questioning various Christians who did counseling about their views on what constitutes Christian counseling. In the interview, I said that I believed that any counseling worthy of the name "Christian" should be *conscientiously and comprehensively Christ-centered.* It will make much of who and what Christ is; what He has done for us in His life, death, and resurrection and in sending the Holy Spirit; what He is doing for us right now in His session at the Father's right hand; and what He will yet do for us in the future.

In Christian counseling, the Christ of the Bible will not be an appendage, a "tack on" for surviving life in the "fast lane." He will be both the center and the circumference of our counseling. Understanding the nature and causes of our human difficulties will include understanding ways in which we are unlike Christ in our values, aspirations, desires, thoughts, feelings, choices, attitudes, actions, responses, and other aspects of our lives. Resolving those sin-related difficulties will include being redeemed and justified through Christ, receiving God's forgiveness through Christ, and acquiring from Christ enabling power to replace unchristlike (sinful) patterns of life with Christlike, godly ways of life.

In his book *Our Sufficiency in Christ,* John MacArthur tells a story about a man who was shut out of a house on a cold night. He suffered some unpleasant consequences during the ordeal, all of which he could have avoided had he known that the key to the house was in his pocket. Dr. MacArthur writes,

That true story illustrates the predicament of Christians who try to gain access to God's blessings through human means, all the while possessing Christ, who is the key to every spiritual blessing. He alone fulfills the deepest longing of our hearts and supplies every spiritual resource we need.

Believers have in Christ everything they will ever need to meet any trial, any craving, any difficulty they might ever encounter in this life. Even the newest convert possesses sufficient resources for every spiritual need. From the moment of salvation each believer is in Christ (2 Corinthians 5:17) and Christ is in the believer (Colossians 1:27). The Holy Spirit abides within as well (Romans 8:9)—the Christian is His temple (1 Corinthians 6:19). "Of His fulness we have all received, and grace upon grace" (John 1:16). So every Christian is a self contained treasury of divinely bestowed spiritual affluence. There is nothing more—no great transcendental secret, no ecstatic experience, no hidden spiritual wisdom—that can take Christians to some higher plane of spiritual life. "His divine power has granted to us *everything* pertaining to life and godliness, through the true knowledge of Him who called us" (2 Peter 1:3, emphasis added). "The true knowledge of *Him*" refers to saving knowledge. To seek something more is like frantically knocking on a door, seeking what is inside, not realizing you hold the key in your pocket.

No higher knowledge, no hidden truth, nothing besides the all-sufficient resources that we find in Christ exists that can change the human heart.

Any counselor who desires to honor God and be effective must see the goal of his efforts as leading a person to the sufficiency of Christ. The view that man is capable of solving his own problems, or that people can help one another by "therapy" or other human means, denies the doctrine of human depravity and man's need for God. It replaces the Spirit's transforming power with impotent human wisdom.[1]

For Christian counseling to occur, the people doing the counseling must be individuals who are *conscientiously and comprehensively Chris-*

tian in their outlook on life. Truly Christian counseling is done by people who have experienced the regenerating work of the Holy Spirit, who have come to Christ in repentance and faith, who have acknowledged Him as Lord and Savior of their lives, and who want to live lives of obedience to Him. Their main concern in life is to exalt Him and bring glory to His name. They believe that because God did not spare His own Son (from the Cross) but delivered Him up (to the Cross and death) for us (on our behalf as our substitute), He will freely give us—through Christ—all that we need for effective and productive living (for transforming us into the likeness of His Son). Truly Christian counseling is done by those whose theological convictions affect, permeate, and control both their personal lives and their counseling theory and practice.

Christian Counseling Is Church-Centered

Another major distinctive of truly Christian counseling that I mentioned to my interviewer was that it will be *conscientiously and comprehensively church-centered.* The Scriptures clearly teach that the local church is the primary means by which God intends to accomplish His work in the world. The local church is His ordained instrument for calling the lost to Himself. It is also the context in which He sanctifies and changes His people into the very likeness of Christ. According to Scripture, the church is His household, the pillar and ground of the truth, and the instrument he uses in helping His people to put off the old manner of life (pre-Christian habit patterns and lifestyles and ways of thinking, feeling, choosing, and acting) and to put on the new self (a new manner of life and Christlike thoughts, feelings, choices, actions, values, and responses—Eph. 4:1–32).

Even a cursory reading of the New Testament will lead a person to the conclusion that the church is at the center of God's program for His people. Jesus Christ, who proclaimed that He would build His church (Matt. 16:18), invested in it authority to act with the *imprimatur* of heaven (Matt. 18:17–20) and ultimately revealed that His plan was to fill the world with local bodies of believers (Matt. 28:18–20).

When trying to capture and project his conception of the role of the church in God's program and with God's people, John Calvin made this impassioned assertion:

> Because it is now our intention to discuss the visible church, let
> us learn from the simple title "mother" how useful, indeed nec-
> essary, it is that we should know her. For there is no other way to
> enter life unless this mother conceive us in her womb, give us
> birth, nourish us at her breast, and lastly, unless she keep us
> under her care and guidance until, putting off mortal flesh, we
> become like the angels (Matthew 22:30). Our weakness does
> not allow us to be dismissed from her school until we have been
> pupils all our lives. . . . God's fatherly favor and the especial
> witness of spiritual life are limited to his flock, so that it is al-
> ways disastrous to leave the church.[2]

This statement about the church by John Calvin was not specifically
directed toward the issue of counseling. It does, however, indicate Calvin's
perspective on the importance of the church in the lives of believers. His
view concurs with the ideas that the church is responsible for providing
counseling and that Christians are responsible for seeking care and guidance for their personal lives. Calvin's study of the Scriptures convinced
him that the nurture, edification, and sanctification of believers was to
be church-centered. I wholeheartedly agree with this emphasis because
I believe that this is the unmistakable teaching of Holy Scripture.[3]

Christian Counseling Is Bible-Based

As I continued to explain my views on Christian counseling, I told
my visitor that truly Christian counseling will be *conscientiously and
comprehensively Bible-based,* deriving from the Bible its understanding
of who man is, the nature of his main problems, why he has these problems, and how to resolve them. For counseling to be worthy of the name
of Christ, the counselor must be conscientiously and comprehensively
committed to the *sufficiency of Scripture* for understanding and resolving all of the nonphysical personal and interpersonal, sin-related difficulties of man.

Questioning the Sufficiency of Scripture

At this point, the individual who had come to ask about my views on
Christian counseling responded by saying, "Well, what you're saying

about all of these things is nice, but what do you think should be done when people have really serious problems?"

Now, consider what this person—who claimed to be a Christian— was implying by that question. She was implying that the factors I had mentioned might prove helpful with people who have minor problems, but certainly they are not enough for resolving the really serious problems of life. She was intimating that the approach I had described was rather simplistic. She was suggesting that the resources that God prescribes in His Word for ministering to needy people are not adequate. She was insinuating that the substantial insights necessary for ministering to people with major difficulties must come from sources other than the ones I had mentioned.

Unfortunately, at least from my perspective, her views represent the opinions of many professing Christians. In a book titled *Introduction to Biblical Counseling,* Douglas Bookman describes the way many professing Christians think about the sufficiency of Scripture in counseling:

> Any Christian who sets out to counsel another individual is aware that the counsel offered must be true. Counseling is by definition and impulse a helping ministry. It assumes that someone is confronted with some measure of confusion, disappointment, or despair and that a second person who endeavors to help by analyzing the counselee's situation, sorting out the issues involved, and then offering helpful and healing advice and direction. But the efficacy of all that the counselor undertakes to do is dependent at least on this one thing: that his analysis and counsel is true. Thus, any thoughtful consideration of the ministry of counseling must begin with the most basic of all philosophical questions, that question articulated by a Roman procurator two thousand years ago, "What is truth?"
>
> Ever since its genesis as a distinguishable discipline almost four decades ago, the school of thought and ministry broadly known as Christian Psychology has been convulsed by the issue of its own epistemological construct. (That is, where ought/may Christians to go to find the *truth* necessary to help people who are hurting?) Because that discipline grew up largely within the

broad limits of evangelical Christianity, there has been a universal acknowledgment of the veracity of Jesus' answer to the question of truth when, as He addressed His heavenly Father in prayer, He stated simply, "Thy Word is truth."

But for most that answer alone has not sufficed. The persuasion continues—articulated, justified, and applied in various ways—that there is truth that is at least profitable and perhaps even necessary to the counseling effort. This truth is to be discovered beyond the pages of Scripture. Christians who are thus persuaded are anxious to affirm Jesus' simple but profound declaration, yet they feel compelled to qualify that affirmation with the proposition that Scriptural truths may (or even must) be supplemented by truths that have been discovered by human investigation and observation. This persuasion lies at the heart of the integrationist impulse of Christian Psychology.

By all accounts, this integrationist tendency is rather recent in origin. Throughout much of the twentieth century a spirit of mutual mistrust and even contempt existed between the worlds of secular psychology and Christian theology. But that hostility began to thaw in certain circles sometime in the middle of this century, and by this last decade of the twentieth century there exists an obvious attitude of reconciliation between Christianity and psychology in many quarters. Indeed, many devotees of Christian psychology evidence a greater measure of fraternity with the secular psychological community than with those Christians who are compelled by their theology to reject the discipline of secular psychotherapy.[4]

The Two-Book Approach

Bookman then proceeds to delineate several ways in which Christians who do not believe in the sufficiency of Scripture for counseling actually do regard and use God's Word in counseling. One approach to the integration issue is called the *two-book,* or the *general-versus-special revelation, approach.* The argument that is often used to support this theory is that God reveals truth to us in two primary ways: through "nonpropositional truth deposited by God in the created order of things," which "must be investigated and discovered by mankind," and through "the propositional truth recorded in Scripture." The idea is that because all truth is God's truth, it really does not matter where that truth is found. Those who hold to this view believe that "the truth accurately derived from the consideration of the natural order of things (general revelation) is just as true as that derived from Scripture." When applied to the area of counseling, the proponents of this approach affirm that "any defensible truth that is derived by means of psychological research into the order of mankind is truth derived from general revelation, thus truth derived from God, and thus truth as dependable and authoritative as truth exegeted from Scripture."[5]

A representative quote from J. Harold Ellens, a defender of this two-book view, clearly illustrates the thrust of this position. He asserts,

> Theology and Psychology are both sciences in their own right, stand legitimately on their own foundations, read carefully are the two books of God's Revelation. . . .
> Wherever *truth* is disclosed it is always *God's truth*. Whether it is found in General Revelation or Special Revelation, it is *truth* which has equal warrant with all other *truth*. Some truth may have greater weight than other *truth* in a specific situation, but there is no difference in its warrant as *truth*.[6]

In another publication, Ellens gives additional information about the nature and rationale for the two-book perspective. In keeping with this idea that *general* and *special revelation* are complementary, serving different purposes and being *equally* authoritative, he makes the following comments:

> I believe the Bible to be an internally coherent testimony of the believing community throughout a 2000 to 3000 year period regarding the mighty acts of God's redemption in the community's experience. I believe that testimony is normative and authoritative for us in matters of faith and life because it is a warrantable testimony and is God's universalized truth. This does not, however, force me to agree that the Bible is authoritative truth in matters which are not the focus and burden of that spirit-inspired,

redemptive testimony of the historic believers. Moreover, because the Bible is a testimony incarnated in the human fabric of historical and cultural material, just as God's testimony in the Son of God himself was incarnated in that same human stuff, it is imperative that its human limitations and historical anomalies be differentiated from its redemptively revelational material. Jesus, for example, . . . spoke quite erroneously in terms of a three-storied universe, an imminent second coming, and the like. Humanness radically conditioned him with cultural-historical limitations as regards issues that were not central to the single truth of God's testimony in him, that is, that God is for us, not against us. Why are those who insist on inerrancy as the only foundation for authority in Scripture afraid to have a Bible that is at least as culturally bound as was the incarnate Son of God himself . . . ?

Sound psychological theory and practice genuinely enhance the patient's personhood. God designed what that is. Christians perceive it to varying degrees. Full-orbed personhood may be achieved by patients to varying levels of functionality. Sound psychology, which brings the patient, for example, out of depression to emotional resilience and stability is just as Christian at that level as at the level affording the final stages of maturity. . . . Even if that deliverance from depression is done by a secularist, it is a Kingdom act and a Christian enterprise. . . .

What makes practice in the helping professions Christian is less the imparting of biblical information or religious practices to the patient, and more the enhancement of healthy functionality of the human as person: in the direction of completeness in body, mind and spirit. That practice of the helping professions that is preoccupied with the final step of wholeness, spiritual maturity, will short-circuit the therapeutic process and put the religious dynamic of the patient or therapist straight into the religious person's pathology.[7]

The No-Book Approach

Another approach to the integration issue might be called the no-book approach, which suggests that we cannot really be sure that our understanding of the Bible is accurate because our interpretive efforts are always colored by our own perspectives. Bookman explains this approach thus:

> All human knowledge is flawed by definition. There is no reason to be any more suspicious of science than of theology (i.e., of the theories and facts derived by human investigation than of supposed truths derived from Scripture) simply because Scripture is no less liable to the limitations of human participation than is any other truth source.
>
> Regardless of the authority and/or veracity of the truth source, human knowing of truth can only approach greater and greater levels of probability; certainty is propositionally unthinkable.[8]

Although this viewpoint might seem incredulous to most Christians, it is likely to become the dominant view of so-called "Christian counseling" in the years ahead. This viewpoint already dominates post-critical hermeneutics and will most likely continue to filter down into the arena of pastoral and religious counseling.

The Filtering-Device Approach

Some Christians who are not comfortable with either of the previously mentioned perspectives assert that the Bible should be used as a rule book or filtering device for identifying counseling truth. According to the advocates of this view,

> All truth claims that are the result of human cogitations, investigations, and theorizing must be subjected to the Word of God that alone will be allowed to pass judgment on the veracity and applicability of those truth claims. The Bible and the Bible alone will be granted the role of falsification; that is, if a truth-claim is discerned to contradict or compromise a truth established in Scripture, that competing truth-claim is to be adjudged false.[9]
>
> Truth derived from the study of any segment of general revelation, whether psychology or any other field, is not as trustworthy as the truth found in Scriptures. This is the reason

that the integrationist will filter psychological truth through biblical truth and will accept only that which is not contradictory to God's special revelation.[10]

This view is sometimes called "spoiling the Egyptians"—a phrase from Exodus 12:36 used in reference to what the Israelites did when they were delivered from their Egyptian captivity. This incident is used to illustrate and give some biblical warrant to the practice of accepting and benefiting from extrabiblical insights in the realm of counseling theory and practice. The idea is that because the Israelites did not reject the silver and gold that came from ungodly Egyptians (in fact, they were commanded by God to take all of the silver and gold they could get— Exod. 3:21–22), we should not reject counseling theories and practices discovered and used by unbelievers.

Although proponents of these three major approaches to Christian counseling differ on some issues, they are all agreed on one major point: The traditional biblical resources for dealing with man's problems are not enough; they simply are not adequate. We must use insights, ideas, and techniques that are neither taught by nor found in God's Word. Bookman and others have written excellent resources that expose the errors of such thinking, and I recommend their writings to you for further illumination and refutation.[11]

The Shortcomings of Extrabiblical Insights

Limitations of Human Knowledge

I have three reasons for rejecting the idea that Christian counselors need extrabiblical insights to do truly effective counseling. The first reason is related to the *finiteness of man's knowledge*. The fact that man is finite necessarily limits the extent and validity of his knowledge. Even Adam, the first man, was a finite human being. He needed God's revelation for a correct understanding of God himself, of what was right and wrong, of what was true and what was false, of what should be believed and what should not be believed (Gen. 1:26–28; 2:15–17, 24).

An old fable about six blind men who all bumped into and felt different parts of the same elephant illustrates the futility of man's attempts to find absolute truth by the usual means of intuition, reason or logic, or empirical research. As the story goes, one man approached the elephant from the front and grasped his trunk and said, "An elephant is like a fire hose." A second blind man happened to touch one of the animal's tusks and said, "An elephant is like a thick spear." The third blind man felt the elephant's side and said, "An elephant is like a wall." The fourth blind man approached the elephant from the rear and, gripping its tail, said, "An elephant is like a rope." The fifth man grabbed one of the elephant's legs and said, "An elephant is like the trunk of a tree." The sixth man who was very tall grabbed one of the elephant's ears said, "An elephant is like a fan."

Which of these depictions of an elephant was correct? None of them! Why? Because each of them encountered or experienced only a limited portion of the whole elephant. Their knowledge of what an elephant was like was restricted and even erroneous because of the limitations of their experience and perception. And so it is and always must be with finite mortal man when it comes to the matter of discerning absolute truth apart from revelation from the living God, who knows all things and sees the whole picture clearly and perfectly.

A recent newspaper article reminded me of the futility of thinking that finite man can discover absolute truth apart from divine revelation. In the "tongue in cheek" article titled "Education's Duplicity, Uselessness," Russell Baker writes,

> Pluto may not be a planet. Can you believe it? Is everything we learn in school a lie?
>
> This Pluto business is the last straw in the duplicity and uselessness of education. Now I have to deal with Plutonic revisionism, and I haven't even recovered from the discovery that you should not eat a good breakfast.
>
> "Always eat a good breakfast." That's what they taught us in school. They said it was good for us.
>
> Well, you know it, I know it, we all know it: they were wrong. We now know a good breakfast is bad for you. Those eggs sunny side up, that crisp bacon, the butter-soaked toast covered with jelly—bad for you.

So now we always eat a bad breakfast because they say a bad breakfast is good for you.

And remember the milk? Remember paying the milk money and having milk served right there in the class room? What kind of milk was it?

Was it skim milk? Was it low fat milk? Hah! You know it wasn't. It was milk with all the evil left in.

And they said it was good for you. Good for you! It was clogging your arteries and hastening your trip to the grave.

And they called that an education!

The older you get the clearer it becomes that education for the young may not only be useless, but downright dangerous.[12]

At this point in the article, Baker goes on to make a few more "tongue in cheek" remarks about the way what we once considered to be truth has been revised. Then, having done this, he concludes,

Many people become as irked as I do about the incessant need to keep up with today's wisdom by abandoning or revising yesterday's. And of course today's wisdom will just as inevitably have to be abandoned or revised as the future bears down upon us.

You can bet the world has not faced the last revision of knowledge about Pluto, or about what constitutes a good breakfast. The revising of what we think of as knowledge goes on forever, and always has.

The truth about knowledge seems to be that its truth is only a sometimes thing, that what we accept as truth this year will have to be abandoned as the world turns.

This endless abandonment and revision is usually said to result from progress. But suppose progress is also an idea doomed to be abandoned. What if there is no such thing as progress, but only change?[13]

In this article, Russell Baker astutely identifies the tentative nature of our humanly discovered knowledge or "truth" as he asserts that "what we accept as truth this year will have to be abandoned or revised." And why is humanly discovered "truth . . . only a sometimes thing"? One reason is that man's finiteness necessarily limits the extent and validity of his knowledge.

Depravity of Human Nature

A second factor that causes me to reject the idea that Christian counselors should welcome and depend on extra biblical insights and therapies connects to the biblical teaching about the *depravity of man's nature* since the fall of Adam in Genesis 3. Any biblical discussion of how man comes to know truth must include a consideration of what theologians often refer to as the "noëtic"[14] effects of sin. Scripture clearly teaches that sin has affected every aspect of man's being. Man's character, speech, and behavior have all been perverted by sin[15]—as well as his emotions, desires, conscience, will, intellect, thought processes, goals and motives, and the way he views and interprets life. None of man's faculties has escaped the corrupting, corrosive, perverting, and debilitating impact of sin.

In reference to the cognitive, motivational, and emotional aspects of man's being, Scripture asserts the following.

> The heart is more deceitful than all else And is desperately sick; Who can understand it? (Jeremiah 17:9)

> God has looked down from heaven upon the sons of men, To see if there is anyone who understands. . . . (Psalm 53:2)

> For the wrath of God is revealed from heaven against all ungodliness and unrighteousness of men, who suppress the truth in unrighteousness. . . . Professing to be wise, they became fools. . . . For they exchanged the truth of God for a lie, and worshiped and served the creature rather than the Creator, who is blessed forever. . . . And just as they did not see fit to acknowledge God any longer, God gave them over to a depraved mind. . . . (Romans 1:18, 22, 25, 28)

The mind set on the flesh is hostile toward God. . . . (Romans 8:7)

You were formerly alienated and hostile in mind. . . . (Colossians 1:21)

To the pure, all things are pure; but to those who are defiled and unbelieving, nothing is pure, but both their mind and their consciences are defiled. (Titus 1:15)

Out of the heart come evil thoughts. . . . (Matthew 15:19)

In commenting on the noëtic effects of sin, Edward Reynolds wrote,

> Look into the mind; you shall find it full of vanity, wasting and wearying itself in childishness, impertinent, unprofitable notions, "full of ignorance and darkness"; no man knoweth, nay no man hath so much acknowledged, as to enquire or seek after God in the way whereby he will be found. *Nay more, when God breaks in upon the mind, by some notable testimony from his creatures, judgments, or providence—yet they like it not, they hold it down, they reduce themselves back again to foolish hearts, to reprobate and undiscerning minds, as naturally as hot water returns to its former coldness.* Full of curiosity, rash, unprofitable enquiries, foolish and unlearned questions, profane babblings . . . perverse disputes, all the fruits of corrupt and rotten minds. Full of pride and contradiction against the truth, "oppositions of science," that is, setting up of philosophy and vain deceits, imaginations, thoughts, fleshly reasonings against the spirit and truth which is in Jesus. Full of . . . fleshly wisdom, human inventions . . . of rules and methods of its own to . . . come to happiness. Full of inconstancy and roving swarms of empty and foolish thoughts, slipperiness, and unstableness. . . .[16]

What a clear description of the effects of sin on the mind of man! "But," you may ask, "what does this teaching about the noëtic effect of sin have to do with whether Christian counselors should accept and use extrabiblical insights in their counseling efforts?"

The answer to that question is simple: Scripture teaches that the minds of unredeemed men have been adversely affected by sin and, as a result, even if they observe something accurately, they are likely to interpret it wrongly. Having the kind of mind (including all of the cognitive, motivational, and emotional aspects mentioned earlier) described in the previous verses, unregenerate—and even to some extent regenerate—men will tend to distort truth. The only way we can think rightly is to allow the Holy Spirit to renew our minds so that we will learn to look at, interpret, and understand life through the lens of Scripture (Pss. 36:9; 119:104; Isa. 8:19–20; Rom. 1:18–32; 12:2; Eph. 4:23).

When he commented on the role that secular disciplines should play in biblical counseling, David Powlison vividly described the noëtic impact of sin on man's thinking processes:

> Secular disciplines may serve us well as they describe people; they may challenge us by how they seek to explain, guide, and change people; but they seriously mislead us when we take them at face value because they are secular. They explain people, define what people ought to be like, and try to solve people's problems without considering God and man's relationship to God. Secular disciplines have made a systematic commitment to being wrong.
>
> This is not to deny that secular people are often brilliant observers of other human beings. They are often ingenious critics and theoreticians. But they also distort what they see and mislead by what they teach and do, because from God's point of view the wisdom of the world has fundamental folly written through it. They will not acknowledge that God has created human beings as God-related and God accountable creatures. The mind set of secularity is like a power saw with a set that deviates from the right angle. It may be a powerful saw, and it may cut a lot of wood, but every board comes out crooked.[17]

Because of our finiteness and sinfulness, our understanding of man and his problems can be trusted only as our thoughts and insights reflect the teaching of Holy Scripture. We simply are not able to ascertain truth apart from divine revelation. In another work, I wrote,

> We have no standard by which we can evaluate whether something is true or false except the Word of God. Thus while we can be confident that whatever we share with our counselees from the Word of God is true, we should have a healthy skepticism about any theory or insight that does not proceed from Scripture. If it is not taught by the Word of God alone, it may be error.[18]

In his book *Every Thought Captive,* Richard Pratt explains man's epistemological predicament apart from Divine revelation this way:

> All that can properly be called truth, not just "religious truth" resides first in God and men know truly only as they come to God's revelation of Himself as the source of truth . . . (Psalm 94:10). . . . This dependence on God in the area of knowledge does not mean that men are without the true ability to think and reason. . . . Men do actually think, yet true knowledge is dependent on and derived from God's knowledge as it has been revealed to man.[19]

"But," someone may ask, "what about those statements that finite and sinful men make that seem to be a reiteration of concepts and ideas taught by Scripture? Must we regard these observations as false because the person did not get them from the Bible?" Those questions may be answered in several ways.

1. People may have been influenced by biblical teaching through various means and not even be aware of it, nor do they give the Bible credit for their insights. But even if this occurs, they will always distort Scriptural teaching and put their own spin on it. They may, for example, talk about the importance of God, prayer, forgiveness, dealing with guilt, of taking responsibility, love, confession, or the

spiritual dimension in life. On the surface, a person's teaching on these concepts may seem very biblical, but on further investigation the theologically, biblically trained person will discover that not everything that sounds the same is the same. People may use the same words or seem to be presenting the same concepts that God does in His Word but fill those words and concepts with completely different meanings. Inevitably, the Bible indicates that men will suppress, pervert, devalue, deny, and distort the truth, even if it is staring them in the face (Rom. 1:18; 1 Cor. 2:14).

2. Extrabiblical statements that seem to reflect biblical truth must be regarded as false because, as Richard Pratt states, "They are not the result of voluntary obedience to God's revelation. . . ."[20]

3. "Beyond this," Pratt continues, "the statements are falsified by the non-Christian framework of meaning and therefore lead away from the worship of God. If nothing else, the mere commitment to human independence falsifies the non-Christian's statements."[21]

The Sufficiency of Scripture

My third reason for rejecting the idea that Christian counselors need extrabiblical insights to do effective counseling is that the Bible says God has given us—in our union with Christ and in His Word—everything that is necessary for living and for godliness (2 Peter 1:3). Scripture clearly says that it contains all of the principles and practical insights that are necessary for understanding people and their problems (as we'll see in a moment). So, apart from the question of whether it is possible to integrate the ideas of man with the truths of God's Word is the issue of whether it is necessary. On this matter, I am convinced that the Scripture's own testimony about its sufficiency, adequacy, and superiority is abundantly plain.

To demonstrate the biblical accuracy of this third truth, I could cite numerous passages of Scripture, but for the sake of time and space, I will refer to only three representative passages: one from the OT and two from the NT. Psalm 19:7–11 makes numerous statements about the Bible that no one would ever consider making about the ideas of any man. This text makes assertions that set the Bible in a class all by itself—statements that unmistakably demonstrate the Bible's sufficiency and superiority over any of man's theories. Consider carefully what this passage declares about what Scripture is and what it can do, and then think of the counseling implications of these assertions. According to Psalm 19:7–11, Scripture

1. is *perfect* (whole, complete, sufficient, lacking nothing) and therefore able to restore (transform, renew) the soul (the inner man, the real self)—verse 7.

2. is a *sure* (trustworthy, reliable, dependable) witness and therefore able to make wise the simple (people who lack a proper understanding of life, of God, of themselves, of others)—verse 7.

3. contains the precepts (principles, guidelines, and rules for character and conduct) that are *right* (correct, in accord with what is just and good, appropriate and fitting) and therefore able to cause the heart (the totality of man's inner nonphysical self) to rejoice (to experience a sense of well being, serenity, tranquility, and peace)—verse 8.

4. is *authoritative* (it gives mandates and directives that are always correct) and pure (clear, untainted with evil or error) and therefore able to bring light into man's chaos and confusion, to replace man's ignorance and lack of understanding with clear direction, perspective, and insight—verse 8.

5. is *clean* (uncontaminated, free from impurity and defilement) and *enduring* (permanent, unchanging, relevant, up to date, never outdated, never in need of alteration) and therefore able to produce the fear of the Lord (a wholesome and incredibly practical and positive reverence for God)—verse 9.

6. *provides insights* about God, man, life, and everything needed for living and godliness that are altogether true (they correspond to and accurately reflect reality, they tell it like it really is) and righteous (they reflect that which is right, good, and holy, that which is truly just and fair) and therefore lead men to understand and practice what is truly real and right—verse 9.

7. being "more desirable than gold, yes, than much fine gold" is able to produce in us a kind of *prosperity* that is more valuable than all of the material riches of the world—verse 10.

8. being "sweeter also than honey and the drippings of the honey-comb" is able to remove the sourness, acidity, and bitterness caused by sin and to produce in us a *sweetness* of life that surpasses anything the world can provide—verse 10.

9. possessing all of the previously noted qualities, is able to infallibly *warn and protect* us from the numerous dangers and disasters of life caused by ignorance of what is truly right—verse 11.

10. possessing all of the previously noted characteristics, is able to *preserve* us from temptation, sin, error, false teaching, and every other threat to the health and well being of our inner man—our thoughts, emotions, affections, and attitudes—verse 11.

Believing as I do in the inspiration, inerrancy, and authority of the Scriptures, Psalm 19:7–11 settles the sufficiency issue for me. If words mean anything, how could I come to any other conclusion? But there's more—much more. And some of that "more" is found in 2 Timothy 3:1–17. In the first thirteen verses of that chapter, Paul delineates a host of problems representative of what counselors often encounter in their attempts to help people. Many people who require counseling do so because they are struggling with difficulties that stem from one or many of the sinful attitudes, desires, and actions that Paul mentions in this rich passage.

Some people seek counseling because of problems that are associated with being "lovers of self, lovers of money, boastful, arrogant, revilers, disobedient to parents, ungrateful, unholy, unloving, irreconcilable, malicious gossips, without self control, brutal, haters of good, treacherous, reckless, conceited, lovers of pleasure rather than lovers of God" (vv. 2–4). Some individuals need counseling because they are "holding to a form of godliness, although they have denied its power" (v. 5). Some people are struggling because they are "weighed down with sins, led on by various impulses" (v. 6). Some severe difficulties that many people experience in their lives are related to pride, opposition to and rebellion against God's truth, ungodly thoughts, deceitful patterns of living, and people relationships.

Unpleasant, distressing difficulties that motivate people to seek counseling occur because they are "always learning and never able to come to the knowledge of the truth" or because they live in the midst of a society of people who are evil and hypocritical, people who are going "from bad to worse" (vv. 6–13). People need counseling either because they are personally experiencing and manifesting sinful attitudes, desires, and behaviors or they are personally suffering from the impact of associating with people who manifest the sinful patterns depicted in this passage.

Where do we turn for resources to minister to these kinds of people? What do we need for understanding and resolving their problems? Paul answers those questions in verses 14–17. At this point in his epistle, he turns from a description of the kinds of problems that people experience in this sin-cursed world to a description of the resources that Christians have for ministering to the people he has just described in the first thirteen verses. In clear and unmistakable words, Paul tells us that Scripture contains the resources we need for ministering to people who live in a 2 Timothy 3:1–13 society. In concise and direct terms, he extols the Bible's total adequacy for ministering to people whose lives are characterized and/or affected by the things mentioned in verses 1–13.

Why Is Scripture Adequate?

Paul emphasizes the total adequacy of God's Word in 2 Timothy 3:14–17 in the following manner.

1. *It is holy or sacred* (v.15). It is set apart from any other writing or literary production; it is unique; it is in a class all by itself. No other writing can compare with what is written in the Scriptures.
2. *It is able* (v.15). It has power to do things to and in people. "It is," as Jay Adams has written, "the Holy Spirit's tool for working in the minds and hearts of men and women to make them like Christ. Being peculiarly associated with the Spirit both in its composition and in its use, the Bible is powerful, able to transform our lives."[22]
3. *It is inspired by God* (v. 16). Literally, the Greek word translated "inspired" means "God-breathed." So Paul is telling us that the Bible is unique and able because its truths had their origin in God; they are not merely some man's opinions, discoveries, or insights. As Peter said, "No prophecy of Scripture is a matter of one's own

interpretation, for no prophecy was ever made by an act of human will, but men moved by the Holy Spirit spoke from God" (2 Peter 1:20–21). That is why when quoting a portion of Psalm 2—a psalm written by David—the early Christians said that the truth found in this psalm came by the Holy Spirit through the mouth of David (Acts 4:24–26). To the early Christians, the words of Scripture were authoritative and sufficient because, though coming through the agency of holy men, they ultimately had their origin in God.

4. *It is profitable or useful* (v. 16). It has utilitarian value; it enhances life; it is profitable in every way—for time and eternity, for our relationship with God and our relationship with our fellow man, for our spiritual and emotional and mental well-being, for our marriages and families, for our goals and motivations, for guidance and direction, for comfort and challenge, for preventing and resolving our inner and interpersonal problems, and for all of life. It is useful *for teaching*; it is the instrument the Holy Spirit uses to provide for us a standard of what is right and wrong, good and bad, and true and false about all of the truly important matters of life. Scripture is useful *for reproof*; it is the instrument that the Holy Spirit uses to convict us of sin and to show us where and how we are wrong in our thinking, motives, desires, attitudes, feelings, values, actions, and reactions. It is the instrument that the Holy Spirit uses to bring us under conviction and motivate us to want to repent and change.

5. God's Word is useful *for correction*; it is the instrument that the Holy Spirit uses to point us in the right direction and correct our sinful thoughts, motives, feelings, actions, and speech. Scripture not only shows us where and how we need to change but also actually tells us how to change and to what we should change. And Scripture is profitable *for training*; it is the instrument the Holy Spirit uses to help us develop new patterns of life. It makes that which is unnatural—living righteously—natural and makes that which is difficult—living God's way—easier. It helps us develop strength in the areas in which we are weak.

6. *It can thoroughly equip the man of God for every good work* (v. 17). Through Scripture, the Holy Spirit thoroughly equips His

servants—people of God—to do everything He wants them to do
in the kind of society described in 2 Timothy 3:1–13. Do God's
people need anything more than the Scripture to minister effectively to the people living in the world he has described? Is anything else really necessary? Absolutely not! Scripture can
thoroughly equip every believer. In Scripture, Christians have
everything they need to understand people and their problems
and to help them resolve the same.[23]

John Murray draws the following conclusion from 2 Timothy 3:15–
17: "There is no situation in which we (as men of God) are placed, no
demand that arises for which Scripture as the deposit of the manifold
wisdom of God is not adequate and sufficient."[24]

Our Sufficiency in Christ

Perhaps no better summary of the Bible's teaching about our complete sufficiency in Christ exists than the one that the apostle Peter gave
when he wrote that by His divine power God "has granted to us everything pertaining to life and godliness" (2 Peter 1:3). "Life" has to do
with everything that we experience on the horizontal plain—in terms of
what it takes to live effectively and biblically in our daily activities and
relationships with our environment and other people. "Godliness" has to
do with our relationship with God—with living a God-centered, God-
conscious life marked by godly character and conduct.

Peter proceeds to define "everything pertaining to life and godliness"
as *"becom[ing] partakers of the divine nature"* (2 Peter 1:4–8, emphasis added). It involves being born again or from above, becoming a new
creation in Christ Jesus; receiving from God a new nature with new dis-
positions, desires, interests, potential, and power; putting on the new
self; and being renewed in the image of God (John 3:1–8; Rom. 6:1–11;
2 Cor. 5:17; Col. 3:10; 1 Peter 1:23; 2 Peter 1:4). It involves the capacity
to "escape the corruption that is in the world caused by evil desires"
(2 Peter 1:4 NIV). It involves developing the qualities of faith, moral excellence, true knowledge, self-control, perseverance, godliness, brotherly kindness, and Christian love (2 Peter 1:4–7) so that you might live a
useful life for Christ (2 Peter 1:8–10).

"Life and godliness" also involves being able to deal successfully with issues that are present in the lives of people who seek counseling. People who need counseling lack the qualities that Peter mentions in 2 Peter 1:4–7 and need help in developing them. It is interesting to observe that people whose lives reflect these qualities do not need much formal counseling. This passage is pregnant with counseling implications.

Notice that Peter says that God has, by His divine power, "granted to us *everything* pertaining to life and godliness" (2 Peter 1:3, emphasis added). *Everything* that is needed to develop and acquire this kind of life and the qualities in verses 4–7 has been granted to us by God. And how do we tap into these powerful, all-sufficient resources? Peter declared that these divine resources become ours through the true knowledge of God and of Jesus our Lord and through the medium of His precious and magnificent promises (2 Peter 1:2–4). In other words, the repository of the *everything* we need for life and godliness is found in our glorious and excellent God and His precious and magnificent Word (2 Peter 1:2–4).

Our sufficiency in Christ is found in a deeper, fuller, applicatory, life-changing knowledge of the glory and excellence of God and the magnificence and preciousness of His promises. According to Green, God has called us to share "something of His moral excellence in this life, and of His glory hereafter. . . . The triple agency of the promises, the power and the Person of the Lord regenerate a man and make him a sharer in God's own nature, so that the family likeness begins to be seen in him."[25]

Worthy of Full Confidence

In light of what we have learned from Psalm 19:7–11, 2 Timothy 3:15–17, and 2 Peter 1:3–7, I ask this question: Could God have stated more clearly the sufficiency of our resources in Christ and in His Word? What more could He have said to get the message through to us that we do not need any extrabiblical resources to understand people and their problems and to help them develop the qualities, attitudes, desires, values, feelings, and behavior that are proper for relating to and living before God in a way that pleases and honors Him?

A consideration of the truths presented in these three passages and many other sections of Scripture forces me to draw the following three conclusions.

1. The inerrant Bible to which Christians are committed as an authority in life teaches that God has provided for us in His Word whatever is true and necessary for successful living. It declares that God has given us, in the Bible, everything we need for being in right relationship with God, ourselves, and other people.

2. Because the first conclusion is true, professing Christians have two options: they must either yield to its teaching on this matter or abandon the idea that the Bible is inerrant and authoritative. Either it is inerrant, authoritative, and sufficient or it is none of these things. If the Bible claims to be sufficient in the ways and for the purposes previously delineated but it is not, then you cannot say that it is inerrant and authoritative. Given what the Bible teaches about itself, you simply cannot have it both ways.

3. The final conclusion is a natural concomitant of accepting the truthfulness of the first conclusion: Because the Bible asserts its own sufficiency for counseling-related issues, secular psychology has nothing to offer for understanding or providing solutions to the nonphysical problems of people. When it comes to counseling people, we have no reason for depending on the insights of finite and fallen men. Rather, we have every reason to place our confidence in the sure, dependable, and entirely trustworthy revelation of God given to us in Holy Scripture. This confidence is because the Bible contains a God-ordained, sufficient, comprehensive system of theoretical commitments, principles, insights, goals, and appropriate methods for understanding and resolving the nonphysical problems of people. It provides for us a model that needs no supplement. God, the expert on helping people, has given us, in Scripture, counseling perspectives and methodology that are wholly adequate for resolving our sin-related problems.

The Need for Caution

David Powlison has stated well the danger of including extrabiblical ideas in the counsel offered to or by Christians:

Let us clarify first what we mean by counseling methodology. A counseling methodology is a *system* of theoretical commitments,

principles, goals, and appropriate methods. It is a set of inter-
connected things; it is not a collection of random and eclectic
bits of observation or technique. A counseling methodology is
an organized, committed way of understanding and tackling
people's problems.

Do secular disciplines have anything to offer to the methodology of biblical counseling? The answer is a flat no. Scriptures provide the system for biblical counseling. Other disciplines—history,
anthropology, literature, sociology, psychology, biology, business,
political science—may be useful in a variety of secondary ways to
the pastor and the biblical counselor, but such discipline can never
provide a system of understanding and counseling people.

God is the expert when it comes to people, and He has spoken and acted to change us and equip us to help others change.[26]

Secular psychology may play an *illustrative* (i.e., providing examples
and details that, when carefully and radically reinterpreted, illustrate the
biblical model) or *provocative* (i.e., challenging us to study the Scriptures more thoroughly to develop our model in areas about which we
have not thought or have neglected or misconstrued) function, but, because of man's finiteness and fallenness, the insights, methodologies,
and practices of secular psychology are, in many instances, dangerously
unbiblical and dishonoring to God and harmful to people. Other aspects
of secular psychology are at best neutral and therefore unnecessary.

None of the illustrations, observations, or details that secularists present
are really necessary for the task of understanding and helping people.
We already have all we need—the authoritative, indispensable, perspicu-
ous, sufficient, and superior revelation of God in His Word (Isa. 8:19–
20). Why, then, would any Christian think that we must turn to or place
our dependence on the extrabiblical theories or practices of men for understanding and promoting change in people?[27]

Endnotes

1. John F. MacArthur Jr., *Our Sufficiency in Christ* (Dallas: Word, 1991), 27, 72. In
   the last paragraph quoted, MacArthur is referring to attempts to help people based

on secular humanistic theories, techniques, and therapies. He is not referring to the kind of counseling being described in this chapter, as is evidenced from many of his other writings, from his coediting a book titled *Introduction to Biblical Counseling* (Dallas: Word, 1994), and the facts that the church he pastors has a very active counselor training and counseling ministry and that The Master's College, of which he is the president, has an undergraduate major in biblical counseling and a graduate program leading to an M.A. degree in biblical counseling.

2. John Calvin, *Institutes of the Christian Religion* (1559; reprint, Philadelphia: Westminster, 1960), 2:1012.

3. More about the role of the church in the lives of believers may be found in the book by Wayne Mack and David Swavely, *Life in the Father's House: A Member's Guide to the Local Church* (Phillipsburg, N.J.: Presbyterian and Reformed, 1996).

4. Douglas Bookman, "The Scriptures and Biblical Counseling," in *Introduction to Biblical Counseling,* ed. John F. MacArthur Jr. and Wayne A. Mack (Dallas: Word, 1994), 63–65.

5. Ibid., 69.

6. J. Harold Ellens, "Biblical Themes in Psychological Theory and Practice," *Journal of Psychology and Christianity* 6, no. 2 (1980): 2, as cited by Bookman, "The Scriptures and Biblical Counseling," 71.

7. J. Harold Ellens, "Biblical Authority and Christian Psychology," *Journal of Psychology and Theology* 9, no. 4 (1981): 320.

8. Bookman, "The Scriptures and Biblical Counseling," 90.

9. Ibid.

10. William F. English, "An Integrationist's Critique of and Challenge to the Bobgan's View of Counseling Psychotherapy," *Journal of Psychology and Theology* 18, no. 3 (1990): 229, as cited by Bookman, "The Scriptures and Biblical Counseling," 91.

11. Important critiques related to integrationist attempts are found in *Introduction to Biblical Counseling,* ed. John F. MacArthur Jr. and Wayne A. Mack (Dallas: Word, 1994), 63–97; Michael S. Horton, ed., *Power Religion* (Chicago: Moody, 1992), chap. 8 by David Powlison, 191–218, and chap. 9 by Edward Welch, 219–43; David Powlison, *Journal of Psychology and Theology* 12, no. 4 (1984): 270–78; Jay Adams, *Competent to Counsel* (Grand Rapids: Zondervan, 1970); idem, *A Theology of Christian Counseling* (Grand Rapids: Zondervan, 1979); idem, *Teaching to Observe* (Woodruff, S.C.: Timeless Texts, 1995); Edward Bulkley, *Why Christians Can't Trust Psychology* (Eugene, Ore.: Harvest House, 1993); Gary Almy, *Addicted to Recovery* (Eugene, Ore.: Harvest House, 1994); David F. Wells, *No Place for Truth* (Grand Rapids: Eerdmans, 1993); John F. MacArthur Jr., *Our Sufficiency in Christ* (Dallas: Word, 1991); idem, *The Vanishing Conscience* (Dallas: Word, 1994); idem, *Reckless Faith* (Wheaton, Ill.: Crossway, 1994); Noel Weeks, *The Sufficiency of Scripture* (Edinburgh: Banner of Truth, 1988), 3–46, 76–90, 167–82; and James Owen, *Christian Psychology's War on God's Word* (Santa Barbara, Calif.: East Gate, 1993).

12. Russell Baker, "Education's Duplicity, Uselessness," *New York Times,* 16 March 1996.

13. Ibid.

14. The word *noëtic* is related to the Greek word *nous,* which in English means "mind." This Greek word denotes "the seat of reflection, consciousness, comprising the faculties of perception and understanding, and those of feeling, judging and determining" (W. E. Vine, *An Expository Dictionary of New Testament Words* [Westwood, N.J.: Revell, 1957], 69).

15. Cf. Romans 1:18–3:23; 8:8; 1 Kings 8:46; Psalms 14:1–3; 51:5; 58:3; Isaiah 53:6; 64:6; and Ephesians 2:1–3.

16. Edward Reynolds, *The Sinfulness of Sin* (1826; reprint, Ligonier, Pa.: Sola Deo Gloria, 1992), 123, emphasis added.

17. David Powlison, "Frequently Asked Questions about Biblical Counseling," in *Introduction to Biblical Counseling,* ed. John F. MacArthur Jr. and Wayne A. Mack (Dallas: Word, 1994), 365–66.

18. Wayne A. Mack, "Providing Instruction through Biblical Counseling," in *Introduction to Biblical Counseling,* ed. John F. MacArthur Jr. and Wayne A. Mack (Dallas: Word, 1994), 254.

19. Richard Pratt, *Every Thought Captive* (Phillipsburg, N.J.: Presbyterian and Reformed, 1979), 17.

20. Ibid.

21. Ibid.

22. Jay Adams, *How to Help People Change* (Grand Rapids: Zondervan, 1986), 23–24.

23. See Adams's book, *How to Help People Change,* for a fuller explanation and application of 2 Timothy 3:14–17.

24. Murray, *Collected Writings,* 3:261, cited by Michael Green, *The Second Epistle of Peter and the Epistle of Jude* (Grand Rapids: Eerdmans, 1968), 64.

25. Michael Green, *Second Epistle of Peter and the Epistle of Jude,* 64.

26. Powlison, "Frequently Asked Questions about Biblical Counseling," 365–66.

27. The purpose of this article has been to demonstrate that the Bible asserts its sufficiency for understanding and resolving the kinds of issues with which counselors (Christian or non-Christian) deal in their attempts to help people. My intention in this article has not been to demonstrate *how* the Scriptures are sufficient, that is, to provide specific examples of how they actually help to understand man and his problems and provide details about a biblical methodology for resolving the variety of problems that people encounter. For those who want to pursue this "how to" aspect more fully, see the following representative resources: John F. MacArthur Jr. and Wayne A. Mack, eds., *Introduction to Biblical Counseling* (Dallas: Word, 1994), chaps. 10–16, 20; I have developed many books, audiocassettes, and videotapes of counseling courses and tapes dealing with a biblical approach to counseling on a variety of specific issues (a catalog listing

these materials is available by writing to the author at 21726 W. Placerita Canyon Road, Newhall, CA 91322); The Master's College offers an undergraduate emphasis leading to a B.A. degree and a graduate program leading to an M.A. degree in biblical counseling (P.O. Box 278, 21726 W. Placerita Canyon Road, Newhall, CA 91322); Christian Counseling and Educational Foundation West has video tapes of several counseling courses and offers numerous training courses (3495 College Avenue, San Diego, CA 92115); Christian Counseling and Educational Foundation East offers courses on biblical counseling and produces an excellent journal, *The Biblical Counseling Journal,* for biblical counselors (1803 East Willow Grove Avenue, Laverock, PA 19118); the National Association of Nouthetic Counselors (NANC) sponsors conferences, produces a biblical counseling publication, and has audio and video tapes on numerous "how to" issues (NANC, 5526 State Road 26 East, Lafayette, IN 47905); Jay Adams has written numerous books and produced many audio and video tapes on various biblical counseling issues (Woodruff, S.C.: Timeless Texts); Gary Almy, *Addicted to Recovery* (Eugene, Ore.: Harvest House, 1994); Edward Bulkley, *Only God Can Heal the Wounded Heart* (Eugene, Ore.: Harvest House, 1995); David Powlison, *Power Encounters* (Grand Rapids: Baker, 1995); Edward Welch, *Counselor's Guide to the Brain and Its Disorders: Knowing the Difference between Sin and Disease* (Grand Rapids: Zondervan, 1991); Richard Baxter, *A Christian Directory* (1677; reprint, Pittsburgh: Soli Deo Gloria, 1990); William Playfair, *The Useful Lie* (Wheaton, Ill.: Crossway, 1991); William Bridge, *A Lifting Up of the Downcast* (1649; reprint, Carlisle, Pa.: Banner of Truth, 1979); Jeremiah Burroughs, *The Rare Jewel of Christian Contentment* (1659; reprint, Carlisle, Pa.: Banner of Truth, 1979); D. Martyn Lloyd-Jones, *Spiritual Depression: Its Causes and Its Cure* (Grand Rapids: Eerdmans, 1965); Michael Bobick, *From Slavery to Sonship: A Biblical Psychology for Pastoral Counseling* (available from Grace Book Shack, 13248 Roscoe Boulevard, Sun Valley, CA 91352); Sound Word Cassettes (430 Boyd Circle, P.O. Box 2035, Mail Station, Michigan City, IN 46360) carries many audiocassettes and videotapes on counseling various problems biblically; Westminster Theological Seminary (Chestnut Hill, P.O. Box 27009, Philadelphia, PA 19118, and 1725 Bear Valley Parkway, Escondido, CA 92027) offers many counseling courses that provide a biblical approach on various counseling issues.

In these resources, you will find information about a biblical counseling methodology for understanding and resolving the problems of people biblically. In these resources you will find case studies and teaching that illustrate the sufficiency of Scripture for people who claim to be suffering from multiple personality disorder (MPD); various kinds of eating disorders; sexual sins such as incest, homosexuality, transvestism, transexualism, and slavery to pornography and lust; depression; anxiety; anger; bizarre, schizophrenic behavior; drug abuse, including slavery to alcohol; and what secularists would call obsessive, compulsive disorders. You will find biblically based information on counseling and the problems of the past, self-esteem problems, chronic fatigue, demon possession, chemical imbalance, victimization, suffering, human defensiveness, women in menopause, women and premenstrual syndrome (PMS), confidentiality in counseling, crisis counseling, guilt, panic attacks, inordinate fears, psychological testing, attention deficit/hyperactivity disorder (ADHD), rebuilding a marriage after adultery, counseling various kinds of marriage and family problems, and many other counseling issues.

CHAPTER TEN

Involvement and Biblical Counseling

Wayne A. Mack

Attempts at biblical counseling sometimes neglect the important factor of establishing a facilitative relationship between the counselor and the counselee. Such a relationship can come through a demonstrated compassion such as Jesus and Paul had for people to whom they ministered, a compassion that is possible for the counselor to develop through controlling his thoughts. The necessary involvement can also develop if the counselor follows certain guidelines in showing respect for his counselee. The facilitative relationship is also possible when built on the foundation of sincerity, when the counselee realizes that the counselor is perfectly honest and has no hidden agenda. The substance of the counsel given is of greatest importance, but the involvement of the counselor with his counselee is most frequently the packaging that makes his advice effective in helping people.

This essay appeared in *Introduction to Biblical Counseling* (Dallas: Word, 1994), of which Dr. Mack is the editor. President MacArthur and the faculty of The Master's College collaborated on this work. The essay is used here by permission. Quotations are from the *New American Standard Bible* unless otherwise noted.

* * * * *

Biblical counseling seeks to solve people's problems. It is about discovering the causes of those problems and then applying biblical principles to them. Sometimes even the best-intentioned counselors err, however, by trying to attain these goals without an attempt to incorporate an indispensable element. That element is *involvement* with the person counseled.[1]

Consider the approach of a counselor described by Adams:

> Clara comes to you stating that she has filed for divorce on the grounds of mental and bodily cruelty.
>
> Clara returns for the third session. "I tried to get him here but he had other things to do," she begins. "You know what his other things are, of course. I told you all of them."
>
> "I don't want to hear such charges behind Marty's back," you respond. "This continuing hostility toward him, even though you told him you forgave him, seems to indicate that you made little or no attempt to bury the issue and start afresh. I don't think that you understand forgiveness. You . . ."
>
> "Forgive him! You know there is a limit. After he has beat me, and his drinking away our money maybe, but when I came home and found him in my bed with that woman, I can never bury that! He is just an immature, immoral, animalistic pig," she declares.
>
> You tell her that it will be necessary for her to change her language about her husband and that you are here to help but not to salve her self-righteous attitude and listen to her ever-increasing charges against her husband.
>
> "Why are you siding with him? I'm the one that belongs to this church!" She breaks into tears.[2]

Why did that third session deteriorate into near hopelessness before it had hardly begun? It was not because the counselor offered bad advice—most of what he said was probably true. Rather, it turned sour, at least partially, because he took what may be called the "auto mechanic" approach to counseling.

When someone leaves a car for repair, the mechanic pulls out the shop manual for that particular model. After putting the car through various diagnostic tests, he repairs any indicated problem as the book prescribes. Sadly, some counselors treat people that way. They restrict their responsibility to finding out what the problem is and what the Book says to do about it and to moving directly to "fix" the problem. They devote little effort to developing their relationship with the counselee.[3]

This neglect in counseling commits the error of treating the counselee as a mechanism, in contrast to biblical counseling, which tries to help the *whole person*. People's problems are important, and counselors should not ignore them, but biblical counselors should come to these painful problems through a genuine care and concern for the total being of their counselees.[4] Efforts to help people should not be exclusively *problem oriented*. They should be *person oriented,* with the resolution of problems flowing from that focus. This sets counseling in its proper context.

In Clara's case, the counselor failed because he was too problem oriented in his approach. Apparently, he had done very little to establish involvement with his counselee. He had not labored to develop a facilitative relationship so that she knew that he cared about her. He could have taken some time to listen to her and sympathize with the pain she was experiencing, but he had jumped right in and addressed her sin.[5] Almost immediately, Clara viewed him as her opponent rather than her ally. As long as she had this perspective, his counsel to her was next to meaningless. His words could be completely true and appropriate to her situation, but she would nonetheless reject them.

Proverbs 27 says, "Faithful are the wounds of a *friend* [emphasis added]" (v. 6) and "A man's counsel is sweet to his *friend* [emphasis added]" (v. 9). People are more receptive to counsel from those whom they know to be on their side. Allies can speak to them frankly about their faults. They might find temporary annoyance with criticism, but they soon realize that sincere concern is behind the criticism and their critics are only trying to help. On the other hand, if a stranger or seeming enemy offers the critique, people tend to react defensively and are suspicious of the underlying motives.

As in any other relational function, *a counselor's impact and influ-*

ence in the lives of people are usually related to people's perception of him. That is why involvement is so vitally important to the counseling process. Usually, the counseling process is most effective after the achievement of an acceptable level of involvement.[6]

With this fact in mind, a consideration of three ways for developing involvement with people seeking help is in order. *Compassion, respect,* and *sincerity* are the foundations for building a facilitative relationship with counselees.

Involvement Through Compassion

A counselee's awareness that the counselor genuinely cares promotes involvement.

Two Great Examples of Involvement

Jesus. Undoubtedly the greatest counselor who ever lived was the Lord Jesus Christ. Isaiah prophesied that "His name will be called Wonderful Counselor" (9:6) and that upon Him would rest "the spirit of wisdom and understanding, the spirit of counsel and strength" (11:2). One of the keys to His success as a counselor was His great compassion for men and women, a characteristic evident throughout the gospel accounts of His life and ministry.

Matthew records, "Seeing the multitudes, He felt compassion for them, because they were distressed and downcast like sheep without a shepherd" (Matt. 9:36). The Greek word for His compassion in Hebrews 4:15 is *synpatheō,* which is the source for the English word *sympathy. Syn* means "with" and *patheō* (or *paschō*) means "suffer." He suffered with the needy multitudes. He felt for them and cared for them with a compassion that permeated all of His attempts to meet their needs (Matt. 9:35, 37–38). Far from being a cold-hearted, "auto-mechanic" counselor who limited his attention to the problems and treated people like statistics, He was a person who had compassion for them.

Mark 3:1–5 says that Jesus noticed a man with a withered hand in the synagogue and that He was both angry and sad over the Pharisees' lack of sensitivity toward the man. He showed His own compassion by restoring the man's hand despite His enemies' objection to His doing so on the Sabbath.

A rich, young ruler came to Jesus seeking eternal life, but he left without it because he loved his riches too much to give them up at Christ's command. Even so, Mark 10:21 says, "Looking at him, Jesus felt a love for him." Even when Jesus had to uphold unpopular standards that repelled people, He did so with compassion.

One day, Jesus was with His disciples when a funeral procession passed near them (Luke 7:11–15). A widow's only child had died, so Christ stopped to comfort her: "And when the Lord saw her, He felt compassion for her, and said to her, 'Do not weep'"(v. 13). He then proceeded to raise her son from the dead.

Jesus' compassion caused Him to shed tears of grief, as Luke 19:41 notes. He wept over Jerusalem as He predicted the future judgment of God to come upon it. When He saw the sorrow of Mary over the death of Lazarus, "He was deeply moved in spirit, and was troubled" (John 11:33-35) and wept with her. She and all the others with whom Jesus interacted throughout His ministry could tell from being around Jesus how much He cared for them. This is one of the qualities that contributed to His being the Wonderful Counselor. He did not just observe problems and dispense platitudes; He epitomized the compassion every counselor needs.

Paul. In the writer's opinion, the second greatest counselor who ever lived was Paul. Many people picture Paul as a staunch defender of the faith and a brilliant theologian, but they fail to realize that he was also a compassionate man who cared deeply for the people to whom he ministered. Paul reminds the Ephesian elders, "Night and day for a period of three years I did not cease to admonish each one with tears" (Acts 20:31). The Greek word for "admonish"—*noutheteō*—also means "counsel" and most often means "correct" or "warn." Even when Paul rebuked Christians for their sin, his tears communicated a genuine, caring, and loving heart.

Paul's great love for his fellow Jews is a theme of Romans 9:1-3: "I am telling the truth in Christ, I am not lying, my conscience bearing me witness in the Holy Spirit, that I have great sorrow and unceasing grief in my heart. For I could wish that I myself were accursed, separated from Christ for the sake of my brethren, my kinsmen according to the flesh." He was on the verge of willingness to burn in hell if that would save them! Surely contemporary counselors have a long way to go to match that kind of compassion!

Paul felt the same compassion for his Corinthian converts. He refers to a strong letter of admonishment that he had written to them: "For out of much affliction and anguish of heart I wrote to you with many tears; not that you should be made sorrowful, but that you might know the love which I have especially for you" (2 Cor. 2:4). He also speaks of the "daily pressure" of concern he feels for all of the churches, and then he says, "Who is weak without my being weak? Who is led into sin without my intense concern?" (2 Cor. 11:29). Paul identified with the problems and weaknesses of his "counselees" to the degree that he experienced them himself.

The Thessalonian church received an especially moving expression of Paul's love for them: "We proved to be gentle among you, as a nursing mother tenderly cares for her own children. Having thus a fond affection for you, we were well-pleased to impart to you not only the gospel of God but also our own lives, because you had become very dear to us" (1 Thess. 2:7–8).

Paul cared for people, and they knew it. His heart was "opened wide" to them (2 Cor. 6:11). That is why he could be so straightforward in addressing their faults without alienating them in any way. If a contemporary counselor is to be effective, he must have the same kind of compassion.

How to Develop Genuine Compassion

Perhaps some people question whether they have the kind of compassion that Jesus and Paul had or wonder how they can develop more of it. Fortunately the Bible tells how to emulate these great examples. Following are some suggestions from Scripture about how to develop compassion toward people who need help. Because any righteous attitude, action, or emotion originates in the mind (cf. Rom. 12:2), these suggestions pertain to how a person thinks.

Think about how you would feel if you were in their position. In many of the previously mentioned passages about Jesus' compassion, the text first mentions His seeing or looking upon people. For instance, Matthew 9:36 says, "*Seeing* [emphasis added] the multitudes, He felt compassion for them." The account of the mourning widow records, "When the Lord *saw* her, He felt compassion for her" (Luke 7:13, emphasis added).[7] That is very significant. Jesus looked thoughtfully at people who were experiencing difficulty, that is, He put Himself in their place and intentionally tried to feel what they were feeling. His compassion for them arose from that empathy. Even now, although He is in heaven, He is "touched with the feeling of our infirmities" (Heb. 4:15 KJV).

Consider again the case of Clara. She concluded that her counselor was not in sympathy with her. All that she sensed from him was condemnation. The counselor should have first listened to her complaints and concerns and tried to understand how she was feeling. Before responding, he could have asked himself, "What would it be like for me to come home to a wife who was wasting all of our money on alcohol? What would it be like to have a wife calling me names, scratching me, and throwing things at me? What would it be like to have a wife who did not care about what I thought or what I said? What would it be like for me to come home and find my wife in my bed with another man? How would I feel? What emotions would I be experiencing?"

The counseling process does not end with understanding the feelings of the counselees, of course. Their sin problems need to be addressed with a view to finding solutions. But the counseling process must *start* with that understanding. In most cases, effective counseling cannot occur until the counselor demonstrates to the counselee the compassion of Christ by identifying with his or her struggles.

Think of them as family members. Paul says in 1 Timothy 5:1–2, "Do not sharply rebuke an older man, but rather appeal to him as a father, to the younger men as brothers, the older women as mothers, and the younger women as sisters." A deliberate effort to treat the counselee as a close relative will contribute toward developing compassion. In reality, counselor and counselee are spiritual brothers or brother and sister if both are Christians. The heavenly Father expects His children to treat each other according to their spiritual ties.

Think about your own sinfulness. Galatians 6:1 instructs and cautions counselors: "Brethren, even if a man is caught in any trespass, you who are spiritual, restore such a one in a spirit of gentleness; *looking to yourselves, lest you too be tempted* [emphasis added]." When counselors learn of sin in the lives of their counselees, they must remember that they are not immune to that deadly disease and can fall into sin just as easily as anyone else. No one has done anything that a counselor could not do, if not for the grace of God. Keeping that fact in mind will guard the counselor against becoming self-righteous or condescending toward those who sin and help him to reach out to them in compassion, as Jesus did to the adulterous woman (John 8:1–11).

Think about practical ways that you can show compassion. Compassion is not so much an emotion as it is a choice of the will. Although a counselor might not *feel* like being kind to someone, he can still do so (cf. Luke 6:27–28). Often, those feelings of love for others result from a counselor's choice to act in a way that pleases and benefits them. Asking the following questions may help determine whether a counselor has genuine compassion for the people he is trying to help.

- Have you told the counselees verbally that you care for them? (Phil. 1:8)
- Have you prayed for them and with them? (Col. 4:12–13)
- Have you rejoiced and grieved with them? (Rom. 12:15)
- Have you dealt with them gently and tenderly? (Matt. 12:20)
- Have you been tactful with them? (Prov. 15:23)
- Have you spoken graciously to them? (Col. 4:6)
- Have you continued to love and accept them even when they have rejected your counsel? (Mark 10:21)
- Have you defended them against those who mistreat and accuse them? (Matt. 12:1–7)
- Have you forgiven them for any wrong they have done to you? (Matt. 18:21–22)
- Have you been willing to meet their physical needs if necessary? (1 John 3:17)

Involvement Through Respect

People need to know not only that the counselor cares for them but also that he respects them. Webster defines *respect* as "deferential regard" and "considering another worthy of honor." The Bible lauds that quality repeatedly. Romans 12:10 tells Christians to "give preference to one another in honor." Philippians 2:3 commands, "With humility of mind let each of you regard one another as more important than himself." First

Peter 2:17 instructs, "Honor all men." To return once more to the counselor who was trying to help Clara, he failed miserably in this area. The way he talked to her implied only disrespect, which no doubt is the major reason their relationship took a bad turn.

In cases when a counselee shows little respect for the counselor, it is often because the counselor has shown little respect for the counselee. The counselor is repaid with what he or she has sown. So when the one seeking help fails to look as he should to the one providing help, the first question the counselor should ask is, "Have I honored him as God commands me to do?"[8]

How to Show Respect for a Counselee

One can show respect in a counseling context in several ways that help establish the necessary involvement.

By proper verbal communication. The counselor can demonstrate respect for a counselee in the way he talks both to and about him. Paul advises, "The Lord's bond-servant must not be quarrelsome, but be kind to all, able to teach, patient when wronged, with gentleness correcting those who are in opposition, if perhaps God may grant them repentance leading to the knowledge of the truth" (2 Tim. 2:24–25). Scripture never condones rude or harsh speech, even when speaking the truth (cf. Eph. 4:15). Proverbs 16 says that "sweetness of speech increases persuasiveness" (v. 21) and "pleasant words are a honeycomb, Sweet to the soul and healing to the bones" (v. 24). So the way a counselor communicates verbally is of primary importance in showing respect to a counselee.

By proper nonverbal communication. The mouth is not the only way to show respect; the rest of the body can do the same. Moses wrote, "Rise in the presence of the aged, show respect for the elderly" (Lev. 19:32 NIV). In the OT, etiquette required younger people to stand when an older person entered the room. That was a nonverbal way of saying, "We honor you; we respect you." This kind of unspoken communication is as important to God now as it was then because it reflects one's opinion of another.

The acronym S-O-L-V-E-R is useful as a reminder of several ways to show nonverbal respect to a counselee. These are traits of a person who is truly helpful, and a counselor should be conscious of them during every counseling session.

S—squared shoulders. Face the counselee in a way that indicates you are alert and giving him or her your undivided attention.

O—open stance. Relax your arms, hands, and shoulders as if to say, "I am here to receive whatever you want to communicate. You have access to me."

L—leaning slightly forward. This posture shows interest in what the person is saying to you.

V—vocal quality. Maintain a volume and intensity in your speech that is neither abrasive nor hard to hear. Let your voice always reflect tenderness and compassion rather than anger and irritation.

E—eye contact. Look at people, especially when they are speaking. Don't stare at them so much that you make them uncomfortable, but show your interest in what they are saying by giving them your rapt attention.

R—relational posture. Coordinate all of your body, head, and facial movements in a way that is most conducive to the comfort of the counselee. Your posture should not be stiff and robotic, but neither should it be so totally relaxed that the person thinks you're about to go to sleep.[9]

In all of these areas, a counselor must keep a good balance so that the counselee does not perceive him as being either too uptight or too indifferent because either perception can build a wall between him and his counselee and interfere with the counseling process.[10]

By taking their problems seriously. Never minimize the problems presented by counselees. A counselor may think, *This is so trivial—why are they making a big deal out of it?* But it *is* very important to them, or they would not be sitting across from you. By taking their problems seriously, a counselor is communicating respect. On the other hand, making light of their problems will alienate them from the start and remove any hope they might have had that you could help them.

By trusting them. First Corinthians 13:7 says that love "believes all things." Applied to counseling, this phrase means that a counselor should believe what his counselee tells him until the facts prove otherwise. He should also believe that the seeker has entered counseling because he wants to please God more. Presumptive suspicion is a worldly, not a

Christian, attitude (Phil. 2:3). One psychology textbook says the following about Gestalt therapist Fritz Perls:

> Perls . . . expresses his skepticism about those who seek therapy and indicates that not very many people really want to invest themselves in the hard work involved in changing. As he points out, "Anybody who goes to a therapist has something up his sleeve. I would say roughly ninety percent don't go to a therapist to be cured, but to be more adequate in their neurosis. If they are power mad, they want to get more power. . . . If they are ridiculers, they want to have a sharper wit to ridicule, and so on."[11]

Believers in Christ cannot approach counseling with that cynical attitude because Scripture says that love believes all things. No doubt, people will sometimes come with insincere motives, but the counselor should not allow himself to think that until he has good reason to do so.

By expressing confidence in them. The Corinthian church had more problems than any other people to whom Paul wrote; nonetheless, he told them, "I rejoice that in everything I have confidence in you" (2 Cor. 7:16). No matter how many weaknesses counselees may have, if they are believers, the counselor should convey the attitude that he is confident that they will respond well to the counseling and grow through it.

Because Scripture states that God is at work in believers "both to will and to work for His good pleasure" (Phil. 2:13) and because Jesus said, "My sheep hear My voice, . . . and they follow Me" (John 10:27), the counselor should have an attitude of relative confidence that believing counselees will respond positively to the directives of the Lord. He should also communicate the same to people he is helping. Frequently—in fact, in every epistle but one—Paul follows this practice through his letters to people he was counseling. In each case, he advises them about serious problems in their midst and in their lives. With only one exception (Galatians), his teaching, reproof, correction, and admonition join with expressions of confidence in and respect for those whom he counsels.

Paul not only knew the problems of the people to whom he wrote but also recognized and appreciated the good qualities and behavior that God had accomplished in them. Furthermore, he gives the impression that he expects them, as Christians, to respond positively to counsel from the Lord. In essence, he respected them and had confidence in them because he respected and had confidence in the Lord and His Word. So it should be with today's counselor as he counsels. He should communicate an attitude of respect for and confidence in his counselees because he has respect for and confidence in the Lord and the promises and power of His Word. As God works in his counselees to produce godly strengths and virtues, it is appropriate for the counselor to praise God and let the counselee know what he sees. When they have done a good job on their homework, it is fitting for him to tell them that. In counseling, he certainly must deal honestly and forthrightly with problems in people's lives, but he must also remember that the counsel of Philippians 4:8 about focusing on the things that are lovely, honorable, virtuous, right, and worthy of praise applies to counseling as well as to the normal routine of life.

The writer of Hebrews provides another good example of this principle in action. In the last part of chapter 10, he warns his readers sternly about the danger of apostasy, into which he undoubtedly feared that they might fall (vv. 26–31). Before leaving the topic, however, he commends them for the good that they have already done (vv. 32–34) and expresses confidence that they will heed his warning and prove themselves to be genuine believers. Verse 39 records, "But we are not of those who shrink back to destruction, but of those who have faith to the preserving of the soul."

By welcoming their input. A counselor can show respect for his counselees by asking them to help him through evaluating the sessions and suggesting improvements. He could say to them, "God has brought us together, and He wants not only to use me in your life but also to use you in my life." This also entails a willingness to receive their negative input without becoming defensive or irritated. Any such criticism or complaint provides him an opportunity to model the godly responses that he wants them to develop in their own lives. Numerous times in this writer's counseling, he has had to respond to criticism by admitting his wrong and asking forgiveness from the counselee.

By maintaining confidentiality. The counselor must show respect to his counselees by guarding their reputations as much as he possibly can without disobeying God. "As much as he possibly can" is as far as he can go because confidentiality is not always possible (or best) in light of the commands that Jesus gave in Matthew 18:16–17, where He says that if a brother is sinning and proves unwilling to listen to private rebuke, a believer should "take one or two more with you, so that by the mouth of two or three witnesses every fact may be confirmed. And if he refuses to listen to them, tell it to the church." Regarding these verses, Adams has written,

> The implication of this biblical requirement to seek additional help in order to reclaim an offender is that Christians must never promise absolute confidentiality to any person. Frequently it is the practice of Bible-believing Christians to give assurances of absolute confidentiality, never realizing that they are following a policy that originated in the Middle Ages and that is unbiblical.
>
> Is it right, then, to refuse any confidentiality at all? No, confidentiality is assumed in the gradual widening of the sphere of concern to other persons set forth in Matthew 18:15ff. As you read the words of our Lord in that passage, you get the impression that it is only reluctantly, when all else fails, that more and more persons may be called in. The ideal seems to be to keep the matter as narrow as possible. . . .
>
> What then does one say when asked to keep a matter in confidence? We ought to say, "I am glad to keep confidence in the way that the Bible instructs me. That means, of course, I shall never involve others unless God requires me to do so." In other words, we must not promise *absolute* confidentiality, but rather, confidentiality that is consistent with biblical requirements.[12]

This kind of confidentiality, along with all of the other ways by which we show respect, is essential to building a relationship of trust between counselor and counselee.

Involvement Through Sincerity

The kind of relationship a counselor should seek to develop with his counselees can exist only when they know that he is genuine and honest.

Paul described his ministry as "not walking in craftiness . . . but by the manifestation of truth commending ourselves to every man's conscience in the sight of God" (2 Cor. 4:2). Concerning this verse, Hughes has written,

> So far from being marked by subterfuge, self-interest, and deceit, however, Paul's ministry was one in which the truth was manifested, openly displayed, outspokenly proclaimed (cf. 3:12f.), in such a manner that none could gainsay the genuineness and sincerity of his motives.[13]

The counselor must be like Paul in his counseling, having no hidden agendas or disguised motives but openly revealing the truth about who he is (and even what he is thinking) to those he seeks to help.[14] Only then will they be able to trust him through the process.

What are some areas in which he can show his sincerity and practice honesty in counseling? Scripture indicates that he can do so in the following ways.

Be honest about your qualifications. It is easy for a counselor to misrepresent his credentials to counselees in an attempt to gain their respect and confidence. His goal might be legitimate, but the method is not. Even the great counselor Paul, who had every right to throw around his title of "apostle," more often referred to himself as merely "a servant of Christ" (Rom. 1:1; Phil. 1:1; Titus 1:1; etc.). The counselor should follow this humble example and represent himself in the same way to his counselees. Certainly he must never exaggerate or otherwise deceive them about his qualifications. A relationship of trust will be highly unlikely if they find out that he has lied to them!

Be honest about your own weaknesses. Openness about his own personal problems and struggles is an effective way of showing others that a counselor is sincere. Paul told the Corinthians, "When I came to you, brethren, I did not come with superiority of speech or of wisdom, . . . I was with you in weakness and in fear and in much trembling" (1 Cor. 2:1–3). He did not present himself as somebody who always had it all together. He was honest about the fact that he had weaknesses and fears. When he wrote to the Corinthians again, he told them that during a time of affliction he and Timothy had been "burdened excessively, beyond our strength, so that we despaired even of life" (2 Cor. 1:8).

That was the man who said in 1 Corinthians 10:13 that God would never allow Christians to be tempted beyond what they are able to bear. Yet, to the same people he admitted to an experience of being so burdened that he did not think he could take it anymore. This is another reason Paul was such a great counselor: he was able to proclaim the truth firmly without leaving people under the impression that he was perfect or unable to relate to their failings (cf. Rom. 7:14–25).

A counselor needs to be careful that his self-disclosure is not inappropriate in nature or in duration. He does not want to make his counselees think that he needs counseling more than they do, nor should he spend an inordinate amount of time talking about his problems when they came to receive help for theirs. But an appropriate openness about himself is very helpful in showing sincerity and thus establishing involvement. And whatever he does, he must never pretend to be something he is not.

Be honest about your goals and agenda. Generally speaking, it is advisable and fitting for a counselor to let counselees know—prudently—from the beginning what he is trying to do and how he intends to do it. He should be up front about his counseling method and standard. He should commend himself to them by being sincere and open. He should not play games with them. He should make clear that God and the Bible are the sources of his authority. He can also let them know that he counsels thus because he is convinced that God's way of describing problems, identifying their causes, and solving them is really superior to any other way.

Occasionally, people come to this writer wanting their problems to be labeled, interpreted, and solved psychologically. His frequent answer to them is something like this:

> I want to serve and help you, and I'm firmly convinced that the best way to do that is God's way. I am resolutely committed to the Scriptures as my sole authority because I believe that God knows far better what our problems really are, why we have them, and what to do about them than anyone else. So, because I'm a Christian who is convinced that God's way of understanding and

dealing with problems is far superior to any other way, and because I want to give you the best help available, my method will be based on Scripture. If you want any different approach, you'll have to secure another counselor. For the Lord's sake and for yours, I can't approach it any other way. [This, of course, is a condensed version of what might involve a considerable amount of time to develop and explain, but it does contain the bare bones of this writer's response to people who are enamored of psychology.]

Over the years, this response has brought appreciation for the counselor's honesty, and the counselees have stayed for help. From the very start they would see that he was going to be honest with them, and that openness did not destroy the necessary relationship; rather, it enhanced it.

A biblical counselor must never follow the example of many non-Christian therapists, who hide their true intentions and play games with people to get them to change. About Haley, one such therapist, Foley has written,

> A third tactic [of Haley's counseling approach] is the encouraging of usual behavior. In this case resistance to the advice can only result in change. For instance, asking a domineering woman to take charge of the family will often highlight her interaction and result in her wanting to recede more into the background. What is important in Haley's approach is the question of control. If the therapist tells the domineering woman to lead, she is no longer leading but following the instructions of the therapist. . . . Like Zen Master the therapist induces change in the client by the use of paradox.[15]

Any kind of such "reverse psychology" is unacceptable for the biblical counselor. It will only create barriers to his desired involvement with the counselee.

Be honest about your limitations as a counselor. When a counselor makes mistakes or has difficulty knowing how to proceed in a particular case, he should admit that fact. Paul told the Galatians that he was "perplexed" about them (Gal. 4:20; cf. 2 Cor. 4:8). Also, he writes, "I am afraid that when I come again my God will humiliate me before you" (2 Cor. 12:21). Now that's being honest! Paul knew and admitted that he was fallible as a minister, an admission that revealed his sincerity and enabled people to trust him.

What role does establishing a facilitative relationship with a counselee play in the counseling process? Scripture underscores its crucial place by exhortation and example. Furthermore, what Scripture teaches, counseling experience illustrates. Following is one counselee's evaluation of some of the factors that she considered to be most helpful in her counseling experience.

> For me the content of the counseling in many ways was secondary. Often it was who the counselor was that laid the foundation for whether I could trust, accept, and do what was presented during the counseling. Admittedly, though, the two cannot be separated. If the counseling is not adequate then whoever the counselor is will not make a difference. But the one has had such an impact on me that I'd like to speak to the issue of the counselor first and probably most, but not to negate nor lessen the importance of the counseling.
>
> It was a big step for me to be under the tutelage of a male. My relationships with both men and women have been so bad that I didn't trust anyone, although it was worse with men than with women. A counselor needs to be trustworthy. For me some of the hardest things in my life did not hit the table until long after I knew my counselor. Much of that was simply that I needed to know that no matter what was happening, he could be trusted. I had many experiences with people who didn't believe me when I told them certain things were happening in my life. I assumed that most people were like that, and feared that they all were. So I did not easily trust anyone. Time was needed and I needed to see that this counselor believed in me. I needed to see that he trusted me. I don't mean to suggest that he never had the right to question the validity of my situation (in fact he did), but I simply needed to see that I was going to be trusted, accepted and believed in.

This also then implies the need for patience, longsuffering, love and respect for the counselee. On one occasion I walked out on the counselor and slipped back down the slide, yet he was patient with me. He hurt with me and even in the midst of my own failings, I sensed the respect from him that helped me start climbing the ladder again. The counselor must not express either verbally or non-verbally the impression that this is just another problem and let's quickly get it solved and move on to more important things or people. My counselor's credibility was built over the long haul—he continued to love when I did not love and tried to run. The counselee is important and this must be conveyed. The problem, whatever it is, is serious simply because it is to the counselee and the counselee needs to know that he or she is being taken seriously.

One counselor I've had seemed to have the answers too available on his cuff. At times he responded too quickly and gave the impression of having a canned approach, and I left feeling that he didn't sense the difficulty that existed and the time needed for rebuilding. Whereas my counselor seemed much more sensitive to my own hurts, and although he didn't hesitate to confront me with hard truths, he did it in ways that I knew without a doubt that he loved and cared for me and my growth in Christ.

One other very big element I needed and looked for was whether or not I was accepted. Even when things would seem to go from bad to worse, did he still accept me? As mentioned earlier, this didn't mean that he condoned everything I had done or still did. It didn't mean that he never rebuked or reproved me or called on me to repent, but it did mean that he did it in a loving and gracious way so that I knew he was my friend and not my enemy. It also meant that my counselor affirmed me when possible—he commended and complimented as well as challenged.

To sum it all up, I would say that the most effective counselors are those who are given to prayer, sensitive, loving, patient, tender, forgiving, trustworthy, giving, compassionate, and they counsel in a way that matches that lifestyle. In a sentence, the most effective counselors are people who know Jesus, reflect Jesus, relate to and counsel people in the way He did.

As that letter illustrates, those who come for counsel are often scrutinizing the counselor to see whether he or she is someone who can be trusted. If the counselor is trustworthy, he can establish and maintain the kind of relationship that will make the counseling a profitable experience for both parties.

Although God sometimes chooses to accomplish His work through unlikely ways and unlikely people, the Bible emphasizes (and the preceding letter illustrates) that God usually changes lives in a situation where a relationship of concern and trust exists between the helper and the one who needs help. Thus, the counselor must do all he can to wrap the content of his counseling in a package of compassion, respect, and honesty.

Endnotes

1. Of benefit would be a lengthy discussion of the necessity of the counselor's involvement *with Christ*. Only when he or she has a vital, intimate relationship with the Lord can counseling be truly effective (cf. Matt. 7:3–5; Acts 4:13; 1 Cor. 11:1). But this essay will discuss primarily the counselor's involvement with the counselee, an involvement that is intended to develop and maintain a facilitative relationship between the two. Ultimately and preeminently, the purpose of that involvement is to enhance the counselee's involvement with Christ. The vertical dimension is what makes biblical counseling different from all other forms of counseling.

2. Adapted from Jay Adams, *The Christian Counselor's Casebook* (Grand Rapids: Zondervan, 1974), 186.

3. The counselor who is guilty of neglecting the relational side of his responsibility lends validity to the criticism that biblical counselors merely "throw out Bible verses" or "shove Scripture down people's throats." As we will see later in this chapter, that kind of "biblical" counseling is patently *not* biblical.

4. A friend of the writer told a story of the time when he had a bad toothache and the dentist he called wanted him to come in for a preliminary appointment so that they could "get to know one another." The friend said that he was not interested in "building a relationship" with the dentist—he just wanted to get rid of the pain in his tooth. What is unnecessary in dentistry, however, is quite necessary in biblical counseling.

5. Clara's sin was of utmost importance and needed attention as the counseling progressed, but the counselor's approach gave Clara the impression that he did not view her husband's sin as a serious matter. That created an immediate wall between them at a time when her husband's hurtful actions so completely dominated her thinking.

6. Of course, the counselor cannot *make* the counselee view him or her as a friend or ally. Some people may be so predisposed against their counselors that nothing can reverse their feeling. Nevertheless, the counselor is responsible to do whatever he can to be the kind of person who deserves respect and trust.

7. Cf. Matthew 14:14; Luke 10:33; 15:20.

8. Not every counselee will respond with the proper respect for the counselor, of course, even when he receives the utmost respect that the counselor has to offer. He might be a person who simply respects no one. The counselor must, nevertheless, exemplify a godly honor for him and trust that God will use his example to convict the counselee of his own pride.

9. Adapted from Gerard Egan, *The Skilled Helper: Model Skills and Methods for Effective Helping* (Monterey: Brooks/Cole, 1986), 76–77.

10. That is why body language is not a light issue. Over the years, the writer has observed many physical habits of counselors—from foot-tapping to slouching to constant yawning—that have in one way or another seriously hindered their relationships with counselees.

11. Gerald Corey, *Theory and Practice of Counseling and Psychotherapy* (Monterey: Brooks/Cole, 1977), 179.

12. Jay Adams, *Handbook of Church Discipline* (Grand Rapids: Zondervan, 1986), 30–32. See also George Scipione, "The Limits of Confidentiality in Counseling," *Journal of Pastoral Practice* 7, no. 2 (1984): 29–34.

13. Philip E. Hughes, *Paul's Second Epistle to the Corinthians,* New International Commentary on the New Testament (Grand Rapids: Eerdmans, 1962), 124.

14. This, of course, does not mean that he should tell his counselees everything about himself or volunteer everything he is thinking at any given moment. Nevertheless, a willingness to share his thoughts and experiences with them is a good indicator of the godliness of his attitudes toward them, toward himself, and toward God. Reluctance to be open and transparent when appropriate and helpful might indicate pride and a fear of man that is unworthy of a Christian, especially a Christian counselor.

15. Vincent D. Foley, *An Introduction to Family Therapy* (New York: Grune & Stratton, 1974), 84–85.

CHAPTER ELEVEN

The Dynamics of Small-Church Ministry

John M. Koessler

Small churches in the United States and Canada are a large proportion of the total number of churches and therefore deserve closer attention. A small church's perception of itself is good in that it helps maintain a family atmosphere, but it can lend itself to pessimism in both pastor and people. Lay influence tends to be greater in a small church, a feature that can be cultivated to advantage through wise leadership. A small-church pastor must accept his administrative responsibilities as well as his relational ones. He must know how to involve his people and impart his vision to them. Small churches that want to grow must ask themselves several probing questions to succeed in doing so. Service in a small church can be very rewarding.

John Koessler has pastored Valley Chapel Bible Church in Green Valley, Illinois, and presently teaches Pastoral Studies at Moody Bible Institute. His struggles and victories in the pastorate are chronicled in "Trapped in an Ill-Fitting Church," *Leadership* 13, no. 3 (summer 1992): 118–24. This essay differs somewhat from the usual subject matter of *The Master's Seminary Journal,* but it is included in this volume because of its special value for contemporary church ministry.

* * * * *

Is the small church really necessary? More than half of the Christians who worship in the United States and Canada do so in just one-seventh of the churches in these two countries. In view of this preference for larger churches, one might think that the day of the small church has passed. However, Lyle Schaller, noted analyst of American churches, reports that despite this phenomenon, the majority of churches in North America are small.

> The small church is the normative institutional expression of the worshipping congregation among the Protestant denominations on the North American continent. One fourth of all Protestant congregations on this continent have fewer than thirty-five people in attendance at the principal weekly worship service, and one half average less than seventy-five.[1]

The small church is seemingly a continuing institution in our culture. According to Schaller's statistics, the majority of people entering pastoral ministry will serve a small congregation. Yet, most training programs seem to gear themselves for the larger church.[2] The role models placed before seminary and Bible college students are usually "successful" graduates who serve in larger churches. In some cases, they are pastors of today's megachurches.

Such role models can be inspiring, but the operating principles that have enabled them to succeed in the large church are often inappropriate for their smaller counterparts. As Schaller observes, the small church is *different.* The pastor who wants to succeed in a small context must understand the dynamics of small-church ministry.[3]

Perception Dynamic

Perhaps the most significant human factor affecting the small church's ministry is the congregation's own self-perception. Large churches tend to see themselves as an institution. They often look to the business world for their role models. The pastor's ability to be an administrator is an important gauge of his effectiveness.

In contrast to this "corporation" mentality, a small church is more likely to see itself as a family. Relational skills are valued more highly than business skills.[4] In these churches, the pastor is normally a "father" figure rather than a CEO. This kind of image can pose a problem for pastors whose training has primarily emphasized skills applicable in an office setting such as management and administration. This point is especially true of pastors who serve in small towns and rural communities where the relational dynamic is a community as well as a congregational trait.

Positive Features

The tendency of a small church to operate as a family is the basis for many of its strengths. It naturally produces a sense of intimacy that larger churches must make a special effort to achieve, usually through the use of special interest groups. A small church enjoys a more easily achieved advantage over a large church in this area. In his study of a hundred successful churches, Salter observed that those people who were part of a large congregation were often anonymous and unaccountable. He contrasted this fact with the experience of the small-town church of a hundred people in which the attender probably feels personally comforted by God's Word and scrutinized by God's people.[5]

Because the small church sees itself as a family, the feeling of personal responsibility is more intense among its members. This situation produces a strong sense of ownership for the church's ministries. This sense of responsibility, combined with the lack of resources and the short tenure of many small-church pastors, results in a high degree of lay involvement.

Negative Features

Smallness has disadvantages, however. In a small church, the tendency to equate size with success and to view size as a measure of potential effectiveness often produces an inferiority complex that can affect both the pastor and the congregation. Because it is overly sensitive to its resource limitations, imposed because of its size, weaknesses rather than strengths tend to shape the congregation's self-evaluation. Churches of this sort are inclined to apologize for their failures instead of celebrating their victories.[6] A pastor's low morale and frequent changes in the pastoral staff aggravate these feelings of inferiority.[7]

Another hidden disadvantage of the small church's family orientation is the difficulty it poses for the assimilation of new members. Small congregations are closely knit. Their members are not only part of the same church but also frequently belong to the same extended, physically related family. New attenders might feel that the only way to gain acceptance is to marry into one of the family clans.

These ties can produce a subtle bias that causes a small church to sabotage its own growth. Members sometimes feel threatened as they watch the congregation's size increase. As a result, they become suspicious of the motives of newcomers. Their frustration increases as attendance expands because the church seems less familiar than before.[8] A pastor, especially one fresh from seminary, who encounters this mentality and who has not yet had his idealism tempered by reality, reacts with outrage when he realizes that he and his congregation are actually working at cross-purposes. He prays and struggles to see his church increase numerically, but the church's members attempt to maintain the *status quo* or even decrease the size of their congregation.

This frustration can enlarge through a pastor's own hidden (or not-so-hidden) agenda. Regardless of whether the pastor is willing to admit it, his calling is also a career the course of which can be determined by the performance of the church he serves. As Walrath has observed, "The favored pastoral career track leads through small congregations to a goal in larger congregations: bigger is better."[9] When the time comes for a change in ministry, a solid increase in attendance generally opens the door for advancement to "senior pastor" status in a multiple-staff church.

No doubt, the pastor's frustration with the congregation springs from a genuine fear that the church's parochialism will hinder the Great Commission. However, the threat that this exclusive mentality poses to his career also contributes to his feeling of futility.

Ironically, when the congregation reacts thus to newcomers, it does so in the belief that its behavior is in the best interests of the church. An awareness that their pastor regards their behavior as subversive to the spread of the gospel would shock and offend the members. Their ambivalence, or even opposition, toward the church's growth stems from their concern that the new members do not share the same common history as the long-term members of the church.

When these newcomers, one of whom is often the pastor, fail to respect the past and the authority of the patriarchal families, the "old timers" perceive a threat to the very essence of the church. In a sense, this is a threat to "family" solidarity. They conclude, perhaps with good reason, that before long the church as they have known it will cease to exist.

Often, the pastor mistakenly decides that the problem with the "old guard" is that they do not care about Christ or the church. In reality, the opposite is sometimes true. Their resistance, however misguided it may be, is an outgrowth of their genuine love for the church and a reflection of their investment in it. They were around when the pastor arrived, and chances are good that they will remain when he moves on.

The pastor is probably correct in his assumption that the church must move away from the past if it is to grow. But it is unlikely that he will be able to make any headway until he first affirms that past. When long-time members see that he is willing to acknowledge the investment they have made and guard their history, they will probably be ready to set their sights on the future.

Leadership Dynamic

Not only is the small church's self-perception different from that of a large congregation but also the dynamics of leadership are different. In many large congregations, leadership tends to be vested in the pastoral staff. In some cases, one is tempted to use the word *authoritarian* to describe them.

For the most part, this approach to leadership is based erroneously on pragmatic considerations rather than correctly on theological principles. This situation can be especially true of the megachurch. A congregation that numbers ten to twelve thousand makes governing by a small board very challenging and actual congregational involvement almost impossible. The strong leadership style of many megachurch pastors may also reflect the important role that their personalities have played in the development of these churches. A church that is largely the result of the vision and energy of one man is going to listen carefully when that man speaks.

Lay Involvement

Certainly, it is possible to find small churches where the primary leadership power resides in the pastor. In general, however, small congregations tend to reflect a higher degree of lay influence. This tradition is largely the result of the shortage of qualified pastors available to the small church.

Lyle Schaller explains:

> In thousands of small congregations there are no seminary-trained and ordained ministers on the scene. Even in those small-membership churches served by a seminary trained minister, the pastor usually has less influence in charting the course than is true in large congregations.[10]

One of the prerequisites for pastoral success in the small congregation is the ability to accept the reality of lay leadership and work effectively with the influences that reside in the congregation. The effective pastor, however, must also learn to be sensitive to the church's changing expectations regarding his role. This can be complicated because these expectations change with both the size of the church and the individual leadership situation.[11]

Small churches numbering under 100 value the personal and relational aspects of pastoral ministry. In churches that average between 100 and 200 the focus is on individual leadership characteristics. In large congregations, the emphasis is placed upon organizational leadership.[12] Even within small congregations, one finds a range of expectations regarding pastoral leadership. Schaller has divided small churches into three basic organizational types.

1. The fellowship of less than thirty-five or forty that uses an informal decision-making process akin to that of the small group. In the fellowship, the individual member's voice is going to carry as much weight as the pastor's, if there is a pastor!
2. The congregation, averaging from thirty-five to ninety that uses standing committees and more congregational involvement in its decision making. Churches of this size expect the pastor to be

more of an initiator than those that could be regarded as a "fellowship."

3. The larger or mid-sized congregation that averages from 85 to 150 the government of which is more representative. Churches of this size expect the pastor to be an initiating leader and an administrator.[13] Notice that some overlap occurs in these designations. Whether a church falls into the category of a fellowship, small, or mid-sized congregation depends upon a combination of factors. A good example of this is seen in Steve Burt's description of two churches, both with a congregation of eighty to ninety people and engaged in similar activities, but whose self perception was radically different. One church described itself as a "mid-sized church with a variety of programs." The other described itself as "just a small church."[14] A major contributing factor will be the leadership style employed by the pastor.

Interestingly, these differing values not only reflect the increasing organizational complexity of the developing church but also seem to mirror the corresponding distance that arises in the relationship between the pastor and the congregation as the church grows.

Administrative Demands

The pastor's role is further complicated by leadership demands that are placed upon him but that might not be a part of the congregation's normal expectation. Despite the fact that small churches value relational skills over administrative skills, the pastor is still required to do the work of administration. Regardless of whether the small congregation views the pastor as a CEO, he is nevertheless required to function as one. Indeed, the ability to balance congregational involvement with strong pastoral leadership skills may be the key ingredient for success in the small church.

The leadership demands placed upon the pastor not only shift as the size of the church increases but also change with the age of the church. In the early stages of the church's development, the entrepreneurial pastor is likely to be the most effective. As the church matures, however, more complex managerial skills are needed, and the pastor's leadership function becomes more maintenance oriented.

This change can create conflict for the pastor whose primary area of leadership strength does not correspond to the church's current need. At this stage, he can choose either to further develop his own skills in the needed area, compensate through effective delegation, or limit the church's development. In some cases, this might be the point at which a pastoral change will take place.

Balancing Personal and Flock Involvement

Successful leadership in the small church is multidimensional. It is made up of two components that, on the surface, would seem to be in conflict with each other: strong pastoral leadership and strong lay leadership. Strong pastoral leadership is needed for casting vision and providing the kind of direction that will help the church steer clear of those innate tendencies that threaten to stifle its growth and development. The right to exercise such leadership is earned.

Strong lay leadership is equally important. Although the small congregation might not be capable of being a "full service church," motivated and active members can provide a surprising number of highly effective ministries. And although the small congregation naturally tends to foster lay leadership, the pastor also plays a critical role.

The pastor who wishes to achieve the highest degree of lay involvement must recognize that effective lay leadership is a matter of empowerment rather than employment.

Steve Burt observes,

> Too many pastors, in their eagerness to bring in the kingdom fast, act like donkey owners, treating their volunteers like dumb asses who refuse to move instead of treating them like the pearls of great price that they really are.[15]

As a pastor, I must ask myself why I want people to be involved in the ministries of the church. There are two possible motivations. One is utilitarian: Their involvement will enable me to accomplish my ministry goals. When the issue is viewed from this perspective, people become the tools the pastor uses to help the church and further his own ministry. In this model, lay leaders serve the pastor. Understandably, members who feel that they are being used thus are often reluctant to cooperate.

A better motivation is one that springs from a desire to see others find complete fulfillment in Christ by helping them develop their full potential. In this model, the pastor serves the lay leaders. Lay leaders who are fortunate enough to be part of a congregation that employs this model are more likely to enjoy their ministry because the church's programs are designed to match their unique gifts and interests. They feel valued because they perceive that the church has a genuine concern for their welfare. The overall quality of ministry is more likely to improve because the church's programs are driven by the interests of those who serve in them. Jesus' observation regarding the Sabbath is equally appropriate for the ministries of the church: Programs were made for people, not people for programs.

Vision

It is also important to recognize that effective lay ministry grows out of a sense of congregational need. The pastor's function as one who casts vision must be balanced with a sensitivity to the congregation's perception of its own needs. The pastor often anticipates a field of ministry that is much broader than that perceived by the congregation. This difference is due partially to the fact that most members view the church as a place to be served rather than to serve.[16] They believe that the church's primary responsibility should be to minister to the needs of its own.

Because of this perception, the thinking of the average member tends to be rooted in the present. The leadership role of the pastor, on the other hand, requires that his thinking be focused on the future. At times, this difference in orientation produces conflicting views of what the church's goals and objectives should be. The pastor, for example, may think that the church's resources would be most strategically used in fostering the strength of the youth ministry because he anticipates that an increasing number of teens will come into the church program in the years ahead. The congregation, however, may think that those same resources would be better used to renovate the kitchen because they are currently being inconvenienced by its inadequate facilities.[17] This difference in priorities does not necessarily mean that the congregation is unconcerned about the youth. It is simply a reflection of their "present-minded" orientation. Congregational priorities are likely to change once the current population of children ages and members become aware of the stress placed upon the church's programs. While such short-term thinking is understandable, it is also dangerous because it can limit the church to a maintenance ministry, or it can force a church to base decisions on selfish priorities rather than spiritual priorities.

Perceived needs must be affirmed and balanced with goals that reflect both the developing needs of the church and its broader responsibility to the community at large and to God's Word. A vision statement can be an effective means of accomplishing this.

George Barna recommends that the church's vision statement be limited to a short paragraph and satisfy at least three key requirements. First, it must identify the type of people to whom the church has been called to minister. Second, it must clarify what the church hopes to accomplish through its ministry to this target group. Third, it should identify the distinctives of the church that have defined its particular ministry niche.[18] Once the church's mission has been defined and articulated, it should be regularly restated to the congregation.

Growth Dynamic

Perhaps the greatest challenge facing the small church is that of growth. Congregational growth is not automatic. It is affected by a complex set of factors, not all of which the church can control. Small congregations that are committed to church growth would do well to ask themselves three key questions.

(1) *Why are we small?* Given the preference that worshipers seem to have for larger churches, the fact that the majority of congregations in North America are small is somewhat surprising. One can only conclude that when a church is small, there is a good reason for it. William E. Ramsden identifies three types of small churches: those that have always been small, those that are new and are on their way to becoming larger, and those that were larger but have decreased in size.[19]

It is not enough for a large church that has shrunk to take into account the dynamics inherent in its smaller size that now hinder its growth. It must also identify and address the elements that originally contributed to the church's decline.

For the new church on its way to becoming larger, the issue of size is primarily an organizational question, especially if it is located in a community that is experiencing population growth. People are more easily attracted to new churches than to those that are already established.[20] The challenge before the new church is to design its organizational structure in a way that prepares for future growth.

The church that has always been small faces the most difficult challenge of the three. The shrinking church wants to be larger. The new church expects to be larger. But the church that has always been small, in the vast majority of cases, falls into that category because it prefers to be small.

(2) *Do we really want to grow?* The longstanding small church must wrestle with this question for a couple of reasons: first, because members must change the attitudes and practices that have kept them from growing in the past, and second, because it needs to work through the implications that growth will have for the church. Lyle Schaller explains:

> Planning to move up off a plateau in size, especially in congregations averaging fewer than 160 at worship, usually is extremely difficult. One reason is growth usually means attempting to bring strangers into a small, intimate, and warm fellowship that is reinforced by longstanding kinship and/or friendship ties. A second reason it is difficult is that substantial growth usually requires changing the basic organizing principle from a network of one-to-one relationships with the pastor at or near the hub of that network to a network of groups, organizations, classes, cells, choirs, and circles and/or to a larger and more complex program.[21]

Schaller adds that moving off a plateau in size is especially difficult because people naturally prefer the *status quo*. In other words, if the small church succeeds in growing, it will lose those characteristics that attracted its members to it in the first place. They love the church precisely *because* it is small.

Despite this preference, the small congregation still has an obligation to seek growth—not because bigger is better but because it is heir to Christ's calling to "seek and to save that which was lost." Evangelism is central to every church's mission regardless of size.

(3) *What must we do to grow?* It is possible for the small church to experience growth. But first the church must develop a strategy that is based on its own unique gifts and tailored to the needs of the community.

One of the reasons people prefer larger churches is that they are capable of offering an array of services. The small church cannot afford such a luxury. If it is to be effective, it must carefully choose its ministries.

George Barna has observed that this strategy is a common feature of growing churches:

> Despite the urge to be all things to all people, the successful churches resisted that impulse to be the answer to everyone's every problem by focusing their vision for ministry, by reaffirming their commitment to quality, and by recognizing their limitations. If they were to devote themselves to meeting every need in their marketplace, they would dissipate their resources and have no impact—the very tragedy that has befallen the majority of Protestant churches in America. In general, these growing congregations refused to be enticed into areas of ministry in which they discerned no special calling. Instead, they concentrated on doing what they knew, beyond a doubt, they were called to do.[22]

The smaller church is especially well positioned to practice this principle. Unfortunately, many churches, both large and small, seem to develop their ministries by default. Programs are developed haphazardly, without first asking if the church has the resources to staff them or whether they are merited by the needs of the community or even called for by Scripture. In many cases, the successful programs of other churches are copied in the hope that "if it worked for them, it will work for us." This attitude often results in a futile attempt to act like a big church.

Specialization has long been recognized as an effective strategy by the business world. It has been the key to success for many small businesses that fill a "niche" left by other larger companies against whom they would otherwise be unable to compete.

Some people might object that such an analogy is inappropriate, arguing that churches ought to cooperate rather than compete. This view is a noble sentiment. However, the blunt reality is that most churches are already competing for the same pool of worshipers.[23] Most church growth comes from new members who transfer in from other congregations rather than as a result of conversion. A niche approach to ministry that is sensitive to the needs of the unchurched can increase the likelihood of reaching prospective worshipers who lie outside the pool of those who are merely being shifted from one church to another.

A niche approach to ministry can also be a tremendous boost to the small church. It demonstrates that a place truly exists for the small congregation that cannot be filled by its larger neighbors. When the small congregation becomes a specialist in ministry, it discovers that a small church can actually do some things better than a large church can.

Such an approach requires a dual focus. First, the church must look *inward* to discover its area of primary strength. This task can be done formally by means of congregational surveys and spiritual gift inventories. Or it can be done more informally by looking at the ministries that the church already has in place. One or two programs will usually stand out above the others, and these ought to be seriously considered as possible areas of specialized ministry.

Second, the church must look *outward* to identify an appropriate target group. Lyle Schaller recommends that the church that is contemplating a specialized ministry ask itself three questions: Who are the people in this general community who are overlooked by the churches? What are their spiritual needs? To which of these needs could we respond if we decided to make the effort?[24]

These questions can be supplemented by demographic information that addresses the following questions: Who lives in our community? How does the demographic profile of this community compare to the makeup of our church? What is the typical lifestyle of the target group we are trying to reach?

Much of this information can be obtained from the latest census report, usually available at the public library. Lifestyle demographics can be culled from observational trips through the community, church-sponsored or professional surveys, and the local newspaper. The local chamber of commerce is often a helpful resource for collecting demographic information.

There is really nothing new about a niche-based ministry. Most churches expect missionaries to employ this strategy as a matter of course. If mission organizations approached their task as inefficiently as does the typical local church, would we continue to support them? So the small church should subject itself to the same kind of accountability.

The Bottom Line

Small-church ministry is not easy, but it does have its rewards. This fact is poignantly illustrated by Walter L. Cook's account of his conversation with a pastor who had served the same small church in rural Maine for eight years:

> He told me he plans to stay even longer, "When I look at the same faces in the congregation each Sunday and often during the week, too, I never fail to find something new in them. It's really more exciting to stay than to travel up from church to church trying to get to the top."[25]

Reflecting on his contentment and the unique privilege of serving a church whose members are closely knit and highly involved, Cook observes, "Maybe he *has* arrived at the top."

Endnotes

1. Lyle Schaller, *The Small Church Is Different* (Nashville: Abingdon, 1982), 11. The definition of *small* is a matter of disagreement. Some people identify a small church by its attendance. In the 1960s, for example, the New York State Council of Churches attempted to establish a numerical minimum as a mark of congregational viability. Another approach has tried to identify the small church in terms of the number of pastors who serve the church; a small church is one served by a single pastor. For the purposes of this essay, *small* is defined in terms of certain shared characteristics that affect the church's identity, leadership dynamics, and patterns of growth or nongrowth. See Anthony G. Pappas, "Let's Talk SMALL," *American Baptist Quarterly* 9, no. 2 (June 1990): 87–90.
2. Editor's Note: Although The Master's Seminary is on the campus of Grace

Community Church, which usually ministers to more than eight thousand people each Sunday, TMS is one of the few seminaries in America to devote an entire course to "Pastoring the Small Church."

3. The differing dynamics in a small church should not obscure the broader consideration that the biblical principles according to which Christ has built and continues to build His church (Matt. 16:18) have not changed with time and remain equally applicable to both small and large churches. This essay will focus on the dynamics of the small church, but the writer presupposes that these foundational principles apply here as they do in larger churches. For a good summary of the principles, see John F. MacArthur Jr., *The Master's Plan for the Church* (Chicago: Moody, 1991).

4. Schaller, *Small Church Is Different*, 25.

5. Darius Salter, *What Really Matters in Ministry* (Grand Rapids: Baker, 1990), 114. Yet, this potential in a small church is not always realized. This writer has observed that an increased awareness of the intimate details of the lives of those who attend the small church may actually keep its members from holding one another accountable. This is especially true in a small town, where social pressure sometimes leads to a pattern of denial when serious problems arise. For example, leaders may sometimes be less willing to exercise church discipline when it is warranted, fearing that other members will take offense and leave the church.

6. Cf. Gary Harrison, "The Making of a Good Little Church," *Leadership* 7, no. 3 (summer 1986): 92–93, has written, "In smaller churches, I have observed what I call the 'attitudes vs. abilities' factor. Organizations that work with churches often offer resources to sharpen leaders' skill levels. Such resources, of course, are both good and needed. Rarely, however, do they address the self-image of the church. It is often that deficient attitude, not the lack of skills, that hinders a small church's development." In reality, it would be better to ask, "What does Christ think of our church?" Contemporary applications of His seven messages to first-century churches in Revelation 2–3 help answer this significant inquiry.

7. Schaller, *Small Church Is Different*, 60.

8. Loren Seibold, "Stretching Your Small-Town Church," *Leadership* 10, no. 3 (spring 1989): 109.

9. Douglas Alan Walrath, "Help for Small Churches," *The Christian Ministry* 14, no. 3 (May 1983): 15.

10. Schaller, *Small Church Is Different*, 28.

11. The situational leadership theory of Blanchard and Hersey points out that the most effective leadership style depends upon a combination of factors that include both the motivation and the task readiness of those for whom the leader is responsible (Paul Hersey and Kenneth H. Blanchard, *Management of Organizational Behavior* [Englewood Cliffs: Simon & Schuster, 1988]). This view applies to only those opportunities that fall outside well-defined biblical mandates or direction.

12. Lyle Schaller, "What Does Your Pastor Do Best?" *The Christian Ministry* 15, no. 2 (March 1984): 13.

13. Schaller, *Small Church Is Different,* 161–63.
14. Steve Burt, *Activating Leadership in the Small Church* (Valley Forge: Judson, 1988), 46.
15. Ibid.
16. A 1991 survey by the Barna Research Group revealed that 15 percent of the adults questioned who described themselves as Christians were also involved in the teaching ministry of the church. Nineteen percent of those surveyed were in positions of leadership. While these percentages are surprisingly high, they still reflect what might be described as a consumer mentality among believers. In the average church, a minority does a majority of the work. See George Barna, *What America Believes* (Ventura: Regal, 1991), 261.
17. The ministry goals of the pastor may also be affected by community needs that are not immediately felt by the congregation. For example, if the congregation is aging, the pastor's desire for a ministry to teens may have been prompted by his awareness that there are a large number of troubled youth in the community.
18. George Barna, *Without a Vision the People Perish* (Glendale: Barna Research Group, 1991), 130.
19. William E. Ramsden, "Small Church Studies: Emerging Consensus," *The Christian Ministry* 14, no. 3 (May 1983): 10.
20. Schaller, *Small Church Is Different,* 129. This fact is probably not because people are attracted by the fact that the church is new so much as because such churches are by nature more inclusive than longstanding congregations. New churches are actively seeking worshipers and have not yet become a closed society. As the church becomes cohesive and develops a sense of its own congregational identity, openness will no longer come so naturally to it.
21. Lyle Schaller, *Create Your Own Future* (Nashville: Abingdon, 1991), 73.
22. George Barna, *User Friendly Churches* (Ventura: Regal, 1991), 51–52. This concept does not bypass the sovereign work of God's Spirit in the church but rather depends on it.
23. George Barna observes that although the number of churches has grown in the past two decades, the number of worshipers has remained the same: "Since 1970 there has been no appreciable change in the proportion of adults who attend church services at any time during the week. This is true in spite of a growing number of churches, increased church spending for advertising and promotion, and the availability of more sophisticated techniques for informing people of a church's existence" (*Marketing the Church: What They Never Taught You About Church Growth* [Colorado Springs: Navpress, 1988], 22).
24. Schaller, *Small Church Is Different,* 74.
25. Walter L. Cook, *Send Us a Minister . . . Any Minister Will Do* (Rockland, Maine: Courier-Gazette, 1978), 80–81.

CHAPTER TWELVE

The Modeling of Ministers

George J. Zemek

An often-neglected part of leading a local church is the element of providing an exemplary lifestyle for the flock to follow. Modeling has its origin in the creation of man in God's image, but through the fall and new creation of man in Christ, it has assumed a renewed importance. NT usage of the tupos ("type") and mimētēs ("imitator") word-groups provides a good idea of the responsibility of church leaders to live as godly examples before those whom they lead. Only when they do so can pastors fulfill the biblical standards of their office.

This essay appeared in *TMSJ* 4, no. 2 (fall 1993): 165–85.

* * * * *

Reportedly, a pastor once said, "Do as I say, but don't do as I do." This frank admission has unfortunately characterized many past and present preachers, many of whom have reputations as great teachers of God's Word. However, when measured by the Bible's qualifications for both communication *and character,* such "ministers" come up woefully short.

Saying-but-not-doing in its multiplied forms and settings has always been particularly detestable in the eyes of the Lord. Jesus spoke to the crowd about the scribes and Pharisees, telling them to follow their instructions from Moses but not to follow their personal example because "they keep on saying and yet are not doing" (Matt. 23:3, note Greek present tenses). His indictment ultimately embraced a whole lineage of dark hypocritical examples throughout fallen mankind's history.

All men are accountable to God for profession without practice (e.g., James 1:22–27); yet certain men, by virtue of their pastoral office, are responsible at the highest level of divine accountability for *prescription* without practice (e.g., James 3:1). Therefore, it is no wonder that Paul emphasized to Timothy and Titus God's mandate for both exhortation and exemplification (1 Tim. 4:12–16; Titus 2:7). Similarly, Peter spotlights the *showing* dimension of shepherding in his directives to elders (1 Peter 5:1–4).

The Scriptures on spiritual leadership are intimidating to contemporary ministers of the gospel. How can we who are not yet perfect hold ourselves up as ethical examples? How can we whose practice does not yet match our position say, "Do as I do"? A consideration of the macro- and microtheological contexts on modeling will bring *some* relief from intimidation, but God designs all theological tensions to be constructive. As in the cases of other equally powerful biblical magnets, the poles of this one (i.e., the revealed reality that we are not yet glorified and the inescapably clear mandate for modeling) should develop in us first genuine humility and then a renewed dependence upon God and His resources.

The Macro-Theological Context of Modeling

This context of modeling is exceedingly broad. It entails some of the most panoramic issues of theology, for example, Christ *as* the image of

God, man's *creation* in the image of God, commensurate issues of Adam theology, salvation history with a special emphasis upon moral re-creation in the image and likeness of God, and the ethical significance of the Lord's operations of sovereign grace primarily through His efficient means of the Word and the Spirit.

The Importance of Image

A theological rather than a logical priority is the best starting point. When viewed from a historical perspective, traditional theologies usually begin with the creation of mankind/humanity (i.e., originally Adam, or from a theological vantage point, the "First Adam") "in"/"according to" the "image"/"likeness" of God.[1] However, the theological Archetype, Christ Himself furnishes the better beginning place. Since He is uniquely the effulgence of God's glory and the exact impress of His being or essence (Heb. 1:3), and since He alone perfectly displays the Godhead (John 1:18, cf. 14:9), the Lord *is* the image of the invisible God (Col. 1:15). Consequently, He is one who fully manifests and represents God and who also concretely stands ethically as the ultimate and perfect Exemplar (cf. 1 Cor. 11:1).

Christ is uniquely the image of God, but in a derived sense God "made" or "created" mankind in His own image and likeness (Gen. 1:26–27).[2] Although "the Bible does not define for us the precise content of the original *imago*,"[3] generally it appears to be "cohesive unity of interrelated components that interact with and condition each other."[4] This vague conclusion is exegetically credible, but it does not consider some of the major extrapolations about the *imago Dei*. In the history of systematic theology, three basic views relating to the image of God in man have surfaced: the substantive, the relational, and the functional.[5] Historically, these views relate to analogy of being, analogy of relation, and dominion, respectively.[6] The following brief excerpts from Erickson describe the general characteristic(s) of each camp.

[1] The substantive view has been dominant during most of the history of Christian theology. The common element in the several varieties of this view is that the image is identified as some definite characteristic or quality within the makeup of the hu-

man. . . . [2] Many modern theologians do not conceive of the image of God as something resident within man's nature. Indeed, they do not ordinarily ask what man is, or what sort of a nature he may have. Rather, they think of the image of God as the experience of a relationship. Man is said to be in the image or to display the image when he stands in a particular relationship. In fact, that relationship *is* the image. . . . [3] We come now to a third type of view of the image, which has had quite a long history and has recently enjoyed an increase in popularity. This is the idea that the image is not something present in the makeup of man, nor is it the experiencing of relationship with God or with fellow man. Rather, the image consists in something man does. It is a function which man performs, the most frequently mentioned being the exercise of dominion over the creation.[7]

The basic shortcoming of both the second and third views is that they are the consequences of the *imago Dei*. They are valid functions, but do not answer the apparently ontological implications of key Scripture texts.[8] It is difficult to eliminate some sort of analogy in man's image-bearing. Yet, as historically expressed, problems have plagued the first view, especially in light of the catastrophic effects of the fall of man. Erickson seems to be on the right analogical track when he suggests that "the attributes of God sometimes referred to as communicable attributes constitute the image of God."[9] Indeed, the moral attributes of God constitute a significantly large dimension of His image in man, a fact that is acutely relevant in a consideration of the issue of modeling.

The Retention of the Image: Devastated but Not Destroyed

After one decides to accept the analogy-of-being view, the haunting question remains, "What about the effects of the fall?" Once again, the biblicist must endure the poles of another scriptural tension. On the one hand,

. . . the fall of man was a catastrophic personality shock; it fractured human existence with a devastating fault. Ever since, man's worship and contemplation of the living God have been broken,

his devotion to the divine will shattered. Man's revolt against
God therefore affects his entire being. . . . His revolt against
God is at the same time a revolt against truth and the good.[10]

On the other hand, "there is some sense in which the image of God
must persist even in fallen man."[11] The *potential* for the communication
and sovereign application of the Word of grace, a restored relationship,
and moral renovation remains. Avoiding endless pursuits through logical labyrinths, Kidner wisely makes the soteriological transition with
his brief synopsis: "After the Fall, man is still said to be in God's image
(Gen. 9:6) and likeness (Jas. 3:9); nonetheless he requires to be 'renewed
. . . after the image of him that created him' (Col. 3:10; cf. Eph. 4:24)."[12]

The Re-Creation of Image

By original creation, man bore the image of God, including its
significantly moral dimension. His fall[13] radically perverted the whole
image, so much so that no hope for any kind of self-reformation remained.
Yet, the Word of God says that the image and likeness continue even
with man in this horrible condition. By God's grace, men redeemed in
Christ have embarked on an upward and onward journey of moral
restoration (cf. 2 Peter 3:18). Their destination is moral perfection—
Christlikeness. Consequently, the overarching challenge to all genuine
disciples is still "Be ye holy, for I am holy" (Lev. 11:44–45, 19:2; 1 Peter
1:16).

The primary means of grace in moving the saved along that highway
of sanctification is the Word of God attested by the Spirit of God, and a
vital constituent of this divine testimony is the incarnate example of
Christ. Indeed, He abides as God's perfect moral manifestation.

The Micro-Theological Context of Modeling

Because of Christ's pattern, the attitude and actions of His people
should mature in integrity and consistency of Christlikeness (cf. Phil.
1:27ff.; 2:5ff.; 1 John 2:6). As they mature morally, some more rapidly
than others, they themselves are to become reflections of His moral model
(cf. 1 Thess. 1:7). Growth should characterize all of His "saints,"[14] but
the NT holds those who are recognized as church leaders especially re-

sponsible to be examples. They are visible and derived moral models for the Exemplar's *ekklēsia* ("church"). This awesome responsibility is the focus of the rest of this study. A semantical background will prepare the way for the rest of the discussion.

The Vocabulary of Modeling

The OT is replete with commands and implicit obligations concerning the holiness of God's people, but it contains no transparent teaching about following the example of God or His chosen leaders.[15] The NT, however, abounds with this concept. As a matter of fact, a whole arsenal of modeling terms surfaces.[16] Of these, the *typos* ("example") and *mimētēs* ("imitator") word-groups are the most important.

In ancient secular Greek, *typos* exhibits the following usage categories: "a. 'what is stamped,' 'mark,' . . . 'impress' . . . 'stamp'" (e.g., of letters engraved in stone, images, or painted images); "b. 'Mould,' 'hollow form' which leaves an impress," . . . and in a transferred sense "ethical 'example'" . . . ; and "c. . . . 'outline,' 'figure'" (i.e., of the stamp or impress).[17] "In the LXX *typos* occurs in only 4 places":[18] for the model or pattern for the tabernacle and its furnishings in Exodus 25:40, for idols or images in Amos 5:26, for the "'wording,' 'text,' of a decree" in 3 Macc. 3:30, and for "(determinative) 'example'" in 4 Macc. 6:19.[19]

In the NT, its full range of semantical usages include,[20]

1. *visible impressions* of a stroke or pressure, *mark, trace* (e.g., John 20:25);
2. *that which is formed, an image or statue* (e.g., Acts 7:43);
3. *form, figure, pattern* (e.g., Rom. 6:17);
4. *(arche)type, pattern, model,* both literally (e.g., Acts 7:44, Heb. 8:5) and ethically as *example, pattern* (e.g., 1 Tim. 4:12, etc.); and
5. in reference to divinely ordained *types,* whether things, events, or persons (e.g., Rom. 5:14).

Of the fourteen occurrences of the noun *typos* in the NT, half relate to modeling, either implicitly as a negative illustration (e.g., the adverb *tupikōs* ["typically"], 1 Cor. 10:6) or explicitly as positive patterns (Phil.

3:17; 1 Thess. 1:7; 2 Thess. 3:9; 1 Tim. 4:12; Titus 2:7; 1 Peter 5:3). Furthermore, one other occurrence has a tangential theological relation:

> In Rom. 6:17 [*typos* refers to] the context, the expressions of the doctrine. . . . However, the original meaning of the form which stamps can still be strongly felt. As previously sin, so now the new teaching, i.e. the message of Christ, is the factor which stamps and determines the life of the Christian.[21]

The efficient means of the Word of God is seen here as a press and die that leaves an amazing mark on the people of God.

Although the data relating to modeling are quite conspicuous, contemporary scholarship is reluctant to attribute to the concept a fully ethical significance. For example, Goppelt refuses to allow that a disciple's life is "an example which can be imitated."[22] His emphases on the primacy of the Word of God and the priority of an ultimate reference to faith are commendable, but, as subsequent treatments of the key texts will reveal, the inescapable overtones are patterns from people. Müller in his discussion of this issue is not quite as one sided. For example, he asserts that the crucial texts "are not simply admonitions to a morally exemplary life. . . . The shaping power of a life lived under the Word has in turn an effect on the community (1 Thess. 1:6), causing it to become a formative example."[23] He carefully interrelates the effectual means of the Word with a derived means consisting of ethical examples.

> The *mimētēs* word-group, the source of the English word "mime,"[24] furnishes a rich semantical heritage also. Generally speaking, the word group *mimētēs* etc., . . . arose in the 6th cent. [B.C.], and came into common use in both prose and poetry. *Mimeimai* has the sense "to imitate," "to mimic," i.e. to do what is seen to be done by someone else.[25]

Bauder subclassifies the classical Greek usages as follows:

a. imitate, mimic . . .
b. emulate with joy, follow

    c. in the arts (plays, paintings, sculpture and poetry), represent real-
    ity by imitation, imitate is an artistic way. . . . an actor is there-
    fore a *mimos,* a mimer. . . . A *symmimētēs* (Lat. *imitator*) is an
    imitator, especially a performer or an artist who imitates. When
    used in a derogatory sense, the words refer to quasi-dramatic "ap-
    ing" or feeble copying with lack of originality.[26]

Significantly, from the earliest stages of this group's history in classical Greek, "the words were used to express ethical demands made on
men. One should take as one's model the boldness of a hero, or one
should imitate the good example of one's teacher or parents."[27] Such
imitations are without a revelational norm, but they nevertheless illustrate a *linguistic* background for usage in the NT.

One particular nuance in classical usage deserves special attention.
Of course, Plato is especially fond of its employment in this sense. Bauder
captures the gist of it: "The whole of the lower world of appearances is
only the corresponding, imperfect, visible copy or likeness *(mimēna)* of
the invisible archetype in the higher world of the Ideas."[28] Such thinking
is antibiblical, but in the process of its development among pagan
philosophers, discussions arose about "divine" imitation.[29] Although
Michaelis concludes "that in such statements the *imitatio dei* is not too
closely bound to the cosmological mimesis concept,"[30] this study
concludes that such ancient references "have quite plainly an ethical
thrust,"[31] albeit without revelational norms.

Because "The Vocabulary of Modeling" cited earlier has alluded to
the Jewish usage of this word-group, suffice it to add that two of the four
occurrences in the Apocrypha speak of emulating heroes of the faith in
martyrdom[32] and that in subsequent history

    . . . the Rabbis were the first to speak of imitation of God in the
    sense of developing the image of God in men. In the
    Pseudepigrapha in addition to the exhortation to imitate men of
    outstanding character . . . one can also find the thought of the
    imitation of God (i.e. keeping his commands . . .) and of par-
    ticular characteristics of God.[33]

Again, apart from any accretions, eccentricities, perversions, etc., in these materials, such usages are a linguistic link in the conceptual chain culminated in the corpus of the NT teachings.

Bauder's breakdown of the word-group is succinct and accurate: "In the NT *mimeomai* is found only 4 times (2 Thess. 3:7, 9; Heb. 13:7; 3 Jn. 11); *mimētēs* 6 times (1 Cor. 4:16; 11:1; Eph. 5:1; 1 Thess. 1:6; 2:14; Heb. 6:12); and *symmimētēs* only once in Phil. 3:17."[34] The deponent middle verb meaning "imitate, emulate, follow" occurs with accusatives of person, and the uncompounded noun form *mimētēs* ("imitator") occurs either with a personal referent or with an impersonal genitive.[35] Also, "it is noteworthy that in all its NT occurrences *mimētēs* is joined with *ginesthai,* denoting moral effort."[36] Indeed, a safe assertion is that "all [words in the group] are used with an ethical-imperative aim and are linked with obligation to a specific kind of conduct."[37]

Michaelis opposes this ethical-emulation thrust of the words and reinterprets according to his chosen viewpoint. He bolsters his contention with a few textual observations, especially pertaining to contextual emphases on faith, suffering, persecution, death, industriousness, obedience, etc.[38] All of these contextual colorings have some credibility, but specific applications do not negate the all-embracing ethical perspective of total character and consistent lifestyle. Much more subjective is his discussion built upon a presuppositional foundation of apostolic authority, although nearly all interpreters will empathize with its apparent motivational tension (i.e., how can any finite and fallible person, including Paul, say, "Follow my ethical example"?). Despite this tension, no exegete should forge a few implicit references into a hermeneutical hammer for driving many round texts into square contexts.[39] The ensuing treatment of key passages will document the fact that the NT evidence "cannot be reduced to a demand for personal obedience."[40]

The Vocation of Modeling

The best way to organize key NT texts dealing with modeling is by an essentially theological development.[41] Whether historically noted or ethically urged, the NT data present God's model to His people, show the moral example of the apostolic circle to all of the churches, emphasize the particular area of responsibility in reference to church leaders, and advocate that all Christians be maturing moral models for the spiritual well-being of the whole body. This plan is basically consistent with both the early church's historical development and special gradations of judgment or reward pertaining to church leaders. It does not, however, dictate some sort of ethical "apostolic succession." Essentially an unbreakable chain, it comes full circle, creating a theological necklace that begins and ends with the sovereign grace of God and Christ's moral model.

God: The Ultimate Model for His Church. Ephesians 5:1 instructs the church to "keep on becoming (or being) imitators of God." Michaelis argues that this passage, along with similar passages "does not speak of true imitation of Christ or God."[42] Yet, it is in a setting that begins with an identical imperative (4:32) inculcating reciprocal kindness, tenderness, and forgiveness based on Christ's example. Furthermore, the *kathōs* ("just as") clause, which bridges to the Lord's perfect pattern, assumes analogy and infers emulation. Immediately after 5:1 comes another continuously binding imperative to "keep on walking in love" followed by another indication of Christ as the Exemplar (*peripateite . . . kathōs,* 5:2). Additionally, the simple adverb of comparison *hōs* (5:1b), "*as* beloved children," points to the propriety of ethical emulation by believers.

On a larger scale, this command to imitate God and Christ is part of a larger section about holy living (4:25–6:20). This, in turn, is a subset of the practical half of the epistle (i.e., the "do" section) beginning at 4:1. All of these exhortations are appropriate responses to the sovereign grace of God, that is, the theologically "indicative" section (i.e., the "done" section) of this great epistle (Ephesians 1–3).[43] On yet a grander scale of inclusion is the comprehensive scriptural challenge to be holy because God is holy. From the reversed perspective, the obligation to "be holy for God is holy" receives definitive resolution through the prevalent indicative/imperative presentation of ethical obligation, with a variety of explicit exhortations as elaborations. This is the natural theological setting of moral modeling (e.g., "Be imitators of God as beloved children").

The Derived Apostolic Model in the Church. The designation "apostolic" pertains to the apostolic circle and allows for God's use of both apostles and transition men such as Timothy and Titus in establishing churches during the first century. The latter group were not apostles of Christ, but they were in a special sense apostles of an apostle. For example, they supervised the planting and the solidification of local NT churches. When doing this, they were not technically one of the pastors-teachers-elders-overseers of a given local church or group of regional churches. So this section treats them as mediate models. However, they apparently in their day-to-day ministries worked alongside and functioned similarly to pastoral leaders. Therefore, it is also appropriate to apply the following statements about 1 Timothy 4:12 and Titus 2:7 to the next major division, "The 'Third Generation' Model of Church Leadership."

(1) Modeling Directly

Paul did not shy away from offering himself as an ethical model for believers with whom he had personal contact (e.g., 1 Cor. 4:16; 11:1; Phil. 3:17; 2 Thess. 3:7, 9).[44] Maintaining an accurate theological perspective first requires a treatment of 1 Cor. 11:1 and Philippians 3.

First Corinthians 11:1, "be imitators of me, just as I also am of Christ," is basic to all modeling on the horizontal plane. Paul was not *the* Exemplar; only Christ can be that. However, that fact did not exempt him from the divine responsibility of being a derived moral example. The contextual application of his statement has to do with not becoming an offense because of one's personal freedom in Christ (10:23ff.). He closes his discussion with a command to comply (10:32), holds himself up as an example (10:33), and then picks up that same thread but repeating it with the vocabulary of moral modeling (11:1a). He is careful to add, however, that when they follow his example, they are following the ultimate pattern of Christ (11:1b).[45]

Philippians 3 has raised significant questions about the propriety of human moral example. After Paul urges the following of his own example (3:17), does he not confess his own finiteness and moral fallibility (3:3–16)?[46] Or, in the words of Bauder, "Prior to the demand to imitate him, he deliberately places a confession of his own imperfection (Phil. 3:12)."[47]

He does indeed assert that he has not arrived at moral perfection. "He does not think of himself as the personal embodiment of an ideal which must be imitated,"[48] but this saint in process *does* urge the Philippian church to keep on becoming (or being) fellow-imitators of (or with) him (3:17a).[49] In addition to Paul, others are consistently living (3:17b) according to the pattern (i.e., *typon*) of the apostolic circle.[50] It is wrong to ignore one facet of biblical revelation because of another equally important truth that raises an apparent logical contradiction.

But is it possible to resolve this scriptural tension? As with most other biblical paradoxes, not fully. Nevertheless, several observations will ease the difficulty that it causes for our limited logic. For example, the major portion of this epistle (i.e., 1:27–4:9) has to do with ethical exhortation. From the beginnings of this section the theme of unity through humility, including the preferring of others over self, dominates. But the supremely important example of Christ (2:5–8) undergirds all subsequent moral responsibilities. The Lord is the primary pattern for attitude and actions. Basing his comments directly on that perfect example, Paul challenged the Philippians to progress in their sanctification (2:12), reminding them that the resources for such a holy calling reside with God (2:13). The Philippian disciples were fully responsible but were not adequate in themselves. Interestingly, following this general challenge to holy living, Paul refers to Timothy and Epaphroditus (2:19–30) as others-oriented examples.

To begin chapter 3, he rehearses his pre- and postconversion experiences (3:3–16). These experiences not only compare and contrast the preconversion Paul (esp. vv. 4b–6) and other genuine Christians (3:7ff.) with some externalists in Philippi (e.g., 3:1–2, 18–19) but also compare especially the postconversion experience of Paul with that of all true disciples. Although both Paul and true believers at Philippi were positionally "perfect" in Christ, neither he nor they were perfect experientially. Consequently, his quest, like theirs, should be one of an intensifying pursuit of moral purity. Such a focus, by the grace of God, qualified one to be a reflected model of ethical development. However, the perfect moral mold remains the one who said, "You are to be perfect, as your heavenly Father is perfect" (Matt. 5:48).

This theological perspective sheds light on other Pauline statements. For example, when he writes earlier in 1 Corinthians, "Therefore I urge you to imitate me" (4:16 NIV), he does not disregard Christ as the ultimate example (11:1), nor does he intend to leave the impression that he had arrived. He has already negated any claims to self-sufficiency, especially in his exposé of all human wisdom (chaps. 1–3). In addition, he has built a solid bridge to genuine ministry (chaps. 3–4), largely from prominent personalities as illustrations. That sets the stage in chapter 4 to challenge Corinthian arrogance. By weaving in positive examples, he exposes the heinousness of their pride (4:6ff.). He also mixes in several testimonials to God's ultimacy and sufficiency to His servants (e.g., 3:5–7; 4:1–4). This situation is hardly the context for a Pauline ego trip. Once again, his personal example in 4:16 reflects the pattern of Christ and His grace.

He wrote to the Thessalonian church to encourage them to follow the apostolic example (2 Thess. 3:7, 9). Paul, Silvanus, and Timothy (2 Thess. 1:1) supplied positive examples as a corrective for any believers who were out of line among the Thessalonians *ataktōs* (i.e., "disorderly," 3:6, 11; cf. the verb form in v. 7b), especially in matters of freeloading and meddling. The disciples at Thessalonica recognized "how it was necessary [for them] to imitate *(mimeisthai)* us [the apostolic circle]" (3:7). Paul and his associates offered themselves as a "model" *(typon)* for the members of body there to emulate (3:9).[51]

(2) Mediately Modeling

First Timothy 4:12–16 is an exceedingly important passage regarding moral exemplification. It equals 2 Timothy 4:2 in importance as a qualification for Christian ministry. In fact, it stresses that in importance patterning the Word is a necessary corollary to preaching it, with the former usually preceding the latter.

Furthermore, the whole epistle places a very high priority on character and conduct. The man of God is always accountable in areas of personal and "professional" responsibility. He cannot be faithful just in teaching the truth; he must live the truth. Heralding God's gospel is a highly motivating and worthy call, yet the human instrument must possess certain qualities of integrity (1 Tim. 3:1–7). As with Paul (e.g., 1:12–17), he must accept both responsibilities with a profound sense of humility and in utter dependence upon the One who commissions. Indeed, by the time 1 Timothy closes (e.g., 6:11–16), the young man of God certainly understood the two primary obligations of spiritual leadership.

But chapter 4 is especially cogent. Verses 7b–8 set the tone for verses 12–16 with Paul's command to Timothy to "work out" strenuously (*gymnazō*, "I train, exercise") to develop spiritual muscle for godliness (v. 7b). For all intents and purposes, the many imperatives in verses 12ff. supply the whys and the wherefores of the exhortation to holiness. In 1 Timothy 4:12–16, three waves of commands pound Timothy with his two general responsibilities. The first wave crashes with an overwhelming reminder of his personal responsibility (i.e., v. 12). As it begins to ebb, commands relating to his professional accountability drench him (i.e., vv. 13–14). For most conservative evangelicals, the professional requirements (e.g., v. 13) are an authoritative given. The same applies concerning personal requirements; however, the application of these requirements is far more sensitive personally. The intimidation factor at times seems to be overwhelming. For that reason, the focus of this brief discussion will concentrate on the modeling requirements.

The first command of verse 12 does not directly address the man of God; it addresses those he leads. Indirectly, it implies that he himself must be irreproachable (cf. the first and general qualification of 3:2). The implication of verse 12a finds confirmation in verse 12b. His obligation is one of being an example before members of the flock: He was to "be (or become) a type (or pattern or model) *(typos)* for the believers."[52] Paul typifies the moral example in five areas: in the language (communications) of the man of God, in his general lifestyle,[53] in his *agapē* ("love," i.e., that unselfish, extending, all-giving variety that exudes tenderness, compassion, tolerance, etc.), in his "faith" (or better, "faithfulness, trustworthiness, reliability," the passive meaning of *pistis*), and in his personal purity. Without integrity of life, his pronouncements and preachings, his proclamations and indoctrinations (e.g., vv. 11, 13) are severely limited.

A second wave of commands comes in verse 15 to remind the man of God to concentrate on both his personal (i.e., v. 15a) and professional (i.e., v. 15b) responsibilities[54] so that his advancement might be clearly visible to "all." The concluding purpose clause of verse 15 stresses the importance of Timothy's modeling.[55] His life was to exhibit significant "progress."[56] Therefore, verse 15 not only reiterates his patterning responsibility but also confirms that it is not necessary for ethical models to be absolutely perfect, but they must be growing in holiness.

Two imperatives in verse 16, Paul's third crashing wave, emphasize the same two areas, "yourself" and "your teaching" (cf. vv. 12–14; cf. also Acts 20:28) but in a slightly different way. Putting person before ministry, Paul writes, "Pay close attention" to yourself and to your teaching (v. 16). Calvin summarizes, "Teaching will be of little worth if there is not a corresponding uprightness and holiness of life."[57] Guthrie expresses it, "Moral and spiritual rectitude is an indispensable preliminary to doctrinal orthodoxy."[58] Paul emphasizes even further Timothy's personal and ministerial responsibilities with his closing injunction to "persist (or continue or persevere) in them."

The rationale for these commands is overwhelming: "because as you go on doing *this* [singular pronoun referring to both duties], you will save both yourself and the ones who hear you." Almost unbelievably, personal example is side-by-side with the ministry of God's Word in a salvific context.[59]

Titus 2 has the same message stated more briefly. Following instructions about appointing elders (1:5–9) and combating false teaching (e.g., 1:10–16; cf. 3:9–11) with healthy doctrine (e.g., 2:1, 15; 3:1, 8a), come directions for how Titus is to handle various groups: older men (2:2), older and then younger women (2:3–5), younger men (2:6), slaves (2:9–10), and the whole flock (3:1–8). A major message was the priority of good deeds (cf. 1:16; 2:7, 14; 3:1, 8, 14).

Among the instructions to young men, probably Titus's age group, Paul reminds Titus of his obligation to be a moral model. Preaching alone was not enough (2:6); he must also live before them (2:7). In other words, he must both exhort *and* exemplify. For the man of God, a pattern (i.e., *typon*) of good works is never optional (cf. Eph. 2:10). It is essential to preaching and teaching.

The "Third Generation" Model of Church Leadership

The same thread permeates the epistle to the Hebrews, from the superior model of Jesus Christ, through the faith's hall of fame (chap. 11), into important statements about church leaders (chap. 13).[60] Accountability of church leaders is the subject of 13:17, but 13:7 deals specifically with their modeling responsibility. The writer instructs the recipients, "Remember your leaders, who spoke the word of God to you.

Consider[61] the outcome of their way of life and imitate their faith" (NIV). Examining the result of their lifestyle (i.e., from *anastrophē*) and emulating (present imperative of *mimeomai*) their persevering faith are parallel efforts. Such concrete examples dovetail with the total thrust of the epistle, which is to "keep on keeping on."

Peter's corresponding message addresses the leaders of the church directly. He commands the elders, "Shepherd (or tend or feed) the flock of God among you" (1 Peter 5:2a; cf. John 21:15–17; Acts 20:28). This is the only imperative in the passage, but its obligatory force permeates all of the qualifiers to follow (1 Peter 5:2b–3). Three contrasts highlight motives for spiritual leadership: Spiritual leaders must not serve because of human constraints *but* because of divine commitments (v. 2b), must not minister for unjust profit *but* with spiritual zeal (v. 2c), and must not lead as prideful dictators *but* as humble models (v. 3).[62] NT shepherds have the binding obligation of being an ethical model for the flock of God. The sheep in turn are to emulate their leaders' lives (cf. Heb. 13:7). This requires genuine humility (1 Peter 5:5b–6).

The Model of the Church to the Church

All believers are to be examples for other believers to follow. For example, Paul mentions two instances of this truth. Paul asserts that when the Thessalonians received God's gospel, they did so in a societal setting analogous to that of the Judean churches (i.e., while being persecuted, 1 Thess. 2:14–16). Paul's words, "for you, brethren, became imitators *(mimētai egenēthēte)* of the churches of God in Christ Jesus that are in Judea," provided an incentive to the church to keep on persevering.

Besides being a reflection of the Judean churches (2:14), the Thessalonians in their persecution modeled both the apostolic circle and the Lord Himself and, in turn, became a pattern for believers throughout the regions of Macedonia and Achaia (1:6–7). Michaelis objects to any form of "conscious imitation,"[63] but the subsequent verses not only document their persecution but also mention continuing evidence of their faithfulness (cf. 1:8–10). These vivid exhibitions were a vital element in the pattern displayed before other believers.

Hebrews 6:12 also speaks of modeling. The exemplars here are all "who are inheriting the promises through faith and longsuffering." The writer urges the recipients of this epistle to join their ranks by mimicking conduct.

Michaelis is correct when he says,

> The admonition of 3 Jn. 11: *mē mimou to kakon alla to agathon*, ("do not emulate what is bad but what is good") is general, but it stands in close relation to what precedes and follows. Gaius must not be ensnared by the Diotrephes who is denounced in verse 9f. He should follow the Demetrius who is praised in verse 12.[64] [translation added]

The Scripture never tells believers to imitate an abstraction. As here, the example is always concrete. This passage furnishes both negative and positive patterns.

The preceding discussion has shown that God's people should emulate not only other mature disciples but also the men whom God has given to them as spiritual leaders (cf. Eph. 4:11ff.). In turn, they in accord with testimonies of the apostolic circle, should strive to model Christ, who alone displays the perfect moral image of God. In the NT, the vital link of ethical emulation represented in church leaders is particularly conspicuous. Consequently, rediscovering pastoral ministry according to God's Word requires that today's church leaders not only recognize and teach the priority of moral modeling but also accept its overwhelming challenge personally and, by His grace, live as examples before His sheep and a scrutinizing world that is ready to level the accusation of hypocrisy.

Endnotes

1. Both the Hebrew terms for "image" and "likeness" and the two prepositions used with them function essentially in a synonymous fashion within the context of the early chapters of Genesis. Cf. John F. A. Sawyer, "The Meaning of *běṣelem 'ĕlōhîm* ('In the Image of God') in Genesis I–XI," *Journal of Theological Studies* 25 n.s. (October 1974): 418–26, on a technical level; and John J. Davis, *Paradise to Prison: Studies in Genesis* (Winona Lake: BMH, 1975), 81, on a popular level.
2. The Hebrew is *'āśâ* ("made") in Genesis 1:26 and *bārā'* ("create") in 1:27. Both verbs speak of the creation of humanity in Genesis 5:1–2.

3. Carl F. H. Henry, *God, Revelation and Authority* (Waco: Word, 1976), 2:125. Chapter 10 of this work is particularly worthy of study.

4. Ibid.

5. Millard J. Erickson, *Christian Theology* (Grand Rapids: Baker, 1984), 495–517.

6. G. C. Berkouwer, *Man: The Image of God* (Grand Rapids: Eerdmans, 1962), 67–118.

7. Erickson, *Christian Theology,* 498, 502, 508.

8. Ibid., 510–12.

9. Ibid., 514. He is also right in making a Christological connection: "The character and actions of Jesus will be a particularly helpful guide . . . since he was the perfect example of what human nature is intended to be" (ibid.).

10. Henry, *God, Revelation and Authority,* 2:134–35.

11. Charles M. Horne, "A Biblical Apologetic Methodology" (unpublished Th.D. dissertation; Grace Theological Seminary, Winona Lake, Ind., 1963), 84.

12. Derek Kidner, *Genesis: An Introduction and Commentary* (Downers Grove, Ill.: InterVarsity, 1967), 51; cf. O. Flender, *"eikōn,"* in *New International Dictionary of New Testament Theology,* ed. C. Brown (Grand Rapids: Zondervan, 1971), 2:287–88.

13. For discussions of Adam theology, that is, the "first Adam" as representative of and in solidarity with the whole race and the "Last Adam" as representative of and in solidarity with God's elect, see John Murray's *The Imputation of Adam's Sin* (Grand Rapids: Eerdmans, 1959); idem, *Principles of Conduct: Aspects of Biblical Ethics* (Grand Rapids: Eerdmans, 1957); S. Lewis Johnson Jr., "Romans 5:12—An Exercise in Exegesis and Theology," in *New Dimensions in New Testament Study,* ed. Richard N. Longenecker and Merrill C. Tenney (Grand Rapids: Zondervan, 1974).

14. A profession without practice constitutes a highly culpable state of pretense. For a discussion of progressive sanctification, see O. Procksch, *"hagiosmos,"* in *Theological Dictionary of the New Testament,* ed. G. Kittel and G. Friedrich, trans. G. W. Bromiley (Grand Rapids: Eerdmans, 1972), 1:113; and George Eldon Ladd, *A Theology of the New Testament* (Grand Rapids: Eerdmans, 1974), 519–20.

15. Michaelis concludes that "on the whole the idea of imitation is foreign to the OT. In particular, there is no thought that we must imitate God" (W. Michaelis, *"mimeomai, mimētēs, k.t.l.,"* in *Theological Dictionary of the New Testament,* ed. G. Kittel and G. Friedrich, trans. G. W. Bromiley (Grand Rapids: Eerdmans, 1972), 4:663. In the LXX, this word-group appears only in the Apocrypha, where it does not refer to divine emulation (ibid.). Yet, in the pseudepigraphical writings some occurrences urge the imitation of OT men of renown and even God Himself (ibid., 4:664). Philo exhibits his same pattern of usage (ibid., 4:664–66). Michaelis's controlling presupposition, however, distorts his interpretation of these data.

16. For a general discussion of the most significant of these terms see W. Mundle, O. Flender, J. Gess, R. P. Martin, and F. F. Bruce, "Image, Idol, Imprint, Example,"

in *New International Dictionary of New Testament Theology,* ed. C. Brown (Grand Rapids: Zondervan, 1971), 2:284–91. Their opening paragraph on essential synonymity is important, and subsequent discussions of the Christological model are worthy of special attention.

17. L. Goppelt, *"typos, antitypos, k.t.l.,"* in *Theological Dictionary of the New Testament,* ed. G. Kittel and G. Friedrich, trans. G. W. Bromiley (Grand Rapids: Eerdmans, 1972), 8:247. Regarding etymology, Müller states "The etymology of *typos* is disputed. It may be derived from *typtō,* strike, beat, . . ." (H. Müller, "Type Pattern," 3:903); cf. Goppelt who is more impressed with this etymological connection (Goppelt, *"typtō,"* 8:246–47). He suggests the development goes from a blow "to the impress made by the below," then "from these basic senses *typos* develops an astonishing no. [number] of further meanings which are often hard to define. By virtue of its expressiveness it has made its way as a loan word [i.e., "type"] into almost all European languages" (ibid.).

18. Müller, "Type Pattern," 3:904.

19. Goppelt, *"typos,"* 8:248.

20. This follows the classifications of W. Bauer, W. F. Arndt, F. W. Gingrich, and F. W. Danker, *A Greek-English Lexicon of the New Testament and Other Early Christian Literature,* 2d ed. (Chicago: University of Chicago Press, 1957), 829–30. Subcategory 2, *"copy, image,"* has not been cited because those words furnish no NT examples; however, two of the extrabiblical references that are cited (i.e., a reference to a master being the image of God to a slave and children as copies of their parents) bear illustratively upon the moral references of category 5. This fifth category encompasses the doctrine of modeling in the NT. On the history of the hermeneutical significance of subcategory 6, see Goppelt, *"typos,"* 8:251–59; and Müller, "Type Pattern," 3:905–6.

21. Müller, "Type Pattern," 3:904–5; cf. Goppelt: *"Typos* is . . . the impress which makes an impress, so that in context the teaching can be described as the mould or norm which shapes the whole personal conduct of the one who is delivered up to it and has become obedient thereto" (*"typos,"* 8:250).

22. Goppelt, *"typos,"* 8:249–50. Interestingly, two sentences later, he comments on 1 Peter 5:3 and 1 Timothy 4:12 wherein he apparently concedes a more direct association with ethical emulation. It would seem that a good share of Goppelt's reluctance is due to Michaelis's quite dogmatic conclusions about the *mimētēs* word-group; cf. Michaelis, *"mimētēs,"* 4:659ff.

23. Müller, "Type Pattern," 3:905.

24. E.g., W. E. Vine, *An Expository Dictionary of New Testament Words* (New York: Charles Scribner's Sons, 1908), 2:248.

25. Michaelis, *"mimētēs,"* 4:659.

26. W. Bauder, *"mimeomai,"* in *New International Dictionary of New Testament Theology,* ed. C. Brown (Grand Rapids: Zondervan, 1971), 1:490.

27. Ibid.

28. Ibid., 491.
29. Cf. Michaelis, *"mimētēs,"* 4:661–62.
30. Ibid., 662.
31. Ibid., 663.
32. Ibid.
33. Bauder, *"mimeomai,"* 1:491.
34. Ibid.
35. Bauer, Arndt, Gingrich, and Danker, *A Greek-English Lexicon of the New Testament and Other Early Christian Literature,* 522.
36. James Hope Moulton and George Milligan, *The Vocabulary of the Greek Testament* (Grand Rapids: Eerdmans, 1930), 412.
37. Bauder, *"mimeomai,"* 1:491.
38. Michaelis, *"mimētēs,"* 4:666–68, passim.
39. Ibid., 667–74, contains eccentric applications and overstated conclusions based on some glaring examples of totality transfers that are always hermeneutically counterproductive. Bauder supports the essential thrust of Michaelis's thesis, but he is usually much more careful in his expressions of it (cf. *"mimeomai,"* 1:491–92).
40. Bauder, *"mimeomai,"* 1:491.
41. Another approach would be to follow canonical order. Still another is a biblical theological approach (i.e., modeling in the Pauline corpus, in the epistle to the Hebrews, in Peter, in 3 John, etc.). Although this method has inductive advantages, it does not lend itself to viewing the total NT picture through a common lens. Another way of organizing the data is the grammatical approach (i.e., noting the passages that historically exemplify modeling and then examining others that command it). Yet, it seems better to employ another organizational category, at the same time calling attention to the indicatives and imperatives.
42. Michaelis, *"mimētēs,"* 4:673; Michaelis's presupposition of utter moral transcendence causes him to reject the implications of the thrust of Paul's argument in 4:25ff. (ibid., 4:671–73).
43. See Ladd, *Theology of the New Testament,* 493–94, 524–25, for a discussion of the indicative/imperative motif related to sanctification.
44. This treatment will discuss only passages explicitly employing "model" or "type" terminology, omitting the many conceptual allusions to Paul's own example.
45. Bauder concludes, "Paul never intends to bind the demand for imitation to his own person. It is always ultimately to the One whom he himself follows" (*"mimeomai,"* 1:491).
46. Michaelis is quite dogmatic (*"mimētēs,"* 4:667–68) and Bauder more subdued (*"mimeomai,"* 1:491).
47. Bauder, *"mimeomai,"* 1:491.
48. Ibid.
49. This is the only NT occurrence of the compounded plural form *symmimētēs.* Here

it stands as the predicate nominative of the now familiar present plural imperative *ginesthe* (cf. Eph. 5:1). The personal pronoun in the genitive refers to Paul.

50. In the context, *hēmas* of 3:17c probably includes Timothy and possibly Epaphroditus with Paul (cf. Phil. 2:19, 25).

51. In this context, the industry of the apostolic circle (3:8) is what provides the example for the Thessalonians to follow (3:9b).

52. Moulton and Milligan (*Vocabulary of the Greek Testament,* 645) cite an ethical parallel to 1 Timothy 4:12 in an inscription from the first century B.C. It speaks of being a model for "godliness" *(eusebeian),* a noun used in 1 Tim. 4:7b.

53. The word *anastrophē* ("way of life, behavior") relates to cognates in Hebrews 13:7 (discussed below); 1 Peter 1:15, 17, 18; 3:1–2; 2 Peter 3:11. Here it connects with *eusebeia* ("godliness"), that is, holiness of lifestyle. This word-group was also ethically significant in Hellenistic Judaism (cf. Tobit 4:14; 2 Macc. 5:8; 6:23).

54. Two present imperatives, *meleta* and *isthi,* point to a continuing responsibility: "keep on caring for" these things and "be" in them. Robertson suggests that the force of the latter is "give yourself wholly to them," and adds, "It is like our 'up to his ears' in work . . . and sticking to his task" (A. T. Robertson, *Word Pictures in the New Testament* [Nashville: Broadman, 1931], 4:582).

55. As Stahlin urges, Timothy's moral and ministerial advancement "is to be visible, for he is to show himself hereby to be a *typos* for believers (v. 12). . . ." (G. Stahlin, *"prokopē, prokoptō,"* in *Theological Dictionary of the New Testament,* ed. G. Kittel and G. Friedrich, trans. G. W. Bromiley (Grand Rapids: Eerdmans, 1972), 6:714.

56. In secular Greek, *prokopē* ("progress") was a nautical term for "making headway in spite of blows" and was employed in an extended ethical way, esp. among the Stoics. Philo picked up the ethical sense and tried to give it a theocentric orientation (cf. Stahlin, *"prokopē, prokoptō,"* 6:704, 706–7, 709–11). The verb form is used of Jesus' "progress" (Luke 2:52).

57. John Calvin, *The Second Epistle of Paul to the Corinthians and the Epistles to Timothy, Titus and Philemon,* Calvin's Commentaries, trans. T. A. Small, ed. D. W. and T. F. Torrance (Grand Rapids: Eerdmans, 1964), 248.

58. Donald Guthrie, *The Pastoral Epistles,* Tyndale New Testament Commentaries, ed. R. V. G. Tasker (Grand Rapids: Eerdmans, 1957), 99.

59. Calvin's theological comments are helpful here (*Second Epistle of Paul to the Corinthians and the Epistles to Timothy, Titus and Philemon,* 248–49).

60. "Third generation" applies to the passing of the precedent from the "second generation" of Timothy and Titus to the permanent local church leaders (cf. 2 Tim. 2:2).

61. The participle *anatheōrountes* is best taken as imperatival in force in light of its subordination to *mimeisthe.*

62. Cp. verse 3b with 1 Timothy 4:12b. Cf. the preceding discussion, especially in reference to the vocabulary of 1 Timothy 4:12b. Goppelt aptly synthesizes the key passages as follows: "Along the same lines as in Paul, the exhortation in 1 Pt 5:3

admonishes those who represent the word to become *typoi . . . tou poimniou,* 'examples to the flock.' The word cannot just be recited; it can be attested only as one's own word which shapes one's own conduct. The office-bearer is thus admonished: 'Be thou an example of the believers, in word (i.e., preaching), in conversation,' 1 Tim. 4:12; cf. Tt. 2:7: 'In all things shewing thyself a pattern (in the doing) of good works'" (Goppelt, *"typos,"* 8:250).

63. Michaelis, *"mimētēs,"* 4:670. Some of his contextual comments are credible, but his controlling assumption that modeling relates only to authority limits his conclusion about the verses by his presuppositional mold (ibid.).

64. Michaelis, *"mimētēs,"* 4:666.

Index of Authors

Index of Scriptures

Index of Subjects